Gigolo

Gigolo

by

GOLDEN

with Amanda Astill

First published in Great Britain in 2008 by Hodder

An imprint of Hodder & Stoughton
An Hachette Livre UK company

1

A CIP catalogue record for this title is available
from the British Library

ISBN 978 0 340 96086 8

Typeset in Plantin Light by Palimpsest Book Production Limited,
Grangemouth, Stirlingshire

Printed and bound by
Clays Ltd, St Ives plc

Hodder & Stoughton policy is to use papers that are natural, renewable
and recyclable products and made from wood grown in sustainable
forests. The logging and manufacturing processes are expected to
conform to the environmental regulations of the country of origin.

Hodder & Stoughton Ltd
338 Euston Road
London NW1 3BH

www.hodder.co.uk

For Mum, Dad and Marcus

Acknowledgements

This book couldn't have been written without the help of the wonderful Amanda Astill. I'm also hugely grateful to my agent, Susan Smith, and to all at Hodder. And most of all, I want to say thank you to all the friends, musicians, artists and bohemians who over the years have helped, supported and encouraged me never to give in to the dreaded 9 to 5!!

Contents

Chapter 1

X-Rated Real Estate

I love my life as a gigolo, but I'm still surprised I got into this line of business: they certainly didn't list it as an option during my careers advice sessions at school. The hours are great, the managers are an absolute pleasure to work with, and the perks are amazing, but the take-home pay isn't anything to shout about, and try getting a pension when your occupation involves knowing your way around a woman's body. The computer definitely says no. Having said that, if I ever even begin to have any regrets about trading security for hot sex, Fate always steps in to remind me that I'm probably one of the luckiest men alive.

Take last week: I was on my afternoon off and was gazing wistfully into the window of an upmarket estate agent's office in Hampstead, imagining owning one of the £1 million town houses, rather than visiting them as a favoured guest. In between the property details for a Dartmouth Park penthouse and a luxury Georgian town house, I spotted a gorgeous woman staring directly at me from the comfort of her important-looking desk. Then she winked. A cheeky, suggestive gesture that indicated she was the kind of person I love to work with. I walked into the office, and before I'd even sat down I knew that not only did we have a connection, but that it was of the high-speed broadband variety. This was more than attraction; this was the unspoken law of supply and demand. Any thoughts of the fragility of my future suddenly evaporated.

So here I am, a week of wild sex later, tracing my fingertip down the curve of her back. She is sighing softly at my touch. As I smile and bend down to kiss the nape of her neck, the scent of her freshly washed hair mingles with the smell of something entirely more decadent, namely the musky aroma of Chai Tongue-Teasing Oil, expertly massaged in by my own fair hands. I like the edible massage oils – so much more fun to lick off. I turn her over, see her expensively highlighted hair fan out like a golden halo over the pillow and part her legs. She sighs again, a soft flutter against my skin, as I start to kiss her breasts, moving slowly down until I get to the edge of her neat Brazilian. I look up and she returns my gaze with a spreading smile. Then she puts her hands on my head, wraps her legs round my neck and pushes me down. She looks as sweet as she tastes, but appearances can be deceptive. Only ten minutes earlier she'd been telling me her favourite fantasies in graphic detail, which is why I'm licking edible oil off her clitoris as she screams commands for me to go harder, faster, softer, to the left – believe me, there are no communication issues here. I make her come in five minutes. Usually I like to spin it out for at least twenty, but with such clear direction it's hard not to hit the jackpot on hyper-speed. To be fair, though, we have already been in bed for at least three hours. While she might have wanted to savour the first orgasm (backwards spoons with her touching herself in tandem with me), it's no wonder that this final climax feels more like a quick, but satisfying, after-dinner coffee.

'You should be sponsored by l'Oréal,' she says, as I pour a glass of wine for her a few moments later.

'Why?' I ask with a quizzical smile.

She takes a sip from her glass. 'Because you're worth it.' She splutters with laughter, almost spitting out her wine.

I try and flick my brown hair provocatively and she screams for me to do it again. Always the showman, I stand on the bed and do a serious of comedy poses with my best Blue Steel power stare, flicking my hair and mouthing, 'Because I'm worth it.' In the end we're laughing so much I can't keep it up and collapse next to her on the bed.

'You're so much fun, Golden,' she muses, as our laughter dies out.

'At your service, madam,' I reply, doffing an imaginary cap.

'I haven't even thought about work all afternoon,' she adds seriously.

'Well, you're in my world now – the only target you have to worry about is your Orgasm Index.' I look at her with a businesslike expression.

'My what? What the hell is an Orgasm Index?'

'It's my very own target scheme. Take today – I've set myself the target that you must have at least seven orgasms. We're four down, so in my world there's still a lot of work to be done.'

'Wow. You're very focused on your job. I admire that in a man.' She lies back and starts touching herself. 'Shall I help you out?' She smiles seductively at me.

'Stop immediately,' I admonish her. 'I never cheat. What's the point of having a man like me around if you have to do a spot of DIY in your own garden? I'm very confident I'll hit today's target, don't you worry. The night is yet young.'

'You're right. What was I thinking?' she replies with faux horror. 'Anyway, I need a rest – you've almost worn me out. I'm going to have a shower and freshen up so you have time to think about how you're going to entertain me this evening.' And with that her pert bottom swings off to the bathroom.

Ms Antoinette (not her real name, obviously, but delicacy dictates pseudonyms in this situation) is not a girlfriend, but she's not a customer either. Rather, we have an unspoken agreement. You see, the world of the modern gigolo exists in the grey area of the female sexual revolution: women want their illicit thrills delivered with the kind of finesse – and fun – your average guy is just not equipped for, but without something as crass as a cold, hard cash transaction. I like to think of it as an experience exchange: I provide the fun and frolics; she picks up the tab. Really, I'm the male equivalent of a Balenciaga, the perfect accessory for today's beautiful, confident woman.

My profession has always relied on the libidinous desires

of the fairer sex. Long before me, the Parisian dandies and the British fops enjoyed the patronage of wealthy women. When ladies have desires that need fulfilling, they do it with discretion and they demand something with much more sophistication than a rent-a-dick. Getting a hard-on is the easy part – it's establishing the right persona that takes work.

Firstly, there's the fashion. Women want an *affair*, to indulge themselves, even if it's only a one-night liaison, and believe me, this doesn't come wearing a trucker cap and an off-white wife-beater vest. Every modern dandy has to choose a style, a look that summarises the sex he's selling. Mine is part smart sophistication, part dissolute rock star. At the moment I'm favouring a vintage leather fitted jacket worn with a PPQ shirt, one of the coolest new labels for the fashionista set. A gigolo's choice of shoes is, of course, essential. Experience has taught me that a bad pair of shoes has approximately the same effect on the female libido as an inexpert tongue. In the past only rich wives and courtesans could afford to treat themselves to men who were as beautifully groomed as themselves. Now everyone from office girls to A-listers are giving two well-manicured fingers to badly dressed men with beer guts and opting for a good-time gigolo who can look great on their arm *and* give them a great time – at a price.

We're not talking a few crisp fifties left on the bedside table in a soulless hotel – women's sex toys are far too evolved to waste money like that. Like I said, women buy into a lifestyle. They want designer clothes, glossy magazines, exclusive restaurant reservations, and they want the man who goes with that life. They understand that just as those Louboutins don't walk out of the shop for the

love of fashionable feet, the good things in life cost money.
There is no such thing as a free lunch – especially if it's
at Bistrotheque, dining next to Giles Deacon. You see, the
women fund my *lifestyle*, not my bank account – they
never pay me directly – which is why I often find myself
in the odd situation of being flown first class to a
rendezvous and then having to play piano in my local
café to pay for a decent meal back home. It does sound
mad, but I've discovered that women are intrigued by this
bohemian life of extremes. I suppose it's a welcome break
from the nine-to-five guy who can't be whisked off for
hot sex and romance without first filling in a holiday-
request form.

The funny thing is, though, I crafted myself into this
personification of what women want because for years I
was the guy they *didn't* want. Not in a bad way. I was
good-looking, sweet and intelligent, but I was naïve. I
didn't understand what made women tick. I was like a
gauche puppy darting around their heels. An image springs
into my mind of a gorgeous girl with thick dark hair, a
beautiful smile and mocking eyes. It's ages since I thought
about Simone D – the first girl ever to break my heart.
I think maybe Ms Antoinette reminds me of her. Both of
them are women who have men totally in their power –
fun, flirtatious, but always with something held back in
reserve. Ms Antoinette might be an estate agent, but I
recognise the steely qualities she shares with Simone D
– as if men are just a footnote on her life's agenda.

I met Simone D at the musical conservatory I studied
at almost a decade ago now. I was an incredibly innocent
nineteen, and she was a worldly, knowing nineteen who
dated older men with Porsches. She probably thought my

mad crush on her was 'cute'. I drive a big old Jaguar now – a 'gift', naturally – and I've become the kind of man she would have given the time of day to back then. It feels good to understand how to turn these girls on – sexually and emotionally. They're very demanding, but that makes it all the more rewarding when you can show them a good time.

'Golden, I'm bored – let's party. What's happening tonight?' Ms Antoinette interrupts my reverie with a mischievous smile.

She has emerged from the bathroom and looks incredibly pretty in the fading light, with the aubergine bed sheet wrapped round her waist, leaving her pert breasts exposed. But see what I mean? Very demanding – a few minutes spent not focusing on the job at hand and she's itching for a new adventure. Luckily, I know exactly how to handle the situation. The trick is to take control straight away, rather than staring slack-jawed like she just slapped you across the face. With my, admittedly vast, experience, I know that she's not bored of me; she just needs stimulating with something new. And this is where the other essential gigolo attribute comes in: not only do I look the part, I *live* the part. She knows I'm hooked up, that I know all the best parties and all the best people, and I'm happy to drive her in my golden carriage right into the heaving throng of it. She wants someone who'll take her on a first-class journey, not some hanger-on riding on her Prada coat-tails.

I pick up my mobile and dial my best friend, and fellow dandy, Rochester. 'It's me – Golden. Where are you?'

Rochester's half Russian and half Belizean. It's a

heady, exotic mix and a seductive alternative to my polished British gent. 'You are never going to believe where I am,' he whispers in that heavy accent women can't get enough of. 'I'm with Celebrity Z.' Rochester disclosed her name, but I'm far too discreet to do the same. 'We've just spent an hour having crazy sex in the Jacuzzi. She is *so* beautiful. We're off to Miami tomorrow. In *her* plane.'

'That's nice,' I reply, smiling.

It's a good feeling when your closest confidant is having a tête-à-tête with a Hollywood actress who is prepared to pay for the pleasure when it would happily be administered gratis. Part of me does feel slightly peevish about it, though. It's not that I'm unhappy with Ms Antoinette – it's just good to have a celebrity to name-drop on your CV. Women like to think they're batting in that league, as it's a great compliment. Obviously, my own CV is sprinkled with a few Hollywood stars, but recently I have felt in need of an update. Rather inconveniently, my last big hitter had a public meltdown, and while women may want to share sexual partners with an *Elle* cover star, ubiquity in the *National Enquirer* doesn't have quite the same aphrodisiac effect.

'Well, have fun,' I say. 'Call me when you land. I'll need all the gossip at our next Dandy Trade Union meeting.'

I wonder whose turn it is to organise our monthly boys-only soirée. I've got a feeling it's me. I'll have to think of something exceptional – it's a point of pride amongst us fellow dandies that the person who hosts our meet-up makes it unique. We trade tips, anecdotes and contacts over a few cold beers (no ladies present means no champagne for once) and then try and out-flirt each other with any women who come across our path. A bit like flexing our muscles. It is truly a sight to be seen when a group of handsome, elegant men pull out their full flirting arsenal and have a charm-off. It's better than Botox for freshening up a girl's self-esteem.

Next on my speed dial is Johan, a Swedish supermodel who is rumoured to charge up to £10,000 for sperm donation to older women wanting offspring with perfect DNA. Face like an angel, hung like . . . Well, needless to say, he's *very* popular with the ladies.

'J, how are you?' I walk into the hallway and sit down on a beautifully upholstered Louis VII chair. I don't like to inflict on my female companions the mechanisms of how the magic happens. If they wanted to hear someone calling to make arrangements, they'd date the maître d'.

'Are you out tonight? No? Why?'

Johan is strangely mysterious about what he's up to. He must have a new lady on the go, I figure. Still, it's unusual for him not to give me some hint, although he's always far too discreet to dish out the juicy details – unlike Rochester. Such a shame he's not out tonight, though. It's nice to sprinkle a few male supermodels in the society you're keeping. As long as your lady doesn't get wandering eyes, it raises the calibre of proceedings. More bang for the buck, as they say.

When I speed-dial a third friend, I don't even have to ask if he's out. I'm greeted by the pounding beat of electro music and the shrieks of a whole lot of fun. 'Zen, where are you?'

In retrospect, I should have gone with Zen first. He's the perfect accessory to a night out: a glamorous, gorgeous *über*-queen who isn't so much *on* the scene as *is* the scene.

'I'm DJing at Sketch. It's a launch party for some perfume. Are you coming down?'

Just what I wanted to hear. 'Put me down for four on the guest list.'

'Are we partying, then?' Ms Antoinette shouts from the bathroom, where I can see her applying make-up through the part-open door. She's still naked, save for a rose lace thong. It's seems such a shame for her to get dressed.

'We certainly are. Perfume launch. It'll be a fashionista frenzy.'

She passes a bottle of champagne for me to uncork to start the night's festivities properly before returning to the bathroom. It's amazing what estate agents in London earn these days. Ms Antoinette must be getting some hefty bonuses. She's living life larger than a lot of the trust-fund girls I frequent. Well, it's good to know all the cash from middle-class property investments is being well spent.

'Wedges or stilts?' She comes to the bathroom door and leans on it adorably, jutting out one sexily curved hip.

'Wedges. Definitely. But with a mini.'

Another perk of a highly trained professional like myself is that I never say, 'Dunno,' or, 'Whatever you think,' upon a request for fashion advice. I make it my business to read *Vogue* and *Grazia* and to know the style tips women want to hear.

'I got a couple more places on the guest list if you want to bring along any friends,' I call to her.

'Cool. I'll call Melinda and Haley.' She smiles at me with an excited little shoulder shrug. I know it's important for her to have maximum fun after slogging all week at work. Partying with her friends and the kudos of getting them on the guest list are all part of the package. The difficult question to ponder is what *I* should wear.

Now, I'm not being needlessly coy here – as much as I put emphasis on the numerous lifestyle benefits of having a man like myself as a companion, of course the engine room of this whole dynamic is sex. Lest I forget this, in between the heady pursuits of shopping and socialising, events always conspire to remind me that the build-up is merely the fine art of foreplay. The difference is, while a proper boyfriend might restrict this to such niceties as 'Give us a blow job', a professional gigolo is expected to lubricate with charm and champagne, and deliver specially tailored off-menu experiences – more a table for two at Nobu than a takeaway from Nando's. However, even I, experienced as I am, was shocked at where I found myself servicing Ms Antoinette later that evening. I've got to admit, though, it was quite a buzz.

What I love about career girls is that they know what they want, which makes it easier to fulfil the number-one rule of dandy etiquette: let the woman make the first move. Now this might sound strange, but if you think about it carefully, it starts to make sense. Women spend their lives being pestered for sex by charmless oafs, being object-ified by the deeply unsexy squint of an unsolicited male gaze. Part of the enjoyment for them is pursuing the object of their desire. It's like boutique shopping compared with bargain shopping. It's about getting it because you *really* wanted it, not just because it's going cheap. This isn't about me playing hard to get, which would be no fun – I'm available and highly flirtatious, and once the game has been initiated, I'm an expert in the art of seduction. It's all about spinning the chase into a teasing dance with the woman, like the piper paying and calling the tune.

'I'm not wearing any knickers,' Ms Antoinette whispers coquettishly in my ear, as we walk past the queue and through the door into the dark, red-hued club. I smile knowingly, taking a look at her perilously short shift dress. It's like my own personal peep show. I love it, and she knows it. At the bar, I place my hands lightly on her waist as she asks for a round of champagne cocktails for the four of us and puts her card behind the bar. As she's being served, I press up behind her and check out the authenticity of her claim. My hands are cold against her skin and she gasps suddenly. The barman raises an eyebrow and she giggles, looks behind her, winks at me and hands me a drink. Oh, the hardship of being at the coalface of my chosen career.

As I chink glasses with her friends, I wonder what they think of me, what she's told them. It's obvious this is no normal relationship. Perfect gentleman that I am, I'm not racing to the bar to get the drinks in or picking up the tab after dinner. I'm the trophy here, which by normal male–female standards is very strange.

Haley smiles at me very flirtatiously and I smile in a friendly manner without giving anything back. Hitting on Ms Antoinette's friends would be very bad form. Unless she invited them along for the ride – and you'd be amazed how often that happens. Not on this occasion, though. I can tell that the two friends are just dipping their feet in the water, while Ms Antoinette takes a long soak in the champagne bath.

'Golden, you look wonderful, as always. And who are

the ladies?' Zen bounds over from behind the DJ booth wearing the tightest black jeans I've ever seen, which match his jet-black dyed hair, cut in an angular style. His smile is infectious, and totally negates any intimidating edge from his super-cool look.

'Hello, you.' He pouts at Ms Antoinette and puts his arm round her. He's never met her before, but I've told him about her. 'I hope Golden is taking good care of you,' he says with mock concern.

'Oh, yes, he's certainly looking after me,' she answers with sparkling eyes, which I reward with an affectionate kiss.

Ms Antoinette slips her arm round my waist and I realise there's an incredible warmth between us. In situations like this, where both parties are utterly frank and honest about what they want, it makes it easy to develop a genuine friendship. It's this connection that gives our relationship an entirely different dimension to casual sex. It actually means something to both of us, even if it's not what the morality police deem to be meaningful.

A massive shriek goes up from the girls behind me as the Gossip comes on and suddenly they all rush on to the dance floor. Taking the opportunity to get me on my own, Zen sidles up to me and whispers in my ear, 'Have you heard about Rochester?'

'I know. Amazing, isn't it? The way he tells it Celebrity Z'll be proposing soon.'

'Yeah, right. I somehow doubt she's on the hunt for a husband.'

'No doubt he's giving her a taste of dirty sex Brit-style in the meantime, though.' I laugh, imagining him with his shoulder-length black hair, tattoos and Chanel Noir nail varnish, lounging around in the pristine white minimalism of a Hollywood mansion.

Ms Antoinette interrupts my thoughts by sneaking up beside me and stroking my back. 'Come to the toilets with me,' she whispers. I get the feeling she doesn't need help reapplying her make-up.

As we walk up the stairs towards the toilets, which are white pods that look like they were designed for extra-terrestrials, I notice how heated the whole atmosphere is. It's as if everyone has been snorting pheromones.

'I've never had sex in a toilet shaped like a pod before,' she giggles, as we lock the door and shrug off the knowing glances as we squeeze in together. 'It would be rude not to take advantage of a novelty toilet, don't you think?'

I kiss her and push up her dress. It doesn't have very far to go, so within seconds I'm inside her. Thankfully, it's a very luxurious toilet, so I'm not put off my stride, though I think it's the down and dirty aspect that's getting her off.

Afterwards, I watch as she reapplies her lipstick and brushes her hair.

'I'm going to make this the best night ever. I want to do *everything* I've never tried before,' she laughs.

'Be my guest,' I reply, before asking, 'What is it your ladyship wants?'

'I want to walk down the aisle knowing that I ticked off everything on my fantasy list and I won't have any regrets,' she muses. 'Sometimes I think I can't stop looking at life like a set of objectives. It just bugs me when I know there's stuff I haven't done. I don't want to feel like I missed out. Is that bad?'

'Not at all. It sounds pretty smart to me. Sow your wild

oats and all that. Men have been doing it for years – why shouldn't you girls get a piece of the action?'

'Exactly,' she says emphatically. 'If someone at work told me I wasn't allowed to do something because I was a woman, I'd sue them – why should sex be any different?' With her increasing outrage, she's worked up quite an impassioned flush on her cheeks, which looks incredibly sexy and inspires me to go for a second round.

My grand finale is greeted with a pounding knock on the toilet door. Somehow we've slipped into a time tardis in our little luxury cubicle. The club is closing and the bouncers want us to leave. It's strange how quickly time passes in these circumstances. It's like light speed compared with normal life. Maybe it's the adrenaline rush of lust. Part of me thinks it's the unreal feeling of being with a woman fulfilling her fantasies with a man she'll never fall in love with. Without that end aim, the moment is frozen in time. The fact that there's no future makes the present more exciting and vivid.

Suddenly it occurs to me that Ms Antoinette will meet someone and have a future with them, while I'm still whirling at light speed on the merry-go-round, travelling too fast and having too much fun to face reality. But the thought doesn't linger for long.

'I've got a plan. A *very* naughty plan,' Ms Antoinette breaks into my reverie with a flirtatious giggle in my ear.

'What? You are *so* bad. In fact, I think I might have to spank you as punishment.' I lean her over the toilet, pull up her skirt to see her knickerless bum and give her a few light slaps. The bouncers continue rapping on the door.

Afterwards we walk out together, grinning provocatively

at each other and holding hands as we waltz past the exasperated staff with a carefree shrug.

Outside, Ms Antoinette hails a taxi and directs it to Hampstead. She places a finger over my lips as I start to question why. 'You'll see,' she taunts me.

I lean over and kiss her passionately, but retain enough decorum so as to not make a scene in front of the taxi driver. I'm not cheap like that – unless she wants me to be.

When we pull up outside the exclusive estate agent's office where she works, what we're about to do dawns on me and I break out into a loud laugh, which sets her off too. 'Sshh,' she hushes me with mock seriousness as she pays the taxi driver. 'We wouldn't want to lower the tone of the area and make house prices drop, now would we?' she says, pulling a large set of keys out of her Chloé Paddington bag.

Inside, she switches on a light at the back of the office, creating a soft glow at the front, where she sits down behind the large desk I first spotted her at and beckons me to sit in the seat opposite. 'I'll need to take down your particulars – the measurements especially.'

I start to snigger and she collapses laughing on the desk, at which point I take over. 'I think this a very fine property, top of the range,' I say, unbuttoning her top, 'but I'll need to do a full tour.'

'Will you now?' she breathes in my ear.

A couple walk past the window. They're easily able to see us, but they're so wrapped up in each other they don't notice. By now Ms Antoinette is sitting on top of the desk with her dress round her waist. 'Wow – the first middle-class couple I've seen who are more interested in each other than the contents of an estate agent's window,' she observes dryly.

'Lucky for us,' I say, as I pull her tightly to me.

'No, wait a minute,' she says, stopping me as I'm about to enter her. 'I might need to take notes.' She pushes me away, turns round and leans over the desk, facing towards the window. Then she looks provocatively over her shoulder and says, 'Every time I look out of the window from now on I'll think of this moment. I much prefer the view from this angle.'

She comes – or should I say 'completes' – while dead-eyeing the details for a £1.5 million house in Belsize Park. Well, to be successful in business I imagine it pays never to take your eye off the prize – even mid-orgasm. That's dedication for you.

When we've finished, she sits down and pulls out her calculator.

'Surely you're not working?' I ask with incredulity.

'I'm totting up my Orgasm Index. You promised me seven, and by my calculation we're still only at six.' She frowns in my direction.

Laughing, I lead her by the hand to the window and, as she faces into the street, hold her from behind and let my pianist fingers do their work. She comes, very noisily, in minutes.

'For that I think you deserve a bonus,' she says, turning round and unbuckling my trousers. 'Don't ever say I'm not a good boss.'

As she goes down on me, I wonder where one should address a thank-you note to God.

Chapter 2

Even Gigolos Have Souls

One of the hardest parts of my job is spending time getting to know women who can never really know me back. I'm a carefully constructed image to them, not a flesh and blood person. They don't want to know that a month of solid partying in Monaco has left me run-down and I'm planning to spend the weekend with my mum, who'll feed me back to health. Let's face it, that kind of detail is off-putting when you're about to invest in the hottest sex of your life. So what happens to me when I'm offstage? Well, take today, for instance: Ms Antoinette is off on a sales conference, somewhere in that funny little place called the real world, and I'm in between engagements with about £20 to my name and a Savile Row suit that needs dry-cleaning. Usually I wander down from my *bijou* – OK, small – apartment (where I might one day be forced to sleep with the landlady to pay my enormous rent arrears, except that she's seventy and has arthritis, so I'm thinking a reverse cowgirl isn't on the agenda) and walk across the street to the Literary Café.

It's a beautiful little place, quintessentially English, combining shabby, faded splendour with cosy charm. The ceiling is decorated with an original cornice, and the battered brown leather sofas face inwards towards a Victorian fireplace, where the fire is always lit on the darkest, coldest winter days. At the back, little round tables pepper the room, decorated with candles and faded floral posies, and in the furthest corner is a jaded old grand piano, which thanks to me is still in perfect tune.

In the daytime, the café is populated by a bohemian crowd of intellectuals – usually students who pore over Dostoevsky, making their lattes last for hours. At night, it's a haven for loved-up couples and people enjoying clandestine trysts. A mixture of faded old paintings and new, arty photographs by local artists decorate the walls. The atmosphere is pure vintage British artisan culture.

In time-honoured tradition, I've struck a deal with the owner – a sweet old gent with mad white sideburns – that in exchange for entertaining the customers on the piano I get a free meal and a fine(ish) bottle of Bordeaux. With a glass of red on standby, I play all the old favourites, like 'Fly Me to the Moon' and 'What Is This Thing Called Love?', sometimes to the delight of a roomful of amiably drunk patrons, and sometimes just to the delight of an old professor sitting in the corner, and Charlotte B, the waitress, who makes sure I always get second helpings with my free meal. Charlotte can play the piano too, and sometimes, when no one is around, we'll play stupid songs together and giggle like naughty schoolkids. She is the only woman I've met who loves music as much as I do. Some nights I wait behind to help her lock up, and we talk about our favourite artists – it turns out her dad is a jazz musician and her childhood was spent listening to incredible live recitals in the same way most kids watched *Blue Peter.*

Today, with hardly any customers around, I prop myself against the bar and chat to her. Our conversations are the closest I ever get to revealing my true self these days.

Alongside her latte is the book she was reading before I arrived. I pick it up and look at the title, *Return of the Native* by Thomas Hardy.

'I've never read any of his books,' I admit. 'What's it about?'

'It's Hardy – it's about lots of things,' she laughs, 'but mainly it's about a tragic love affair.'

'Why's it tragic?' I ask curiously, wondering why affairs in novels are always doomed, rather than the shameless fun they're supposed to be.

'Well, Clym Yeobright is a man of the world who returns home from his decadent life in Paris to his native Dorset in search of the rural simplicity of his childhood. He falls in love with Eustacia Vye, a woman who symbolises everything he's looking for – a pure, simple country girl, in contrast with the debauched city socialites he's been hanging out with.'

'So what goes wrong?' I ask, noticing how her eyebrows form a perfect arc over her dark-brown eyes.

'Eustacia is only a simple country girl because she's had no choice. She dreams of living the decadent city life he's left behind and thinks Clym is her ticket there. She's wrong. They get married and it all ends in disaster when they both realise they aren't who they thought they were.'

I ponder what she's told me for a moment and then say, 'That's the problem with love. How can you really know someone? No one is ever what they seem to be.'

Charlotte sighs and leans on the bar, looking into the distance. 'That's true. But it's a risk you just have to take. That's why it's so important that people are honest with each other. Imagine getting involved with someone and then finding out down the line that they have a secret life, and desires, you knew nothing about.'

'Very true.' I nod in agreement, feeling uncomfortable as I think about my own alter ego and how I'm already deceiving Charlotte, even though we're only friends.

'That's what was so weird about my childhood,' she carries on. 'We lived in the heart of Soho,' she tells me, smiling at the incongruity of raising a child there. 'Can you imagine that? I'd read *The Enchanted Forest* and *The Magic Faraway Tree* and then walk out of my front door and bump into hookers, strippers, pimps and dealers. My bedroom window looked on to a brothel, and night after night I'd see respectable men, most of them probably in relationships, go in there. I'd daydream about getting married and living happily ever after, and then I'd see a man coming out, looking all shifty, hoping no one had seen him. That's how someone else's fairytale ended, I'd think to myself – what a reality check. A promise to love honour and obey that ends up in the arms of a twenty-pound hooker on a seedy back street.'

'That is an awful thought,' I admit, feeling forlorn about the bleak picture she's painted. But part of me also sees a different side. Life is too complex to make black-and-white judgements on these situations. In the past, it may have been the clichéd husband looking for extramarital infidelities – and paying for them for convenience's sake – but in the modern world, the axis has turned, and more often than not it's the woman looking for a discreet way to indulge in this type of sexual moonlighting, while the hapless hubby sits at home. In my experience, sex and love aren't always the natural bed partners they're assumed to be. Married women have often confessed that a dalliance with me has saved their relationship. It seems the hands-on approach is sometimes the only solution to marriage-guidance counselling – and not always with the hands of the husband in question. Another part of me wants to believe in Charlotte's innocent view of the world. I wonder to myself what it would be like to kiss her, then instantly dismiss the idea. If she knew the truth about me, she would despise me. It occurs to me that while I'm servicing the sexual whims of women who will eventually marry someone else, or rekindle the spark with their husbands, I will be left behind. At this depressing thought, I try to steer the conversation back into safer territory: music.

'There must have been an up-side to growing up in Soho, though. Wasn't it amazing being surrounded by so many great musicians?' I ask, sipping my wine.

'Of course. I can't imagine any other life. My dad always encouraged me musically, so I'd spend hours practising on my piano. Sometimes I'd even get a class from some visiting player, and then years later find out I had had a lesson with one of the century's great masters.'

'That sounds incredible,' I reply, leaning closer. The scene she's painting is my dream childhood. 'Tell me more about what it was like.'

'There was always music playing in the house. I'd wake up on a Monday morning to hear Stravinsky on the stereo. It felt like living in some amazing old music venue, and at night there'd always be some tunes drifting through the wall to soothe me to sleep. That's the great thing about music – it means you never feel alone . . .' She trails off just as my phone beeps. It's Johan.

Johan has been distant with me and my other fellow gigolos lately, and tells me he needs to meet up and talk. I make my excuses to Charlotte and depart, feeling strangely reluctant to leave the warmth of the Literary Café and Charlotte's presence.

All the time she was telling me about her childhood, I'd felt the urge to talk about mine. To tell her about the strange mixture of influences that make me who I am. But, ironically, the one person to whom I feel close enough to tell these stories is the one person who wouldn't understand. She has no clue I'm a gigolo by trade, figuring I'm a penniless musician. Thanks to her loathing of debauchery, I realise it would be a terrible mistake to reveal my secret. So here I am, unable to share myself, past and present, with anyone. It's a shame, because all the clues to my current occupation are scattered along the road I've taken.

My path to gigolodom is something of a contradiction. On the one hand you could say I was genetically predisposed to my profession, and on the other my working-class upbringing was an unlikely start on the road to sexual hedonism. The truth is, I didn't simply step out of a vintage sports car one day with the looks and sensibilities of a playboy. Like a grow-in-the-bag persona, it took a lot of nurturing to reach full bloom.

Despite my formative surroundings (unglamorously, Woking and the Isle of Wight), I always knew there was bohemian blood running through my veins, and quite a sizeable libido running through somewhere else. My mother is a talented painter and I inherited my creative streak from her. Actually, I inherited much more than that: I inherited a spirit of rebellion and an anarchic attitude that meant I was far more comfortable lounging around salons in Paris not knowing where my next meal came from than listening to the boring advice of career counsellors or a petty-minded boss.

They say mothers pass emotions on to their unborn babies, not just nourishment. If that's the case, then every cell of mine was infused with memories of my mother's despair at growing up in Havant, knowing that there was more to life, but not knowing how to tunnel an escape route out. At sixteen, despite her dreams of going to art school, my grandparents insisted she leave school and get a job. They weren't being cruel, just sensible. Mum ended up working in a bank in Portsmouth. She was young, beautiful and was eaten up with boredom behind a counter that might as well have been a prison door.

At eighteen, as soon as she was officially an adult, she packed her bags and left. Her determination to find adventure took her all the way to Germany, where she worked as an au pair. It's strange how history repeats itself. I dropped out of school at sixteen and worked as a labourer. When I think back to myself then, working on building sites with my tapered fingers and a soundtrack of jazz music playing in my mind, asking myself how I would find a way out, the similarities between myself and my mother are striking. And like her, I did find my own exit sign – just not the one I expected. I saw myself playing in concert halls, bringing pleasure and aural delight to an audience of devoted listeners, but in the end it turned out my greatest talents were best played out to an audience of one, with oral delights top of the bill.

And that's the thing, there's a terrible duality inside me – one that ultimately makes me the perfect gigolo. You see, after all the romance and high art passed on by my mother, come the gifts passed on by my father. This is a man known admiringly to his friends as 'the Wolf', someone who before he met my mother is rumoured to have received a Nobel Prize for seduction.

Mine is a potent combination. A bohemian poet without a sex drive is only a lame fop, and a playboy without a sensitive side is a sad sex addict who could leave a lady feeling slightly soiled afterwards. But, as I've found, if you can hit the G-spot with the same finger you can hit a G note and talk the language of poetry as well as pleasure, you're a valuable commodity.

In his youth, Dad was a proper character – a lovable rogue who would entertain the prettiest girls in the back of his vintage sports cars (the spoils of the building trade in the 1960s – not just for toffs with trust funds, as it turns out) and still make them feel like a princess when he moved on to the next conquest. One of nine children, he was a laid back guy with an easy charm and a Cheshire Cat grin who went to work in the family trade – building and plumbing – along with his six brothers. His friends always insinuate that the housewives booked him for building jobs because of the after-hours service he provided. Whenever I ask him he just winks and laughs; he doesn't deny it.

As a child, I remember going on jobs with Dad and he'd always flirt with women. I didn't understand what he was doing. It confused me. From a young age I understood that there was this magical other half to life that I had yet to figure out. There was a frisson to relations between men and women that seemed to provide the electricity that lit up ordinary life. At that point, however, I had no clue where the light switch was, and believe me, it would be a struggle to find it – I was literally fumbling in the dark for a long, long time.

Dad was more than a playboy – he was a true gentleman with a profound respect for women, and a big heart that believed in true love. When he fell for my mum he gave up chasing women for good, even though he was a natural flirt. Maybe that ran in his veins too. His mother, my grandmother, was reputedly the daughter of a lord who lost all his inheritance for marrying an actress. Rare for the aristocracy, he married for true love and never regretted it – even if it did mean his grandson became, essentially, a brickie.

My parents met at a New Year's Eve party, and that was that. Mum had been over from Germany visiting for Christmas. She flew back, but Dad deluged her with love letters and three months later they were driving home together back through the *Straßen* of Germany. OK, so maybe she didn't expect her knight in shining armour would be riding a white van, but they were madly in love. Their favourite love song, Santana's 'Samba Pa Ti', was even played on Simon Bates's radio feature 'Our Tune' – the pinnacle of romance, 1970s-style. Three years later I arrived.

One summer, when I was ten, Dad took on a job renovating the house of one of Bonnie Tyler's friends in

Mumbles, so we all went to live in Wales for a while. God forbid, I even developed a Welsh accent, which certainly isn't something a gigolo would endeavour to have. Talking dirty via Swansea is more likely to earn you a comedy award than an orgasm Oscar.

We'd often go round to visit Bonnie, who used to babysit me, and Dad, as always in touch with his spiritual playboy side, would drive to the house in his silver Porsche. I remember feeling pretty smooth pulling into the driveway of a pop star's mansion in a sports car and thinking, This is the life. The monotony of the slate-grey skies of Woking and the parochial Isle of Wight seemed a world away. This was my first taste of showbiz, and frankly, I loved it. This sprinkling of stardust was the start of the rot that would eventually corrode my ambition to become a world-famous classical jazz pianist.

Bonnie's house was big and modern – everything you could hope for from a 1980s pop star who personally destroyed a chunk of the ozone layer with her hairspray. On the walls of the grand staircase, which swept up the centre of the house, was the gold disc for 'Total Eclipse of the Heart'. Being a kid, my first thought was simply, Cool, but there were more showbiz delights to come. Bonnie indulged me with chocolate eclairs and SodaStreams. I thought it was all very posh and exciting, and that she was amazing. I was sold. Later on, as Balzac's Lucien Chardon (a beautiful provincial poet who moves to the metropolis and lives off the favours of courtesans to pursue his art) became my hero and I began frequenting the boudoirs of famous actresses, I'd laugh to myself remembering that in the past all it took was a SodaStream and a bit of hairspray rock to impress me.

To this day, I still recall the pale canary-yellow E-type Jag parked in Bonnie's driveway – how I coveted that car. I still do. This experience fused something in my developing mind: the idea of women, exotic women, who drove fast cars and lived in big houses, women who doted on me and treated me to things I liked – even if my tastes had only evolved to fizzy drinks at that point. I realised there was a world outside the parameters of my childhood, where women called the shots and took what they wanted. I just hoped that one day they would want me.

Because of my dad's profession, popping in on the rich and famous became a habit. We went to the home of Kevin Godley from 10cc and fell in love with the swimming pool. I spent my time splashing around in there. Years later I found out that Kevin had bought the house directly from Keith Moon, and that it was the same pool he famously drove his Rolls-Royce into. My hedonistic antennae must have picked up on something straight away.

Once, I was taken to Tom Jones's house – Dad was building a swimming pool for him. After we had stopped off in the E-type Jag, the same model as Bonnie's that I'd admired so much, for scampi and chips in a local pub, we made our way to Tom's house. As we pulled into his driveway, Dire Straits were playing on the radio. With the lyrics 'That's the way to do it, get your money for nothing and your chicks for free' pumping out, it was quite a moment. Maybe it mesmerised me, because I never got over the feeling that there was an alternative way to live your life, one that was infinitely more fun than sitting behind a desk or working on a building site.

It seemed like there were these amazing clues all around me left by Fate, pointing me towards my destiny, telling me that the Isle of Wight, with its local Ritzy and dreams of 2.4 kids, was not for me. Not that there was anything wrong with that life; I just knew I wanted to go on an adventure before I settled down. Which is all very well if I had felt like a gigolo in training, but I didn't – I felt like an outsider.

The problem was, I was different, and while 'different' is great once you're grown up, 'different' in school is not pleasant. Not that I cared to conform. I was happy being an outsider. I romanticised my sense of alienation and whittled it into a sharpened weapon in my quest to get the hell out of there.

For a start, while all the other boys had cropped hair (the arty look wasn't fashionable at my Isle of Wight comprehensive school), I had a long, foppish style like my musical heroes. Even more crucially, Mum was a political activist, so I spent weekends on Greenpeace marches, wearing stickers saying, 'Ban the bomb', rather than playing football with the local boys. It's hip to be green now, but in those days wearing sandals and picketing the Japanese Embassy was definitely not cool, even though I enjoyed the excitement of doing something different. Looking back, it was a good training ground for my profession. Walking through the streets of London with my mum and her activist friends, and watching them wave banners and talk animatedly about complex political issues, gave me a great counterbalance to the training of my dad's 'boob antennae'. I learned that women were more than just beautiful creatures put here for men to ogle. I didn't realise it at the time (I was probably too busy reading 1960s science-fiction books), but later on it made it easy for me to grasp the idea that women were only sex objects if they chose to be, because I had seen powerful women using their heads and standing up in public for what they believed in. A sexual persona was a game played for their own amusement, something they could switch off and on. There was a kaleidoscope of facets to their personalities, depending on which angle you were looking from, and what side of themselves they had chosen to display – though of course back then I didn't see their sexual side. Ten years later, when I was entertaining super-successful women who might want to play whore in the bedroom but would kick your butt if you didn't show them respect afterwards, I had the full picture – which was a great advantage.

At school, unlike the other kids, I developed strangely dandyish tastes and obsessions. For me, the perfect Saturday afternoon was spent looking in old curio shops – I was particularly fond of antique fountain pens. While the other kids would get out their Bic biros to take notes, I would produce my ornate antique pen and write in beautiful swirls. It was almost as if I'd been a Parisian dandy in a past life, dedicating hours to writing seductive love letters in elaborate calligraphy, using the curve of my pen to describe in detail the curves of my paramour. My nature tended towards indulgence, opulence and luxury. I hated the idea of quick convenience (a taste I transferred to my sex life years later), whether it was a plastic pen or a tacky TV show. I preferred to take the time to read books, play old records and surround myself with objects of beauty.

At that point, though, when it came to sex I was a slow starter. Or more like a non-starter. My inherently decadent nature manifested itself in music and daydreams, not the pursuit of female charms. Alone, I could create my own fantasy world, but women exposed me for the gawky, confused teenager I really was. I waited until I was seventeen to have my first French kiss. We spent hours in the back row of the cinema, ostensibly watching a movie but mostly kissing, in the extensive manner that only virgins can.

The night I lost my virginity hardly heralded the champion seducer I was set to become. It was upstairs in my simply furnished bedroom, and I performed with all the finesse of a boy who'd rather be out buying records. I decided to give her oral sex – or my own haphazard version of it (long before I'd finessed my technique). She seemed to be pleased with the fumbling explorations my tongue was making, but I'd no idea what a female orgasm sounded like, so she could have been mentally devising shopping lists for all I knew. When she offered to give me oral sex, I felt strangely repulsed, which of course confused her no end. I think I was probably in shock.

Afterwards, we went for a walk on the beach and I strode along in total silence trying to figure out how to extract myself from the situation. Dad gave us a lift home and I ignored her for the whole journey. I never saw the girl again, and weeks later when I told my dad what had happened, and why I had behaved strangely, he was incensed with me. He told me he was disgusted with how I'd treated her. There was my first real lesson: not only was it was important to treat women with respect, but after sex it was doubly so. No matter what occurs in the bedroom, however filthy, impeccable aftercare is a must. To have dirty sex, you must always have whiter-than-white manners. If a woman feels guilty after you've slept with her, then you've failed – good sex should never make anyone feel bad.

My thoughts are interrupted by a beep on my mobile. 'It's me – Ms Antoinette.'

'Hello,' I reply, genuinely pleased to hear from a woman who wouldn't know a sexual regret if it sued her for compensation.

'I'm in a hotel, we've finished for the day, and I'm naked. Well, not exactly *naked* – I'm wearing an extremely fetching pair of handcuffs. I'd like you to come and investigate.'

'I'm on my way,' I almost purr into the phone.

I put Charlotte and my sense of unease about deceiving her to the back of my mind. If one thing can get my thoughts straight, it's dedicating myself to the pursuit of someone else's pleasure.

Chapter 3

Daddy, I Want That One

Of course, women like Ms Antoinette often pick me up and drop me like a plaything, but some clients see keeping a gigolo as a more long-term endeavour. One of my most enduring and intimate relationships is with a lady I shall call Trustfundista – a moniker that is pretty self-explanatory – and yes, this is a woman whose only hard day's work is done on Bond Street. But there is far more to her than that. Anyone can spend money – it takes someone born into wealth to know how to do it with class, and that is something she has in spades – as an heiress, she's the polar opposite of Paris Hilton.

Travelling first class is one thing, but voyaging across the class boundaries is quite another. Becoming a gigolo is like a crash course in how the other half lives – and how to cruise into their life without appearing as if you came through the tradesman's entrance (excuse the pun). It's quite a feat to swap working on building sites for the boudoirs of women who think the working class are just a figment of Charles Dickens's imagination. This is why my dalliances with ladies of impeccable breeding are such a novelty to me, and extremely rewarding. The contrast of where I come from adds that little touch of deliciousness to proceedings. I'm not saying it's a permanent destination; it just makes a unique vacation.

The night I met Trustfundista was a revelation in what 'upwardly mobile' truly means. Her father owns a bank. In Monaco. She buys a £3,000 designer handbag in the way most of us drop a few pennies in a busker's hat: almost like a thoughtless act of charity to the recipient. You see, a woman like Trustfundista actually believes she's doing the designer a favour by carrying their bag on her well-groomed, well-bred arm. But for all that dazzling wealth, and assumed importance, there isn't a trace of arrogance.

On the night we met I was instantly won over by Trustfundista's unassuming charm. It made me realise that if you're born with it, you don't need to shout about it. Without the usual financial insecurities, such privileged people can be very sweet and giving. Not that Trustfundista's insecurities don't surface elsewhere – even a private education can't purchase a perfect psyche. Like all of us, she has issues. As I found out when we moved things to the bedroom.

But before we even got as far as the boudoir, fraternising with Trustfundista proved to be an education in itself. What struck me most during my encounters with her, which often ran parallel to other engagements (a gigolo doesn't pledge fidelity), was the realisation that the sexual secrets of society have barely changed since the dandies and fops of the eighteenth century. Much is made of men and their illicit mores, but women have been merrily securing a handsome face and an experienced bedside manner for centuries – with little or no publicity. Like the society ladies of Paris and London in their decadent heyday, when all the lunches, diamonds and wardrobe finery have been bought, what is left for the modern woman to indulge herself with? Well, a dashing young gentleman of course. And just like long ago, modern women are split into two camps: the working girl made good, looking to spend her hard-earned money, and the society lady born with it, looking to spend her husband's or father's hard-earned money.

But there is one crucial update for the twenty-first century. While the high-society lady who marries a suitable match and outsources her sexual indulgences remains unchanged over centuries (creatures of habit, those aristos), the working girls have evolved from the courtesans of yore, who headed to the city to make their fortune, to the career girls of today, who can flourish on merit alone.

I get to – quite literally – straddle both strata of society. This is the most fascinating aspect of my work – seeing the entire spectrum of women, from every facet of circumstance and class. Like my dandy predecessors, however, discerning who is the better catch is impossible. Even with a pistol to my head I couldn't choose between the earthy energy of a Ms Antoinette and the cerebral class of a Trustfundista. Luckily, I don't have to. My job is to enjoy the kaleidoscopic experience of womankind and tailor myself to each of their circumstances and tastes. Which is what I did with Trustfundista – quite by accident.

A fellow gigolo had invited me out to dinner at Cipriani. I accepted on the unspoken understanding that a rich lady would pick up the tab. When the aforementioned lady walked through the door, the genetic profile of the restaurant went up a notch or ten. She had expensive honey-blonde hair, which swished like the manes of the thoroughbred horses I imagine she grew up riding. Her outfit was exquisite – a tailored cream trench coat with matching light-tan gloves, Chloé shoes and a ridiculously expensive Chanel handbag.

I was instantly relieved I'd worn a suitably stylish outfit – a smart Crombie overcoat, a three-button tweed hunting jacket, leather gloves and loafers, with vintage Emilio Pucci sunglasses resting in my pocket. There was an instant attraction between us. As soon as we were introduced, her eyes twinkled with a naughty glint. Over dinner she commented that I reminded her of the famous French actor Jean-Paul Belmondo. It was a massive compliment and I knew that I was top of her private menu – for dessert.

I tried to keep the conversation as witty and light-hearted as possible. The more playful I was, the louder she laughed and the keener she appeared. I endeavoured to ensure the dinner was as enjoyable as possible for her. Then came the disaster.

The bill arrived. It was huge – a monster that had gobbled its way through the finest dishes and guzzled on the best champagne. In my trade, you learn to brazen these moments without missing a beat, but just then Trustfundista's phone rang and off she swished to answer it in privacy – totally forgetting about a silly little thing like paying the bill. You see, when you're that wealthy, money becomes something of no consequence and it's hard to imagine the dire significance it has for others less fortunate, like a poor gigolo.

Unless the manager was female, I imagined I might genuinely have to wash the dishes and consign my career to the bin. Luckily, my fellow gigolo had just finished a profitable engagement and agreed to sub me, on the understanding I would return the favour when the time came. The incident left a sour taste. Despite my initial attraction to Trustfundista, I decided that I couldn't take it any further. If she didn't understand gigolo etiquette, she obviously wasn't in the market to take one on.

Outside the restaurant, her face lit up on seeing me approach. It was such a sweet, beguiling smile that on impulse I picked her up and twirled her round until she was breathless with giggles. The close proximity of our bodies was electric. When I set her down, she asked if I could call a cab and escort her home. Remembering the bill incident, and not wanting to get involved with someone who wasn't aware of the rules of engagement, I instead suggested that my fellow gigolo take her home as I had business to attend to.

I didn't realise it at the time but I might as well have administered an intravenous love potion there and then. I had unwittingly tapped into her biggest predilection. They say women are subconsciously attracted to men who remind them of their father, and suddenly there I was, the jocular, charming but unavailable man – just like her loving but incredibly busy father. After a lifetime spent trying to get his attention, her efforts instantly switched to getting mine.

No sooner had her cab pulled away, with her looking forlornly out of the back window like a little girl packed off to boarding school, than my phone rang. It was my fellow gigolo, to say that Trustfundista wanted to take us out for dinner again the following night. With the emphasis on *take*.

The next evening was like an action replay – with one major difference. During coffee Trustfundista announced she had to leave early – *business to attend to*, as she rather cleverly phrased it, just to let me know she hadn't missed my slight of the previous evening. Before I could inwardly panic about the bill, she strolled by my chair and tossed a blank signed Coutts cheque in my lap, along with her phone number, telling me to pay the bill and call her later. With that she casually walked out, her expensive heels clicking on the wooden floor. She didn't even look over her shoulder to see the expression on my face. I was smiling. I liked her style. And I would *definitely* be calling her.

Now, almost nine months later (which is the equivalent of a decade in gigolo years), I am preparing to give her the best birthday treat ever – and no, I'm not even talking about *that*. Usually Trustfundista visits her father in Monaco every other weekend by private jet, but this weekend, which also happens to be her twenty-fifth birthday, he's away on business.

'Can I have you for the entire day – and night?' she had asked with the beseeching tone of a lonely little rich girl.

'Certainly. I'll make it the most amazing day ever,' I'd replied chivalrously.

So here I am, waiting outside the Tate Modern to start

the day off on a cultural foot. I had remembered that Dalí was one of her favourite artists, so when I saw the Tate was exhibiting his work, I knew it was the perfect starting point.

'Hello, Golden,' I hear her call and see her waving and smiling sweetly as she steps out of her chauffeur-driven car. I stroll up and peck her on the cheek. French kissing in public would be too tasteless. 'Shall I ask the driver to wait for us?' she asks enquiringly, eager to discover what I have in store for her.

'No, we won't be needing him,' I assure her, putting a guiding hand on her back as we start to walk in the direction of the Embankment. Truthfully, I prefer to take cabs. Living a first-class life is one thing, but having what I perceive as servants is quite another. Over the years I've developed a healthy disdain for buses and Tubes – but a *driver*? Well, you can take the boy out of Woking, but you can't take the working-class roots out of him.

As soon as we approach the entrance to the Tate, she squeals, 'Dalí – my favourite,' and turns round to hug me, overcome with excitement and a hint of gratitude. We walk through and I sign her in as a guest – I have membership, kindly donated by another female companion.

I look at her admiringly as she walks down the glass-sided corridors of the gallery. She has a very European ambience about her, probably thanks to her international education in Switzerland and Monaco. Something about her flawless skin and perfect posture seems to be framed beautifully by the clean lines and muted colours of the gallery, and her innate sense of entitlement is enhanced by the hushed reverence hanging in the atmosphere.

We walk past a striking painting that could represent a golden-yellow, pitted womb, a riddled angel's wing or a monstrously large lump of cheese. I imagine it isn't the latter.

'Oh, that's my favourite,' she says, stopping to examine it carefully.

'*Enigma of Desire*,' I read out from the sign adjacent to the painting.

'It was inspired by his mother,' she tells me, looking at it with a closed expression.

'Was she a fan of Edam cheese?' I joke, to which she responds with shrieks of laughter, attracting the censorious stares of our fellow visitors.

'Sshh.' I stifle my own laughter and gesture for her to stop giggling, which only makes things worse. Instantly she is reduced to a naughty schoolgirl misbehaving on a field trip, with me cast as the authoritarian teacher. 'Actually, why shouldn't we laugh? You know, Dali was a big fan of silent comic films – he was inspired by Buster Keaton and Charlie Chaplin,' I inform her.

She looks at me incredulously. 'I *did* know that, but I'm surprised you did too.'

I feign mock offence. 'Well, I don't store *all* my expertise below my belt.'

'Oh, I wasn't trying to imply—' She breaks off from trying to excuse her assumption and instead gives me a cheeky smile. 'What a bargain, a man who knows his Dali *and* knows how to . . .' Once more she doesn't finish the sentence and treats me to that naughty smile.

I stroke her hair, and laughing, we carry on walking.

I actually know nothing about Dali, but I spent last night doing a little light revision on the subject. This is the kind of service expected from a gigolo, but I never reveal the truth – that would spoil the magic.

'This is already the best birthday ever and it's only just started,' she says, her voice tinged with sadness.

Hard as it is to believe, belonging to the idle rich isn't all it's cracked up to be. Her peers are mostly married to dull men with money, and her more bohemian friends fill their days with earning a living. As far as I'm aware, Prada and Marc Jacobs have yet to design a handbag that dispels loneliness. Shopping as a solo sport isn't as fulfilling as it might seem. That's where a gigolo comes in handy – on standby twenty-four hours a day to amuse, entertain and play with. Worth the price, surely?

Outside the gallery, we stroll arm in arm alongside the river. The water is bathed in sunlight, and a slight breeze makes us grip each other tighter.

'How far are we walking?' she asks.

'All the way to Westminster – to see Big Ben.'

She looks at me quizzically.

'You'll see,' I reply enigmatically.

I'm strangely unsettled by the intimate romance of the situation. It feels like a day to fall in love. But I know our relationship is based on something entirely more pragmatic.

The clock towers above us and we crane our necks to look up. It chimes three o'clock. 'Now count to sixty,' I instruct.

'Why?'

'Just do it,' I assert, in the slightly domineering, fatherly tone she loves.

Together we silently count to sixty, watching the black minute hand of the clock, which points towards the perfect blue of the sky.

'Happy birthday,' I whisper in her ear.

Suddenly it dawns on her. She is genuinely taken aback.
'How did you know?'

'You told me when we first met and I remembered.'

She was born at one minute past three. I keep a note-book on my long-term ladies for moments just like this. A real lover remembers such details as this out of devotion, but a gigolo retains them out of prudent administration. Luckily, it all worked out to the very minute. If she'd needed a loo break before we got here, the romance of the situation might have soured a little.

'Now for the next leg of our adventure,' I say, hailing a black cab.

'Where are we going now?'

'Yours,' I say, finally giving her a long, lingering kiss in the back of the taxi, and pushing my hand up her expensive skirt.

'You are the birthday present that keeps on giving,' she whispers happily.

On the way, I ask the driver to pull over outside an upmarket delicatessen and wait for us. Inside, we browse the aisles like a society couple, stacking our basket with the most expensive, luxurious nibbles we can find.

'I'll prepare you a picnic feast,' I tell her as she swipes her platinum American Express card, otherwise known as the hotline to the trust fund.

'You're such a sweetie,' she exclaims, looking around for someone to carry our shopping bags to the taxi.

'Local delis don't do concierge,' I chastise her, as I grab a bag in each hand.

'You'll be telling me people travel in tubes that run through underground tunnels next,' she says, laughingly having a dig at how removed she is from the real world.

'No, darling,' I tell her with mock seriousness. 'Even cleaners get chauffeur-driven to work, don't you know? Tube travel is just a figment of science fiction's over-active imagination.'

We get back in the taxi and Trustfundista is overcome with an air of pensiveness. 'I'm not proud of being so spoiled,' she suddenly blurts out. 'I do want more out of life than to be a lady who lunches.'

'I know,' I comfort her reassuringly, feeling terrible that my joke has hit a sore spot.

'I'm not saying "poor me" at all – I know how incredibly lucky I am – but a trust fund is like a pair of golden handcuffs. I get so frustrated with the superficiality of my life – the shopping, the spending, the days that drift into one another with no structure – but I can't motivate myself to do more, because the truth is, I don't *have* to. That's what motivates people, isn't it? Survival, the need to pay the rent. I don't have that, so eventually life bores me. Even *I* bore me . . .' She trails off and bites her lower lip.

'Well, you don't bore *me*,' I tell her. 'I find you endlessly fascinating. Believe me, life is not guaranteed to be more fulfilling and interesting lower down the social scale, where necessity boots you out of bed every morning into an underpaid job.' I cut my speech short. I have wandered dangerously out of gigolo territory and into the backyard of my inner being. How very remiss of me. This is panning out to be a most unusual day and I have been caught unawares.

She looks at me with a curious expression on her face, as if an amusing zoo animal has suddenly bared its teeth

and forced the realisation that its origins are far from the
gilded cage it currently parades in.

I kiss her, then say, 'You are perfect as you are.
"Superficially Deep", as *Grazia* would say.'

She laughs and the moment passes, but I am reminded
how hard it is to conduct a relationship with the coldness
of a transaction. Sexual connection needs heat, but such
a flame can fan dangerously out of control. My job is to
maintain the balance.

Trustfundista's apartment is everything you would
expect from a property purchased by a rich father who
simultaneously wants to make an investment *and* make
his daughter happy. Everything is sleek, top of the range
and quietly exudes wealth and taste. The colours are muted
creams and chocolate browns. It could sell for a song in
a minute, but for now it is what Trustfundista calls home.

'Go and change into something *far* less comfortable,'
I tease her. She has bought some fantastically sexy and
indulgent underwear as a birthday gift to herself, with me
as the inadvertent recipient.

Usually the women I entertain like to be in control,
making sure I am very much their plaything, but
Trustfundista is different. She likes me to be in charge,
and to treat her in a very authoritative way – even, dare
I say, in a *fatherly* fashion.

As a last thoughtful little touch to the proceedings, I
put on a CD I have specially prepared for her. It's a
personalised compilation; every song contains a mention
of her name.

With the same regal poise she has when wearing a cashmere twinset, she walks out in black stockings and
suspenders trimmed with pink lace. I have laid out a

beautiful deep-red blanket on the plush living-room carpet
and created a banquet of erotic food, including strawberries and cream.

The first song plays and she hears her name. 'You are
so clever!' She claps her hands and sets herself down like
a graceful foal. Her legs are beautifully long, with narrow
ankles and toned thighs.

We feed each other strawberries and kiss each other,
the sweet taste of the crushed red fruit on our lips. I
unhook her bra, smooth the whipped cream over her small,
pert breasts and then proceed to lick it off teasingly. She
closes her eyes as I begin to remove the rest of her underwear. I am just about to attempt the same tongue-trickery
on somewhere altogether more delicate when she pulls
away and leads me into the bedroom.

She has something different in mind – fun as oral sex
with an edible aperitif is, Trustfundista isn't particularly
into sex games. She likes it straight, vanilla-style. Well, not
quite. There is a little kink in her sexual repertoire, but it
is altogether more cerebral than clitoral.

Inside the bedroom, the blinds are drawn shut. A
king-size bed dominates the centre of the room, its soft
coffee-coloured sheets and pastel cushions adding subdued
decoration. In the centre of the bed a gentleman's suit is
laid out. I can tell even without examining it that the fabric
is extremely expensive. While it is beautifully finished,
the style isn't something I would wear – it's far too old-
fashioned and straight-laced for my taste. It is the cut for
a distinguished, older businessman, not a dandy.

'Put it on,' she tells me with a smile.

As I undress and put on the suit, I notice her hands
are trembling with excitement. The suit fits perfectly. I sense

it was custom-made to my measurements. She lies back on the bed, by this time totally naked, revealing a neat Brazilian. She doesn't have to tell me what she wants; I know. I tell her to spread her legs. She consents instantly. I unbuckle my belt but don't remove my trousers.

The feeling of her naked body under my fully clothed, suited one is extremely seductive and she moans as she pushes her face into my lapel. The sex is straightforward, missionary position. Neither of us utters a word. Then, at the final moment, a little yelp from her punctuates the silence of the room. 'Daddy!'

'Good girl,' I tell her afterwards, and kiss her gently on the forehead.

She gets up and walks into the en suite, and I change back into my clothes. When she returns, wearing a rose-pink silk robe, we kiss each other and smile, but mention nothing about what's just occurred. I instinctively realise that her 'birthday treat' is better left unmentioned.

In the living room, I grab a bottle of champagne from the fridge and we raise a toast.

'Happy birthday,' I say, chinking her glass.

'Well, it is – thanks to you,' she replies, smiling knowingly.

Her phone goes – it's her father, calling to wish her happy birthday. Her present, I overhear, is a cheque for £10,000.

After the conversation, she comes back to the sofa, snuggles up and says, 'You know I'll end up marrying someone exactly like my father, don't you?'

'Will you?' I reply cautiously.

'I'll marry someone rich who works in finance and will keep me in the absolutely luxurious style I'm accustomed to,' she says, with a hint of coldness – almost to put me in my place.

'You could abscond from all this and elope with me,' I tease.

'Wouldn't it be lovely if we could,' she exclaims, her frostiness disappearing. Then, with a hint of regret, she adds, 'But we live in different worlds.'

'I know how to make our worlds collide,' I tell her, stroking her hair.

'I'd love to, but Daddy says he's on the plane on his way over now. His meeting got cancelled so he's decided to take me out for dinner. Shall I get my driver to take you home?'

'No, a cab will be fine,' I say, sipping my champagne and reclining on the sofa with my arm carelessly round her.

'Oh, I insist on my driver taking you home.'

Of course I acquiesce: a gigolo must never descend to bickering over practical arrangements, like a married couple might. Her wish is my command.

But as I'm driven home, with the dusk setting in, I realise that it isn't so much the novelty of *me*, the bohemian antithesis to her normal life, that she is attracted to; it's the novelty of financing me, just like her father finances her. She has the power.

As the car pulls up outside my apartment, a text message beeps through from her. 'Dinner at Nobu next Thursday? Your dear friend x.'

I smile and reply, 'It would be my pleasure. x.'

In fact, I'm sure it will be *both* our pleasures. And while pleasure might not be permanent, it's certainly a good place to start.

Chapter 4

Essex Girls Do It Better

Much as I love spending time with women, I also enjoy hanging out with my gigolo co-workers. Once a month we all get together for a boys' night out – kind of like an unofficial trade union meeting, but with drinking and trading sex tips on the agenda. Tonight, however, my fellow dandy Rochester doesn't want a boys-only meeting – he wants to party.

That's the funny thing about my life. If you work in a bank, do you pop into your local branch and ask if you can process a few money transfers for your own personal amusement on your day off? My guess is you don't. But things are a bit more complex in my line of work. A night clocked off often involves pretty much the same things as a night clocked on. It's lucky I enjoy what I do so much.

Take tonight, for instance. I had planned a quiet night

in, but somehow sitting on the sofa and listening to jazz doesn't quite cut it. The truth is, I feel like a night out. And that's where the problems start – especially with a partner in crime like Rochester on standby.

'C'mon, Golden, let's have a wild night out – like the old days.' It's 9 p.m. and I've just got out of the shower to answer the phone. It's Rochester, already half a bottle of vodka down, begging me to tour the swankiest clubs and bars of the West End with him. He must have read my mind. The trouble is, being an off-duty gigolo is the same as being an off-duty cop – you can't help but still be on the job. And I don't want to burn myself out.

'Think of the girls,' Rochester tells me. 'Beautiful, sexy, *wealthy*, just looking for a couple of handsome good-time boys to come their way,' he says, tongue in cheek.

'Look, I don't need a night on the prowl.' I desperately try to find a towel before the neighbours catch sight of me wearing nothing but a mobile pinned to my ear.

At the start of my career, hitting the town with Rochester kick-started my client list, but now I prefer discreet friendships with added benefits to carousing the town on the make. When I walk into a club, I've usually got my date for the evening, even though, truth be told, I'm a natural at hustling. I am up for a night out – I'm just hesitant because I know the kind of mischief Rochester will get me into.

'I spent all night with Ms Antoinette – I'm exhausted,' I tell him, unconvincingly.

'Why, what did you get up to? I need details,' exclaims Rochester, who loves nothing better than to disclose all of his dirty deeds.

'Sorry, client confidentiality, I'm afraid. The Golden

files are restricted access – well, to you and your big blabber mouth,' I laugh, knowing that what little resistance I had is crumbling. One thing about Rochester, he may be trouble, but he's fun and he's got a good heart underneath his mad, bad and dangerous to know exterior. How can I say no?

'Well, the Rochester files are open to the public and I've got the most amazing gossip about my latest exploits. But you're obviously too tired to hear about them. Never mind,' he responds, calling my bluff. I can almost see him smirking down the phone.

'Well, I'm not *that* tired. If I rest here on the sofa, I'm sure I can muster the energy to listen. Anyway, where have you been for the last few weeks?' I ask, starting to feel extremely curious.

'Oh, well, as you know, I've been hanging out in LA with one of the hottest actresses in Hollywood, but I don't suppose you'd want to hear the details.'

'You can't manipulate me like that. I'm still not coming out. I told you, I'm tired,' I say, intrigued to hear his gossip, but still in two minds.

'O-*K*. Call me if you change your mind.' And with that he puts down the phone.

I walk into the kitchen and open the fridge door. Empty. Then I walk back into the living room and flick on the TV. *Friends* reruns on E4. Again.

I type 'R' into my speed dial. 'OK, you win. Count me in on tonight,' I say to Rochester, who answers his phone in a nanosecond. 'Were you waiting by the phone?' I ask, incredulous.

'Of course. I knew you'd change your mind. It'll be fun – we haven't had a boys' night out for ages. And I can tell you all about what I've been up to – honestly, it's been the weirdest, most incredible few weeks of my life.'

'OK. I can't wait to hear. But promise me, for once, no girls tonight. I really do need a night off. Where shall we start?'

'Boujis. I feel like hanging out there first. See you at ten o'clock.'

I drive down in my vintage Jaguar, a gift from a former client, and pull up outside Rochester's Soho apartment, still bemused at how he manages to afford somewhere in central London. Like all gigolos, he's very secretive about his financial affairs. I can only think he's been helped out by a generous benefactress. But who? Rochester is more short-term fun than long-term commitment. He bounds out of his apartment, literally grinning like the cat that got the cream – and much more besides.

'OK, so tell me everything,' I say, as he slides into the passenger seat beside me.

'I'd been planning to save it for the Dandy Trade Union meeting, but this is too hot to sit on.'

He starts to explain, but I interrupt him. 'Look, before you begin, tell me how you actually met Celebrity Z,' I say, wanting to get the full picture.

'Well, about a month ago I met an American lady who was over for business – and pleasure, as it turns out. When it was time for her to go home, she flew me back to the US with her as a British souvenir.'

'First class, right?' I check.

'No, premium economy. There were no other flights left. Anyway, it turns out she's a top events director so she's literally hooked up with all of the Hollywood elite and has a VIP invite to all the best parties.'

I try to keep my eyes on the road but I can't help staring at Rochester incredulously. What a stroke of luck.

'She's into some pretty wild sex, which of course I was happy to oblige with. Then she tells me she's got a friend who would love to meet me – a girl who loves to party even more than she does. She wants to set up an intro-duction. At this point I am starting to feel like a joint that's getting passed around, but you know me, always up for an adventure. So the next night we go along to a discreet little party in East Hollywood, and there she is. Honestly, I almost choked on my champagne when we were introduced. I mean, the last time I saw this girl she was about twenty foot tall on an Odeon cinema screen.'

'I hope you kept it together,' I admonish. The first rule of gigolodom is never to go all fanboy on a lady.

'Barely. I knocked back my drink, and then as she held out her hand, I grabbed it, pulled her close to me and whispered in her ear.'

I groan with horror. 'What did you whisper?' I ask, expecting the worst.

'"Hello, pussycat." She loved it, and whispered back at me, "Down, boy – save yourself for later," then swished off into the party to mingle. Everywhere I looked there was someone famous, and in the outdoor court the palm trees were back-lit with neon green, framed against the glow of the Hollywood night. Honestly, I felt like I was in a film.'

'So what happened next?' I ask, hooked.

'The lady that brought me there leaves and gives me the address for an after-party and some cash for a cab.

At the end of the night I turn up at this place, near Whitley Heights, where all the stars of the silent screen lived. It's a beautiful old mansion, Spanish-style and pure Hollywood – massive swimming pool and a marble hallway.

'Celebrity Z is there already, waiting for me, with another guy on her arm – a young model. Pretty soon, after pouring us some drinks, she invites us *both* to join her in the Jacuzzi. She strips off in front of us, and let me tell you, that's *no* boob job, whatever the gossip magazines might say. She looks incredible. Then she laughs, flicks her long hair back and beckons us in. The young guy is starting to look a little nervous, so I tell him to grab a bottle of champagne. Then she straddles me and whispers in my ear how much she loves my British accent.'

'What's the young guy doing?' I ask.

'He's looking awkward and nervously swigging on champagne like a total amateur. After about ten minutes I can't hold back: the situation is too much of a turn-on. Then she turns to the young guy and says, "You're next."'

I laugh loudly. I like the sound of Celebrity Z already – she sounds like a woman who knows how to get what she wants.

'The poor thing is either so drunk or so scared that he can't get an erection. She gives him a withering look and tells him to get dressed, then turns back to me, saying, "Well, it looks like you'll have to give an encore."'

'What? And could you?'

'She was *so* sexy it gave me the impetus for a repeat performance. It would be totally unprofessional to let a woman down in a situation like that. Before she left, she said she'd pick me up at noon the next day to head for Miami.'

'Wow – you must have really impressed her,' I exclaim.

'Well, not quite. The smart move would have been to get some beauty sleep in preparation for the next day, but, you know, there was free champagne, young starlets on standby . . .'

'Oh, God, what did you do?' I ask, shaking my head.

'Celebrity Z called at about a quarter to twelve to say she was on the way in her limo and to tell me to wait discreetly on the street. The man who owned the place was some hot-shot director who'd recently made one of those historic epics. Unfortunately, I'd had so much to drink by that point, and was so delirious from lack of sleep, I decided it would be fun to put on a Trojan outfit I'd found in the house and wait for Celebrity Z in the middle of the road, brandishing a life-size replica sword. The limo pulled up, then drove straight past me – actually, it virtually mowed me down. She called from the limo and went ballistic down the line, saying I could "ruin her career", that if the paparazzi got hold of a picture like that it would "destroy" her. Then she hung up on me and I never heard from her again.'

'Idiot – you blew it,' I said. 'You're a disgrace to the gigolo profession.'

He smiled mischievously, 'But it was *so* worth it.'

We pull up outside Boujis and hunt for a parking space. I'm starting to think that bringing the car and banking on a quiet night was a mistake. We eventually find a space and head towards the club.

As we saunter past the doorman, who ushers us straight through to the VIP section with a welcome smile, I resign myself to the fact that the night won't be a woman-free zone. Since the place became the favourite haunt of the young partying princes, Harry and William, by royal command the beautiful, stylish lady count has shot through the roof. The place is packed with so many hot pashmina princesses that Rochester's jaw is virtually doing a waltz around the floor. My look for the evening, as always, on- or off-duty, is refined gentleman with a twist of modern dandy. I'm wearing my favourite PPQ shirt and a classic Ozwald Boateng overcoat. It's a style that the PPs *love*. It's cool but still suggests someone they wouldn't be ashamed to introduce to Daddy (very important, seeing as Daddy is usually the finance director of their lifestyle). As we walk to the bar, I notice a few appraising looks and smile warmly back at the women, who flirtatiously maintain eye contact.

Rochester has attempted a chic makeover for the Knightsbridge leg of our evening tour, and failed. This is a man who could out rock 'n' roll Pete Doherty while wearing a tweed two-piece. His white shirt, which looks to be vintage Dior to me, is in dire need of a good press and the collars and cuffs are ingrained with the residue from the spoils of a million crazy nights out. His skintight trousers, black pencil tie and All Saints cropped leather jacket are screaming, 'What goes on tour stays on tour,' rather than, 'I can work my way through the *Kama Sutra* backwards and still be seen in Sloane Square.' The fact is, PPs just don't get Rochester. Sure, they chat and hang out, but they wouldn't want to get their expensive sheets dirty with such a blatant bad boy. My look, on the other hand, fits in no problem.

I order us two shots of premium vodka, while a large, rotund Hooray Henry type to my right orders a magnum of champagne. He's about fifty and is sweating so much his face looks like it might explode. As he strides across the club, I notice he's sitting in one of the superior seats, flanked by at least three beautiful young women. I grab Rochester and steer him towards the table.

'You want it to be like old times?' I ask him mischievously.

His eyes light up. 'What do you have in mind?' he whispers back.

'Let's play Robin Hood. I think I've found our Maid Marians.' I nod discreetly over to the girls, who are already surreptitiously glancing in our direction.

I sip on my vodka, feeling more relaxed by the second. As always, the rule is to let the women make the first move. Within minutes one of them has brushed past on her way to the toilet and smiled. Then, from out of the crowd bounds over the exuberant daughter of an *über*-famous ageing rock star. If it's legal for her to be drinking, then it's only just so, and she seems extremely inebriated and determined to draw as much attention to herself – and by proxy us – as possible.

'Hello, gorgeous boys,' she announces in a super-confident manner as she bounces up. Now, drunken teenagers are really not what I'm in the market for, but politeness is a must, so I greet her with a charming hello.

'Ooh, haven't you got beautiful hair,' she gushes in a loud voice, coming in close to stroke it.

I smile indulgently and say nothing (laughing to myself that any softness is thanks to the Kiehl's miniatures I liberate from luxury hotels). Embarrassing as the situation is – because by now of course the gaze of the entire club is pointed in our direction – it suddenly starts to work in our favour. The teenager marches over to the nearby table, pulls one of the women we've had our eyes on towards us and demands that she touch my hair. 'Look, stroke it – see how soft it is,' she commands.

The woman's look is a combination of amusement and mild disdain. She looks to be about twenty-seven, with very expensive honey-coloured hair and a discreet watch that looks like it's out of the new Garrard collection: it's worth at least £5,000. She looks straight into my eyes and unexpectedly curls my hair round her fingers in the most seductive manner imaginable.

'Yes, you're right. It is *very* soft,' she concurs with the drunken girl, turning to give her a withering look, her fingers still entwined in my hair.

The wannabe celeb, knowing she's been outclassed, skulks off into the crowd and everyone turns back to their tables or dates.

'I'm off to the bar. Could I get you two gentlemen a drink?' the remaining lady asks.

Rochester is still looking slightly miffed that no one has commented on the tactility of his own mop, but perks up at this attention.

'That would be lovely,' I reply, wondering at the noughties role reversal in which, after essentially being cooed over like a sex object, I'm now negotiating accepting a drink as a subliminal invitation to go to bed.

I hesitate before I name my preferred choice of drink, and in that space she leans in and whispers, 'It's not on my tab, so treat yourselves,' brushing my arm as she pulls away.

I laugh inwardly and reply, 'I think a bottle of Belvedere would be perfect on a night like this.'

She nods imperceptibly and summons me to the bar.

Ten minutes later, as Rochester and I sip on the finest

champagne, I subtly raise my glass in her direction. I don't mind that she's sitting back with her (as it turns out) extremely rich aristocratic husband, because her well-manicured hands have carefully placed her number in my trouser pocket. Robin Hood indeed – robbing from the rich husband and giving one to the poor sex-starved wife.

'I'm bored,' says Rochester impatiently. The PPs are not giving him any attention and he suggests we move on to Paper, where his charms will be better appreciated. I agree.

Outside on the street, the night feels fresh and young.

'Where's the car?' asks Rochester.

'I thought it was right here,' I reply, looking around in a bemused fashion. I'm worried that I've misplaced the only enduring asset of my career.

After ten minutes of searching, we sit on the pavement like a pair of down-and-out gigolos.

'How can you forget where you parked the car?' Rochester asks in an accusing tone.

'Well, it's not like we can drive – we've been drinking,' I retort, kicking myself for not having taken a taxi into town.

As we both sit looking glumly on to the street, almost simultaneously we look towards the other side of the road. There it is, in all its glory. Not that it's much use to us.

'I think we're far more refreshed than we realise,' says Rochester, laughing. I grin in agreement.

I'll have to pick it up tomorrow, I think to myself.

There's no cab in sight, so we set off on foot for Paper. In a weird way, leaving the car behind and walking the streets of South Kensington reminds me of the old days with Rochester. I feel quite nostalgic thinking back to when we were rookie gigolos. It's good to get back to your roots sometimes. Mind you, after about ten minutes it's also good to get into a taxi. We're both looking forward to the next stage of the evening.

Inside Paper, which is glamorously furnished and has rouge-tinted lights dimly illuminating the proceedings, I think to myself what an altogether different scene it is here, despite being only ten minutes' drive from Chelsea, where we've just left. The club is full of wealthy bohemian women, media darlings and the upwardly ascending working class. Rochester is finally getting the attention he craves. As we walk through the crowd, he virtually seems to be secreting an animal musk that mesmerises women. He exudes excitement and danger, and women who aren't enslaved to a financing father can't get enough. The PPs like boys they won't get disinherited for associating with, and quite frankly Rochester would get a shotgun in his face if he ever came to the attention of someone's father. Luckily for me, my persona operates easily in both worlds, with either tribe of women, as it's neither bad boy nor total toff.

Walking through the club, we don't even make it to the bar before we're grabbed – manhandled – and pulled into a dark booth packed with a group of glamorous women. Their sense of style is *very* different to the PPs – much more glamorous, with *lots* of sex appeal. I notice at least two pairs of Manolos straight away and a dress from the new Cavalli collection. These ladies are far more likely to idolise Carrie Bradshaw than Jemima Khan. And they're *lots* of fun. On the table are three ice buckets containing bottles of Moët purchased by their own fair hands. Within seconds we're sat in between them with a glass in our hands. Rochester already has his arms draped round a rather pretty blonde, whose cleavage is putting on such a show it deserves its own round of applause.

A pouty brunette with a cute upturned button nose asks my name.

'Golden Boy,' I reply, smiling and looking directly into her grey-green eyes.

She throws back her head and snorts with laughter. 'Love the name. I just hope you can live up to it.'

The great thing about a stage name is that it helps create your persona. It's like method acting; it makes it far easier to get into character. The name 'Golden Boy' sets the tone for carnal frolics rather than commitment.

'Don't worry, I come with a full money-back guarantee,' I joke, as she puts her hand on my knee.

'You're very good-looking. Why haven't you got a girl-friend?' she asks quizzically, examining me with narrowed eyes.

'You're very beautiful. Why haven't you got a boyfriend?' I reply as a touché.

'Who says I haven't?' she laughs, looking at me very directly. Then she adds, 'No, I'm single. I don't have time for boyfriends – what a prehistoric concept, *a boyfriend*?'

'Are you all single?' I ask, stroking her hand under the table.

'All of us, except Sienna – the blonde with your friend.'

I look over at Rochester, who appears to be lascivi-ously licking the aforementioned girl's neck as she giggles wildly.

'She's planning to end her two-year relationship

tomorrow,' she tells me. 'Tonight is all about celebrating being young, free and – for her – almost single.'

'Well, let's hope she's met the right man to celebrate with,' I reply, looking back over at them apprehensively. Rochester has now moved into get-a-room territory. 'So how long have you been single?'

'A year and a half,' she says, adjusting her scarlet shift dress so the hemline rides up seductively high.

'And are you enjoying it?' I teasingly ask her.

'I'll tell you in the morning,' she says to me, smirking.

I can't help but laugh. 'You've got all the best lines,' I tell her, and put my arm round her.

She leans over me, stage-whispering to her friends, 'I think we should take this party home.'

All five of them agree and start knocking back their glasses of champagne and turning the bottles over in their buckets to indicate they're finished.

'Your friend seems to have taken a liking to Rochester,' I tell my brunette, as the blonde looks at Rochester with wide, blue eyes that look more dangerously smitten than admiring.

'That's the trouble with serial monogamists – they're always on the lookout for their next victim,' she mutters, almost to herself.

As the girls make their way to the cloakroom, Rochester whispers in my ear, 'I've got to go to the toilet. Wait for me by the door.'

I nod. When the girls return with their coats, I usher them outside.

'Where's Rochester gone?' the blonde asks anxiously, looking around.

'I'm afraid he had an urgent call, so he's had to go

home,' I answer. I quickly realise I've made the right choice
when I see her crestfallen face. I can tell she's feeling
vulnerable about the imminent break-up of her relationship and has developed a speed-dial soft spot for
Rochester. He isn't the kind of man you want to have
wild sex with if you're hoping for a cuddle in the morning.
Her friends are savvy singletons looking to hook up, not
fall in love. I don't want to put this girl in a situation
where, on the rebound, she might fall for an unavailable
gigolo – that isn't part of the game. It only works if both
parties metaphorically sign the same disclaimer, and feel
the same way beforehand.

'OK, here's a cab,' my brunette shouts, and we all
pile in.

Two of them squeeze together on the front seat, and I
sit in between the other two in the back. As the taxi drives
off, I turn my head, look out of the rear window and see
Rochester looking around him, bemused, on the pavement. I know he'll figure things out and move on to the
next stage of the party. He plays by the same rules as me,
after all. We can swap stories tomorrow. For now, I'm
concentrating on the matter in hand. I turn my gaze back
to the girls. The two next to me each place a hand suggestively on my knees. I almost gulp, sensing that this is a
situation that could spin out of control.

Later, walking up the stairs of a semi-detached house
somewhere in Essex (I don't catch the whereabouts), I'm
surprised at how suburban the surroundings are. Not that
there's anything wrong with that – it's a really lovely house
– it just isn't the setting I'm used to for debauchery. Tales
of suburban decadence are true, it turns out.

One of the girls flicks on the stereo and a sexy R&B

tune pumps out. This seems to set the right mood and we all start dancing around in the living room, pouring drinks, giggling and generally being silly. After ten minutes of general mayhem and fun, the brunette leads me upstairs, signalling for the others to follow.

The bedroom is littered with the usual debris of girls getting ready to go out. Straightening irons are discarded on the floor, piles of clothes are scattered on the bed, and make-up and perfumes are stacked high on the boudoir-style dressing table. The light is on a dimmer switch, which helps to create a sexy ambience. I feel like I've stumbled into a hybrid of a girls' pyjama party and a sexually charged Ann Summers' soirée. Just as this thought crosses my mind, the brunette – whose house it appears to be – opens a drawer and pulls out a dazzling array of sex toys and kinky outfits. Interestingly, even a skintight PVC Pocahóntas costume, which she proceeds to wriggle into. Two of the other girls, who were previously twirling round the room with me and giggling, race to the cabinet and start claiming outfits as their own.

The blonde is hanging back by the door and I see my brunette walk over to her and whisper, 'Are you sure you want to do this? You can go home.'

A big, filthy grin breaks across her face and she whispers back, 'This is exactly what I need. God knows, I haven't had sex with my boyfriend for about six months – I might tear this guy apart!'

I sit back on the bed, resting on the rose-patterned duvet and surveying the scene. Four drunken, sex-crazed women seem to be conspiring to commit a sexual felony against my person. Life couldn't get better. The brunette calls my name, then winks as she pulls out a spanking paddle and what appears to be bondage tape. I sit bolt upright, wondering what she's planning. As I look around trying to take in my good luck, the girls all walk in a line towards me, telling me that I'm in safe hands. Then, after a brief – and, on my part, not very wholehearted – struggle, they sit me on the dressing-table chair and proceed to lash my arms to it with bondage tape.

The blonde then gets on her knees and, almost tauntingly, starts to unzip my trousers, tussling with the belt buckle to get them undone. Two of the other girls assist her in removing my trousers and underwear. My brunette looks on smiling as I sit there, helpless, with nothing to conceal my huge erection. More is to come. From behind her back she produces a black satin blindfold, which she ties over my eyes. I am totally at their mercy. The sensory deprivation of losing my sight seems to be compensated for by a heightened awareness around the groin region.

'OK, Golden, we're going to play a little game with you,' my brunette informs me, as I sit in a state of excitement, my feet digging into the soft carpet. 'It's our own personal sexual Olympics, with you as the judge, and us four as the competitors. Each of us girls will perform oral sex on you in our own unique style, and you have to guess who's who and then declare the winner.'

'It sounds like *Blow Job Idol*. I hope I'm not cast as Simon Cowell,' I joke, before one of the girls puts her hand over my mouth and informs me that I can't speak or give instructions during the competition.

Unable to see, the next thing I feel is a soft tongue doing its very best to scoop the title. I moan and then try and gather all my gigolo powers to ensure that the competition isn't cut short by an unexpected commendation from myself. That would be too uncouth.

Finally, the last girl gets to work. By this time I'm in such a pleasure vortex I'm finding it difficult to remember how many have been before and, frankly, what my name and address is. This girl has got a technique that most high-class hookers would give their expensive boob jobs for – a mixture of fluttering tongue movements on the tip and take-no-prisoners deep throat. It's too much. I'm all over the place and have begun to lose my professional cool. (After all, these are *exceptional* circumstances.) 'The winner,' I shout hoarsely, convinced it's my cheeky brunette.

The blindfold is slipped off and I see the blonde, still on her knees, grinning in a highly saucy way in front of me. She turns to the other girls, saying, 'See, I've still got it!' Her friends fall about laughing. The blonde starts to pull off the tape – not even that gently – then leads me into another room, announcing, 'Now it's time to claim my prize and have some *real* fun.'

As I'm led to the other bedroom like a show pony, I turn round to see them taking pictures on their mobile phones, giggling and clapping.

I believe sexual equality died at that very moment, with womankind declared the winner of the battle of the sexes and taking me hostage as a trophy.

Much later the brunette calls me a taxi and gives me a crisp £20 note to cover my fare. The shock of the cold air in the black night gives me a sharp moment of clarity. A smile spreads slowly across my face. Did that really happen? I wonder to myself.

As the cab drives through the deserted streets of suburbia, lit only by the homely yellow glow of streetlamps, it becomes harder and harder to believe what has just occurred behind closed curtains.

I switch on my mobile. I've a missed call and a message from Rochester wishing me good luck and telling me about an after-party he's found. I've also got a message from Charlotte. I delete Rochester's message, then listen to Charlotte's voicemail, smiling to myself as she suggests we meet up to work on a piece of music together. I've had the most amazing night, but this makes me feel happy in an altogether different way. Suddenly I can't wait to spend time with her, playing piano and writing music.

The taxi pulls up in Kensington and I get out, hand over my money and look around for my car. Then I see the empty gap. It's been towed. Every silver lining has a cloud, I think to myself, and grimace at the thought of the £250 penalty charge.

No lady wants to deal with my parking fines – that's something strictly for the confines of marriage. There's more likelihood of a benefactress buying me a new sports car than helping to release this one from the pound. I sigh and start to walk in the direction of home. The night has been a fun diversion, but I vow to stick to more profitable endeavours in future.

Chapter 5

Sex and the Celibate Gigolo

I've been thinking about sex solidly for the last three days, but there isn't a lady in sight. And no, I haven't been locked in my bedroom like some rampantly hormonal teenager having long, philosophical conversations with my right hand. I'm on the gigolo equivalent of a training course.

I'd felt for some time that the 'Other Skills' section of my CV needed updating, but it took a long lunch with one of my gigolo icons to hit upon a new technique for me to develop. So here I am learning tantric sex.

It all started a week ago when I met Shiva, my gigolo guru, for lunch at the Little Earth Café, a vegetarian eatery housed in an exclusive yoga centre on Primrose Hill. Not my normal choice of venue; I'm an expert in lots of positions, but none of them is named 'downward dog'. In a strange twist of Fate, however, the man who introduced me to the gigolo way, and helped transform me from a gawky teenager into an experienced playboy, has now swapped a life of sex for one of spirituality. I still find it hard to believe that the man who once espoused the pleasure principle to me has now been celibate for over two years. And I'm talking *properly* celibate, not just the 'if I don't mention it, it doesn't count' type of celibacy common among my other colleagues who try to go cold turkey.

I must confess the longest I've gone without sex is a week, and then only on account of a terribly incapacitating bout of flu. You see, for me this is far more than a career; it's a calling – I consider my love of women and sex a spiritual pursuit in its own right. Shiva disagrees. He now talks reverently about the 'sanctity' of sex. He's sworn off sleeping with women until he's found his 'sexual soul mate'. And when he finds her, he plans to practise strictly tantric sex – a communion of two bodies dedicated to one aim: enlightenment. Every time we meet, Shiva tries to lead me to what he believes is the right path. I think Buddha himself would have a hard time convincing me to wear a 'True Love Waits' wristband.

'Sex is far more than just a physical act – it's a spiritual connection too,' Shiva tells me, as he stirs his fresh mint tea with a silver spoon.

I look suspicious as a goat's cheese and quinoa salad is placed in front of me by a beatific blonde wearing ink-blue sweatpants with 'Om' embroidered on the back. The salad tastes surprisingly good and I smile at her to say thank you.

'I just don't see why sex has to be about saving your soul,' I reply to him, sipping on my beetroot and carrot juice. 'Isn't it enough for it to be just a source of primitive, unbridled pleasure?'

'No, that's where you're wrong,' he answers, waving his spoon at me in a slightly didactic fashion, looking ever more evangelical by the second. I trust I'm not about to be stabbed to death by a spoon-wielding yoga convert in a spiritual centre. The irony would be too much. 'You're a typical victim of the conspiracy to conceal the true meaning – and power – of sex,' he carries on preaching. 'To speak on your level, tantric sex is a broadband connection to a spiritual high, and casual sex without love is like using a faulty landline. OK, so you might come through normal sex, but during spiritual sex the blissed-out feeling of peace and love is often delivered by a ten-minute orgasm that will literally blow your – and your partner's – mind.'

'Carry on,' I say eagerly, my interest suitably roused by his claim. A ten-minute orgasm? I know a lot of ladies who would love to be on the receiving end of that.

'OK, here's the deal,' he explains. 'Because of the innate power in meaningful sex, authorities have tried to suppress it for centuries. That's why religion says sex is a sin. By creating this duality, whereby hedonists have sex with no spiritual context and religious puritans remove the pleasure, the truth has been concealed from the population. Eastern religions are far more open to reconciling the pleasurable and spiritual sides of sex – just look at the *Kama Sutra*. When you combine the two strands, the results are explosive, both physically and spiritually.'

'Well, I'm liking the sound of hot sex as the route to heaven,' I say, 'but tell me more about this ten-minute orgasm.'

Just as we get to the good stuff, a lithe yoga teacher

interrupts our conversation. 'How lovely to see you, Shiva,' she says, hugging him as he stands to greet her. 'Are you taking the kundalini workshop next weekend?' she asks, with a gently melodic inflection to her voice.

'I certainly am. I can't believe such an amazing teacher is coming over from LA – it's going to be incredible.'

'I know. I can't wait! We should have a herbal tea afterwards. Will you have time?'

'Definitely – that's a plan. See you next week,' confirms Shiva, as the yogini walks away, revealing the most incredible physique I've ever seen.

'She's amazing,' I tell him. 'Could she not be your soul mate? How can you associate with all these beautiful, spiritual-seeking women and not, well, want to seek a bit further with them.'

'Look, Golden, this is your problem. You're obsessed with sex.'

'I'm not, I'm just *normal*,' I say, trying to defend myself.

'So you think it's normal to dedicate your life to pleasuring women who pay you in kind?'

'Not normal maybe, but definitely desirable. It hardly merits the UN sending a peace-keeping mission to my underpants.'

'I'm being serious, Golden. Are you really fulfilled?' he asks, looking at me with an earnest expression.

I can feel the smile fading from my lips. That's a tough question to answer over afternoon tea, but it is something that has increasingly been on my mind recently. My adventures with Trustfundista – as with all my clients – will end with her driving into the sunset with someone else, so the thought playing on my mind is, where do I find the woman *I'll* sail away with? And is this even possible? Can a gigolo ever really reform his ways, and would he want to? That said, I haven't seen much demand for geriatric gigolos recently. My looks won't last for ever, and what do I do then? Is there a retirement home for men like me? I doubt it. It seems ridiculous that old age is casting a shadow over me in my twenties but these are the realities of my profession. Like many despairing women before me, I realise, whatever they might say, no one is interested in a good personality alone. When my looks fade, so does my gigolo lifestyle. If anything, that's the time to go to the spiritual side – and not a moment before.

'Is anyone *really* fulfilled?' I reply to Shiva, trying to avoid the question.

'Not all the time maybe, but I think you know when you're on the right path to becoming fulfilled,' he says thoughtfully.

His question has aroused similar feelings in me as my exchanges with Charlotte have. 'I admit I do have doubts,' I concede. I notice I'm unsettled enough to be tracing my finger round the rim of my glass. 'My problem isn't that I'm unhappy in the present, it's that I worry what will become of me in the future. But don't your Zen masters say we should live in the present, not the future?' I ask.

'Of course. To unlock the secrets of the universe, you need to live in the moment, but you also need to discover the *truth* of the present moment. Are you being true to yourself? Is there truth in your life?'

Again, another difficult question to answer, I ponder to myself. In a sense there is more truth to the way I live my life than people conducting normal relationships. Yes, there is a lot of artifice in the situations I get myself in, designed to conceal the sometimes unpalatable reality of what's happening, but there's also a great deal of honesty. It's a simple exchange, with no promises for the future and no recriminations about the past. In taking pleasure from each other, candidly, with no illusions, we are totally in the moment. For me, that is more honourable than false declarations of love and broken promises of fidelity. A gigolo will never break your heart, because he has never sworn to treasure it above all else. But he *will* deliver on his promise for pleasure.

'You're looking thoughtful,' Shiva observes. 'Have I struck a chord?'

'Yes, but maybe not in the way you intended. As Oscar Wilde said, "The truth is rarely pure and never simple."'

'Look, I'm talking from personal experience here. You have to leave this lifestyle behind you, otherwise it will destroy you. Even a gigolo has to settle down at some point.'

'You're starting to sound like a match-maker,' I laugh. 'You'll have me registered with the marriage bureau before I know it. Listen, I do take your point. I just don't think I've reached that stage yet. But I'm definitely interested in hearing more about spiritual sex.'

'We'll get to that. I just want to check that you're OK. I've been hearing some worrying stories about Rochester on the gigolo grapevine.'

'Well, there's a man who wouldn't know spiritual sex if it mugged him in a church,' I admit. 'We're all worried about him, but he's determined to live the rock 'n' roll dream. I don't know what could save him now.'

'The love of a good woman,' replies Shiva, looking pointedly at me.

'You're probably right,' I muse, feeling strangely relaxed by the peaceful atmosphere of the yoga centre, 'but where is he going to find her? And frankly, who'd have him for keeps? He's too wild.'

'Maybe I need to meet up with him,' ventures Shiva.

'It might be worth a try,' I concede. 'I might mention it at our next gigolo get-together. But let's talk about the wonders of tantric sex. You've got me intrigued.'

'I really think you should try it. If you can't be celibate, at least you're in the perfect position to become an enlightened gigolo, using sex to create the highest connection possible. Think of your clients as being like the dragon ladies of ancient China, women who perfected the practice of esoteric bedroom arts – using a well-trained stud like yourself to help them gain lustrous looks and longevity.'

'Tell me more.' I'm loving the sound of sexually demanding dragon ladies. This is a spiritual doctrine I can definitely subscribe to.

He waves the yogic waitress over and orders a pot of green tea for us to share. I don't know how much more healthy refreshment I can take, but to find out secret bedroom techniques of ancient China, it is more than worth it.

'Well,' he begins, 'the first thing to understand is the different nature of the male and female orgasms. When men orgasm, they lose life-giving essences and deplete their energy. When women orgasm, they generate *more* of their life-enhancing essences – gifts they pass on to the man. So the first rule of sex is to make sure you give a woman an orgasm, ideally multiple ones. That way, any essences you lose are more than compensated for by the miracle essences she is creating.'

'So what you're saying is that women are sexually superior?' I ask with enthusiasm.

'I suppose I am. That's why macho men try and put

women down – because deep down they know, at least when it comes to sex, they're at the mercy of women.'

'That makes sense,' I say, thinking about the oafs I've met who treat women with contempt because secretly they feel inferior.

'Men need to restrict – or at least delay for as long as possible – their ejaculation and focus on female pleasure instead,' Shiva continues.

'That's already a gigolo commandment,' I comment. 'No woman wants to go to bed with a man whose technique amounts to three shoves and a squirt.'

'There's a famous legend in China about the Empress Wu Tze-Tien, who was notoriously sexually rapacious. After her husband died and she took the throne, she proceeded to work her way through all the virile men at court to cultivate the sexual energy that kept her young and beautiful. After tiring of these suitors, she asked her generals to comb the land for a man who could really satisfy her. Eventually a general came back with a forerunner of the modern gigolo, who pleased her so much she barely let him out of the bedroom for two years.'

'What happened to him?' I ask, curious to know the fate of my ancient predecessor.

'He died of exhaustion, and she retired to a mountain in mourning, with four hundred young men to attend her,' Shiva laughs as he finishes the story.

'I can think of worse ways to die,' I observe with a grin.

'Here's a book for you to read, *The Tao of Health, Sex and Longevity*, but I warn you, until you know what you're doing, you have to practise celibacy. Can you do that?'

'I've never even contemplated trying until now,' I admit,

'but I'll give it a go. God knows what this could do to my reputation, though, if anyone finds out.'

'When you master the art of giving ten-minute orgasms, I'm sure your reputation with be greatly enhanced, not ruined,' Shiva points out, not unreasonably.

'Very true. Right, I'm off home to start on my homework,' I say, flicking through the pages of the book. 'And you're sure I can't study by practising on someone? I was always best at practical exams.'

'No!'

Back at home, lounging on my bed, surrounded by books on the subject (I took a detour by an alternative bookshop), I sigh, resigned to the fact that the life of a celibate gigolo is not going to be quite as eventful as a practising one. I pick up my phone, hoping that Trustfundista will call, then put it back down, determined at least to serve three days of my sentence. A minute later, as if by psychic intuition, a message beeps through from her: 'Want to do Nobu again tomorrow? x.'

I hesitate as I reply. It goes against my nature, if not my whole work ethic, to say no. I want to comply but instead find myself typing, 'Sorry, busy with a special project. Will be in touch when it's finished. Kisses.'

Instantly a rejoinder comes through: '????'

'I'm sworn to secrecy,' I reply cagily. 'I'll tell you all when it's over. x.'

I can almost feel her annoyance crackling through the telephone line, but given her daddy fixation, I know it will only fuel her affection for me. Luckily, Ms Antoinette has been too busy to see me for weeks. She wouldn't have tolerated such an absence without leave.

The fading light of the afternoon sun entices me to sprawl on my bed like a basking tomcat. I try to practise the deep-breathing exercises I've been reading about, but instead I find myself gazing at the frothy clouds passing by, lost in old memories. Once more my thoughts drift back to my transition from building sites to boudoirs – and the pivotal part Shiva played in my makeover from man at work to man of the world. Although my formative influences had laid the groundwork for my metamorphosis, I doubt I could have crossed the boundary without a helping hand from my gigolo guru.

In the beginning, my days and nights were polarised between two worlds. By sixteen I'd left school in the Isle of Wight, not knowing what I wanted to do with my life. I loved music, but at this point it didn't occur to me that studying it at college was an option. In the meantime, I decided to join the family business, working on building sites and doing the manual jobs nobody else could be bothered with. I'd wake up at six o'clock, bleary-eyed, blinking at the alarm clock in disbelief and drag on a pair of tattered old jeans, a scruffy T-shirt and a pair of roughed-up, ancient trainers. I'd look in the mirror as I left and cringe: my appearance was that of an embryonic white-van man – everything my decadent inner life railed against. Working on the site was really demoralising: my tasks were always of the most menial nature – anything that didn't require particular skill or strength. Often it was just lugging wheelbarrows of cement around or carrying bricks. Sometimes I would be able to undertake something more complex, like painting doorframes. I'd treat the knots in the wood with a special solution and then paint them white. The worst was when I graduated to loft insulations;

the fibreglass was incredibly itchy and I had to wear a mask, which left me hot and sweaty at the end of the day. It almost broke my spirit.

My workmates were good people, just not what I aspired to be. During breaks they'd sit around boasting about 'shagging birds'. Ironically, I hated that kind of talk. I felt it demeaned the delicate relationship between men and women, and what sex was capable of being. Instinctively I already knew that there was more to what went on in the bedroom than just 'shagging'. Looking forlorn in my tatty, dirt-stained clothes, with my foppishly curtained hair at odds with my attire, I'd sit in the foreman's office to eat my packed lunch in solitude. Inside, left in peace with music compositions drifting through my head, I'd slip into my own dream world, although my reverie would often be shattered by the boss. He'd poke his head round the door and jibe at me mockingly, saying, 'There ain't no pianos in here, son. Get back to work.'

Even though I knew becoming a builder could be a lucrative career, working as a manual labourer made me feel like primitive man, and I was desperate to evolve. By night my world transformed into an entirely different place, thanks to Shiva. We were introduced by one of my family and he instantly sensed I was one of his kind, but in desperate need of liberation, not only from my job, but also my ineptitude with women. He was four years older than me, exceedingly handsome and had an innately winning way with the opposite sex. Our evening adventures would involve sports cars, beautiful women, cool parties and the intangible air of endless possibilities. I could almost live my life vicariously through him.

For me, it was beyond exciting to be part of his world.

One night he picked me up in his sports car with the most incredibly beautiful, worldly woman by his side. She had long, dark hair and exotic looks. She was a successful photographer, independent, fiery and *very* forward. Her manner was overtly sexual towards him, caressing him and teasing him with innuendo-loaded suggestions. For a shy, sweet sixteen-year-old like me, it was quite an eye-opener. I sat in the back of the car, rooted to my seat, barely able to say a word, not knowing how to join in the banter.

At a party later that evening, I had my first encounter with the kind of experienced, liberated women I desired. After drinking whisky for the first time ever, I ended up reclining awkwardly in bed between two women, who were teasingly flirtatious – obviously enjoying that fact that I was awestruck. With cringe-worthy clumsiness I tried to talk to them. There was no sexual activity; we were just literally all lying in bed together. I had no clue how to adopt an easygoing banter and instead came out with over-sincere lines. At one point Shiva walked in and heard my embarrassing efforts at seduction. He nearly fell about laughing, with the girls joining him in his mirth. Afterwards, he said it was like watching a game of tennis – with the girls playing me for their own amusement. I was mortified to think they'd been making fun of me and became determined to understand the rules of seduction.

The next day, after work, Shiva took me out for a coffee and promised to initiate me. My first lesson was about my demeanour: I learned that I was far too serious and intense. 'Make them laugh' was his motto. He stressed the importance of being easygoing and fun. 'Being serious implies you take *yourself* seriously,' he would say. 'Take yourself out of the equation and entertain them instead.'

It was quite a wake-up call. Being a teenage boy, wrapped up in myself, I'd naturally seen the world as revolving round me. It was a revelation to realise that I had to stop thinking about my own feelings and instead focus on someone else's.

Watching him in action was a lesson in itself. He had bouncy brunette curls and, as an avid surfer, a naturally laidback manner. Around women he was charismatic, and his extrovert nature and easy laugh made him magnetic to women. With him they knew they were guaranteed a fun time. He explained that that was the magic formula. Serious relationships were hard work. The key to being a gigolo was making sure the lady was having fun 100 per cent of the time.

At first, trying to fine-tune my persona, I often misunderstood his instructions and would play class clown. 'Make them laugh, don't act like an idiot,' he chided. 'Women want a man with sex appeal *and* a sophisticated sense of humour,' he would lecture. 'Watch how I behave.'

Like anyone with a true talent, he always made seduction appear effortless. He had naturally good energy socially and sexually. The only way to describe him was as an all-round good guy. 'Women don't want a cad,' he would explain to me. 'It's disrespectful and demeaning to her *and* you.' I came to understand that even the most casual encounter must be conducted with integrity and finesse. Women are happy to be candid about sex – they just don't want to be conned.

For two years I continued my education – by day as a

trainee builder and by night as a trainee gigolo, embracing my hedonist's curriculum with relish. At eighteen, emboldened by my after-dark adventures, I announced I was off to study music full-time. I was in love with two things – music and women. I hoped the bohemian environs of the music conservatory would bring me closer to both. The day I left, Shiva waved me off like a proud parent, wishing me luck as I made my way in the world. But it proved harder to succeed in the rarefied world of jazz music than it was to seduce women. So I focused more on the talent that paid the most dividends.

Years later, at the height of my own gigolo success, I received a call from my former guru announcing he was forsaking the pleasures of the flesh for a spiritual life. He had secretly fostered spiritual leanings thanks to his love of surfing and its communion with nature, but his final epiphany came about after he broke the number-one gigolo rule: he fell in love. In the real world of emotions, 'make them laugh' isn't enough to sustain the good times. He had his heart broken, did a lot of soul-searching and decided it was now time for him to retire from a sensual pursuit of women and wait for his soul mate to appear. 'After being in love, you just can't go back to being a playboy,' he explained to me when I reacted with shock to his news. Finally I understood. Even though it wasn't yet a concept I could embrace.

Maybe that was the moment when I lost my certainty about gigolodom – a little fraction of doubt began to creep in. I could still enjoy the spoils of my profession, but in the back of my mind I knew there was a moment when it all had to end.

★

For three days I alternate tantric-breathing exercises and reading research material. I also spend a lot of time thinking about how Shiva set me on the gigolo path – and is now trying to steer me off it.

During my self-imposed internment, my phone is burning with the wrath of Trustfundista, who is infuriated at my refusal to give her the attention she demands. I try to be as soothing and apologetic as possible, but nothing – bar putting in a personal appearance in her bedroom – will suffice. It is a sharp reminder that the whole appeal of having a daddy-substitute plaything is the ability to dictate my schedule, rather than be at the mercy of it.

On the third day of my temporary retirement her patience snaps – just as mine is seriously bending. Knowing my sartorial weakness, she couriers over one of the most beautifully crafted Dior suits I've ever seen, which fits perfectly. I lay it out on my sofa, admiring my bounty, and look around my apartment. The floor is scattered with books bearing strange-sounding titles, and cups of half-drunk Earl Grey tea are perched on the table as if I'm a student working on my final thesis. I miss Trustfundista's high-pitched laugh, the taste of champagne and, well, the opportunity to road-test my newfound skills. I'm not made for the life of a studious hermit.

Out of the corner of my eye I notice a note peeking out of the pocket of the suit that has been gifted to me. I have a good idea what it will say – and I know my power to resist is seriously wavering.

'My driver is picking you up at three this afternoon. We're going on a shopping trip. I won't accept no for an answer!' I read, unable to contain the smile spreading over my face. My time as a celibate gigolo has come to its conclusion. Trustfundista hoped to manipulate me by appealing to my weakness for expensive clothes, but the truth is, she doesn't have to. I would be more than happy for her driver to deliver me directly to her bed.

A gigolo must live up to his reputation, so I immediately send a text saying, 'Looking forward to our shopping expedition. x.'

An hour later I'm lounging happily in the back seat of a Mercedes and contentedly looking out of the window, as the silhouettes of central London whizz by. I soon arrive at my rendezvous.

'Well, hello. Lovely to make your acquaintance again,' Trustfundista greets me in a good-humoured, teasing tone.

'Before you chastise me, you might want to hear what my top-secret mission was,' I say with a grin. She gives me a quizzical look, and I lean in to whisper, 'I've been studying the art of tantric sex. I'm afraid I'll be testing my technique out on your good self later tonight.'

Her eyes widen with disbelief. 'Tantric sex? Really?'

'I promise,' I reply. 'I can now officially "do a Sting".'

She laughs, then strokes my cheek, saying mischievously, 'In that case I may have to postpone our little shopping trip.'

'Don't be hasty,' I reply with mock seriousness. 'I'd take this opportunity to buy the new Dior Samourai handbag before I sexually enlighten you into consumerist cold turkey.'

'That's quite a promise – I hope you can keep it!'

Two hours later we are locked away in her bedroom and I am taking my role as sexual sensei *very* seriously. The room is lit by vanilla-scented Diptyque candles (I drew the line at incense), and the sounds of waves gently breaking on the shore is drifting out of the state-of-the-art sound system.

Trustfundista is naked, save some essential oils I have massaged all over her body. She is sitting astride me and I have my hands on her hips so that I can slow her movements down. We are focusing on synchronising our breathing, emptying our minds and feeling the sensation of pleasure throughout our bodies. The rule is no sexual fantasies – we must concentrate on being present to the moment.

'Oh, my God, it's starting,' Trustfundista starts to moan, making the most velvety noise I have ever heard. It is quite different from any sound she's made before.

'Don't fight it,' I urge her. 'Submit to the feeling.'

'I'm trying . . . Oh, God!' Her moan is almost guttural.

I am amazed at how much control I have over myself, and don't have to resort to counting sheep to delay my denouement. I must admit I've never enjoyed myself quite so much.

All of a sudden Trustfundista's moaning stops; it is replaced by an intense look of concentration – almost like she is clinging to a cliff edge with just one perfectly manicured nail. Her fingers grip into the side of my hips and words form on her lips but never make it out.

I watch awestruck underneath her as this continues for the next ten minutes, a time span that feels like an eternity of pleasure. Then her facial expression suddenly transforms, as if a white light has been shone from inside, illuminating her features and softening the lines of her face. It is a look of total serenity – and total surrender. The most enchanting, low hum of an outward breath reverberates around the room as she reaches orgasm nirvana. I cannot delay myself any longer. We come together, like a pair of highly trained bedroom Buddhas.

'I've just seen God, and He's wearing nipple tassels,' I joke, to break the enormity of the moment.

Trustfundista lies back on the pillow and lolls with a look on her face I haven't seen since Marc Jacobs opened his London store. 'That was simply beyond words. I actually felt like I was falling through trapdoors into some endless abyss of orgasmic pleasure. Every part of me was consumed with it – I think even my elbow found its G spot.'

I laugh and run my fingers through her tousled hair. 'Are you *still* cross I took a three-day sabbatical?' I ask with a wink.

'No word of a lie, that was the best investment of time ever made,' she replies, still slightly flushed and breathless. 'It's the biggest breakthrough since Einstein discovered his theory of relativity.'

'Well, I'm like a cutting-edge sexual scientist, experimenting with the alchemy of orgasms,' I laugh.

'More than happy to be your laboratory guinea pig,' Trustfundista sighs contentedly.

Once more I realise my gigolo guru is a step ahead – even speaking from beyond the grave of celibacy – when it comes to knowledge of the bedroom. I am just grateful to have studied with such an accomplished master.

Chapter 6

Hot Sex, Hollywood-Style

Today is shaping up to be a *very* good day in the office, so to speak. I'm in New York, on the right side of the VIP rope, indulging in the kind of celebrity access people without a high-powered Hollywood agent can only dream of. Getting extremely up close and personal with the super-famous – the aristocracy for the new millennium – has to be one of the best perks of the job.

'Lower East Side,' I instruct the taxi driver, who is failing to live up to the reputation of fast-talking, hardbitten NY cabbies. 'It's a place called the Dark Room,' I add, as he returns a less than eloquent grunt.

Half an hour earlier I stepped off a British Airways business-class flight filled with an intuitive expectation this would be an out-of-the-ordinary adventure – even by my own standards. Now I say 'intuitive' because on the surface of things the possibilities of the situation are limited. I have been flown over not as a gigolo, but merely as a walker. A dear friend, almost like my dowager aunt, has requested that I escort her around New York Fashion Week. The expectation is that I will decorate her arm on the front row, entertain her and shield her from the horror of making a solo entrance that requires soliciting small talk with virtual strangers.

The booking couldn't be more perfect – or have come at a better time. Not only is our relationship uncomplicated by the nuances of sexual engagement, but I also feel a breath of fresh air from the self-generated smog of the London scene is needed.

My lady companion, whom I shall call 'Aunt', is a sharp, intelligent woman in her mid-forties whose natural beauty has developed over the years into a sophisticated allure. She belongs to that strange category of the once-famous whose star, after ascending, slips into a holding pen somewhere on the far side of the A-list, rather than descending back down to the dregs of the D-list: an artist who, once the illuminating flashbulb of fame fades somewhat, goes back to getting on with being fabulous. We were introduced by music contacts and instantly struck up a friendship.

So here I am, on my way to meet her, looking out of the window at the exhilarating verticality of the city streets, having what can only be described as a 'New York moment'.

As we pull up, I see Aunt standing on the pavement smoking a cigarette with the kind of regal worldweariness only people who've been there and *really* seen it all can manage.

'Hello, darling,' she cries, as I step out of the car and kiss her on both cheeks. There's a chill in the air and her hands are ice cold as she embraces me. 'We have such a fun time ahead of us,' she tells me, as I grab my luggage from the trunk of the car and ask the driver to pick us up in an hour. 'I need to rest soon, but not before we have a drink together,' she says, putting her arm round me and walking me to the bar.

Inside, the bar is achingly hip, small and dark, and is flirting with the glamorous side of sleazy. We order two bourbon on the rocks, chink glasses in a toast and then knock them back. The barman produces two more without being asked. These we take slower.

'We'll save the champagne for later,' she whispers laughingly in her husky voice.

'So what's the plan?' I ask, leaning on the bar with a smile.

'Marc Jacobs. He called and invited me to his show. He's such a darling. I can't wait to see the new collection.'

'Fantastic. You know I'm a big fan of his too,' I say, anticipation rising in me.

No matter how many times you attend, New York Fashion Week has a frisson all of its own. To be front row at Marc Jacobs is the fashion equivalent of the Pope popping round to say evening prayers with you. I look at Aunt's face, studying the beautiful line from her perfectly straight nose round to her fashionably arched eyebrows and wonder what it must be like to have a hotline to the likes of Marc Jacobs. If physicists want to prove the existence of parallel universes, they need only travel among the elite of the fashion and enter-tainment industries to validate their theories. I am just glad to have the opportunity to peek behind the celestial curtain.

The taxi arrives, so we leave the bar and head back to the hotel to freshen up.

'OK, I'll see you in the lobby in an hour,' says Aunt, waving as the elevator doors close in front of her.

I'm left to check in by myself. It feels incredibly strange as I'm shown up to my room and the sumptuous double bed I'll sleep in alone. Solitude is not something a gigolo encounters often, especially not in the kind of swanky hotel room he can't afford to finance himself. But sexual liberation is as much about women choosing to have platonic relationships as it is indulging in sexual pleasure.

With an hour to go, and no lady to please, I'm slightly at a loss as to what to do with myself, so I hang up my suit to get rid of any creases and hop in the shower. Afterwards, lounging on the bed and feeling slightly lonely, I decide to text Charlotte. We've arranged to meet up to work on some music together, so I write her a little message about my impressions of New York and how they could inspire us musically.

She replies almost instantly: 'Sounds good. Can't wait for our session! x.'

I try not to smile at her inadvertent use of sexual innuendo. I know it would never occur to her that it could be read a different way, which I find quite endearing.

Sitting on the bed, the thought of having her here by my side suddenly pops into my mind. I instantly dismiss it. If I were the type of man who had that sort of relationship, I wouldn't be in New York enjoying the opulent spoils only available to the elite. The romantic image of us being together doesn't feel quite so charming when visualised in my cramped little London apartment. Even so, the thought lingers.

Half an hour later the hotel phone rings. 'Your car is downstairs,' the concierge says with android efficiency. I head towards the door and check my reflection quickly as I walk out. Knowing what to wear when attending a fashion show is just as hard for men as it is for women. My cream two-button herring-bone suit looks very dapper. I think it hits just the right note – eye-catching, fitted, but nothing that will outshine my companion.

Aunt is waiting in the lobby, wearing the most vertiginous Marc Jacobs black patent heels I have ever seen. Her Jean Harlow-style hair is curled and pinned back, and her black dress is so pinched at the waist I wonder if I might have to offer mouth-to-mouth resuscitation at some point. She looks simply stunning.

As the car pulls up at the fashion show, I can almost feel the crackle of anticipation in the air. Crowds are gathered hoping to catch a glimpse of their favourite celebs, and the paparazzi are jostling at the front, determined to get the perfect shot of the hottest stars. There is a red carpet leading its way up to the entrance, and a beautiful PR guarding it fiercely, clipboard in hand. She smiles at my companion as we sashay past and doesn't even bother to check her list.

A firework display of flashbulbs erupts as we start our ascent to the main entrance. A reporter from *E!* stops us to chat for a few minutes, and a photographer grabs me, asking who my fashion icon is.

I look over to Aunt, who is smiling at me, gesturing for me to answer. I feel slightly uncomfortable with the attention focused on me. Scene-stealing isn't good etiquette for a gigolo. I say Aunt's name and nod in her direction gallantly. She smiles broadly to let me know I gave the right answer.

As we walk in, I catch sight of an *über*-famous actress in her thirties. She has the kind of delicate, fragile beauty that actually makes me take a sudden inward breath. I instantly turn my gaze away. Even though my relationship with Aunt is strictly platonic, it would be bad manners to be blatantly ogling another lady – especially one so exquisite. Nevertheless, as we are led to our prominent front-row seats by a fawning PR, I can't help hoping the actress will be seated near us.

As we sit down Aunt engages me in some chit-chat about the collection we're here to see, and I give her my full attention, unable to scan the room and see where – let me call her Celebrity X – is. Another household name sits next to us, joins in our conversation and briefly distracts me from my would-be object of desire.

We all converse together about everyday things, and I'm struck once again by the surreal nature of these events. The atmosphere on the front row is a real buzz. It feels like stepping into your favourite movie, pulling up a chair and chatting to stars who only a moment ago seemed tiny figments of your imagination.

With Aunt now deep in conversation, I glance up and find myself staring directly into Celebrity X's deep, liquid brown eyes. She holds my gaze for a moment, smiles shyly, then looks back down at the programme she was previously studying. Shivers run down my spine. As a man of the world, I can decode a look in the same way Francis Crick could decode DNA. There was something there far beyond a polite exchange of glances; there was definitely the electricity of attraction. I also notice she is alone and instantly sense she is someone in great need of my services.

I vow not to get distracted from my current obligations, but feel slightly downcast that nothing can come of the connection between me and Celebrity X. I allow myself one last snatched glance in her direction. She looks like Snow White – her jet-black hair frames her porcelain-white skin, and her slender frame is flattered by a simple fuchsia dress that finishes at the knee.

I focus on the runway as the lights go up and the models start to strut, pouting, down the catwalk. They are almost within touching distance as they swish by.

Afterwards, we jump into a yellow cab and zoom off to a trendy downtown location for the official after-party. When we arrive, the scene is one of chaos: *everyone* is trying to get in, and the queue is running almost a block down the road. The poor door staff are being blagged and begged to within an inch of their lives. Once more we walk straight past those standing in line, a series of imperceptible nods are exchanged by the door and security staff, and we waltz in.

Inside, I am immediately overwhelmed by the noise and heat. The club is packed with exuberant fashionistas showing off and talking loudly. A waitress clad sleekly in black breezes past with a tray of champagne cocktails and I grab two for me and Aunt.

'Cheers, darling,' Aunt toasts me, and then shouts over the roar of the crowd, 'Let's get a seat.'

I glance around and see a booth surrounded by ten butch bodyguards. Beyond them, I see the tiny size-zero frame of one of Hollywood's young hellraisers, who, incongruously, is sitting with only one friend, sipping free champagne. I don't fancy our chances of muscling in on their territory. We walk to the back of the club and by luck bump into a young PR from Marc Jacobs, who jostles people out of the way to find us a seat.

'That's better,' sighs Aunt, as we slide into our seats and commandeer a tray of sushi canapés.

I'm too polite to mention the height of Aunt's heels, but I'm guessing it feels like walking around on dagger-tipped stilts. We try and talk, but the music is too loud. It's full of young hipsters, dancing and screaming with laughter or jabbering on their mobiles in a bottleneck at the doorway. We wisely decide to people-watch in silence and indulge in the free champagne. After five minutes a text beeps through on Aunt's mobile.

'At last – thank God,' she shouts in my ear. 'Let's go.' I look at her quizzically. 'It's the *after*-after-party. That's where everyone will be,' she informs me.

I've been discreetly trying to spot Celebrity X, but with no luck, so my ears prick up when Aunt tells me that there's another party. It makes sense: only a publicity-hungry star like the size-zero celeb in the booth would be at a party as conspicuous and crazy as this.

We make our way to the exit and a doorman hails a taxi for us. 'To the Mercer Hotel,' Aunt instructs him.

I try to keep calm, but I can't help tingling with excitement.

The scene that greets us at the after-after-party couldn't be any more different from the one we just left. The atmosphere is laidback and relaxed, with the rich and famous lounging around on comfy sofas among bookshelves and flattering back-lighting. Bottles of incredibly expensive champagne are left on the oak tables, free for anyone to take.

As soon as we walk through the door, I see Celebrity X standing at the bar with a younger-looking girl. Once more our eyes meet. This time the electricity is unmistakeable. After a few seconds she averts her gaze, but with none of the shy submissiveness of earlier. I'm almost spellbound and struggle to get myself together.

'Are you OK?' asks Aunt with a sly smile.

I've been caught out, and kick myself for my thoughtlessness. Aunt tactfully doesn't mention what or who diverted my attention. We sit down, open a bottle of champagne and casually start to discuss the show, analysing which outfits Aunt should place an order for.

After twenty minutes the young girl who was previously chatting to Celebrity X walks over. At first I'm sure she'll walk straight past us, but instead she stops dead right in front of me. 'Come outside for a cigarette,' she asks – well, almost instructs.

Without thinking, I reply, 'Sorry, I don't smoke.'

'Come outside for a cigarette, *anyway*,' she says, more forcefully.

Just as I'm about to be plunged into total confusion, I catch a look in her eye. I realise she's not asking me, she's *telling* me. I have no choice. There's a plan afoot but I'm not quite sure what it is.

Before I can reply, Aunt answers for me. 'I'm so tired I'm going to head back to the hotel. You stay and enjoy the party – and your *cigarette*,' she says, like an indulgent mother. There's a twinkle in her eye.

I insist on seeing Aunt out to her car, then make my way to the outside smoking area. The girl appears by my side, lights a cigarette and starts to make small talk about the show. After ten minutes I wonder if I've got the whole thing wrong. Then Celebrity X appears at the doorway. The light from inside almost casts a halo around her. She walks over with a swaying grace and pulls a cigarette from her designer bag. Without missing a beat I produce my lighter – kept for occasions such as these – and light it for her. It's almost postmodern – I'm lighting the cigarette of a film star in a scene that could have been stolen straight from the movies.

She nods at the girl, who obviously takes it as a sign to leave. 'That's my assistant, a lovely girl,' she says lightly, before reaching out her tiny milk-white hand to introduce herself. The whole thing is a set-up, as I'd suspected.

I try to keep calm. In gigolo terms, this is like a soldier who has never been in combat hearing his first round of real gunfire.

'Lovely to meet you. What did you think of the show?' I ask. First rule of celebrity engagement: wherever possible, always pick a topic of conversation about a shared experience; this way, you subtly establish that you're on an equal playing field. Under no circumstances should you come across as a star-struck member of the general public.

'Absolutely wonderful – I adore Marc,' she says softly, maintaining eye contact and smiling playfully at me.

I'm spellbound by her little rosebud lips as she starts to chatter away about the show.

Over the next hour we drift back inside and our conversation shifts effortlessly from one topic to another – everything from fashion to where you can buy good bagels on Broadway early in the morning. What we *don't* mention is her super-wattage celebrity status, that I've seen her countless times on the silver screen or that if she called her bank for a balance, it would register in the millions.

As the evening starts to wind down, our body language gears up. I suspect something is on the cards, but I can hardly believe it's really going to happen. I don't want to be presumptuous, but on the other hand I'd hate to miss the kind of opportunity a gigolo dreams of.

Across the room, the sound of people saying goodbye peppers the air and farewell air kisses flutter around us. Suddenly another gigolo waltzes up, trying to muscle in on my territory. He's a different breed to me, though – all buffed muscles and over-whitened teeth. Even his tight white T-shirt is a cliché. He almost elbows me out of the way and starts to flirt overtly with Celebrity X. The lines that drip out of his mouth are so cheesy they could virtually be melted and put on toast. I know I have nothing to fear – here, in America, the charms of an English gentleman gigolo are far more coveted than the blatant boorishness of our yank equivalent.

'Why doesn't he leave?' Celebrity X mouths at me, rolling her eyes theatrically.

At this I step in and save her from his smarm. As he walks away forlornly, Celebrity X looks at me provocatively and says, 'Hey, it's just you and me. I've got all this champagne in my room – why don't you come upstairs and help me drink it?'

I nod in acceptance and smile at her. In this situation, it's like being a surfer; when you're on the crest of a wave, you don't think about what you're doing, you just keep paddling.

We walk towards the elevator and I deliberately avoid

looking round to see if anyone has noticed us leaving together, which I'm sure they have. I have a slight insight into the complexities of her life – I don't want there to be an audience to the personal details of our encounter.

On the way upstairs, I continue to be amazed by the sheer professionalism of her charm. Usually I'm the one facilitating the flow of the conversation, but she keeps the rapport going, making sure there are no awkward pauses. I imagine this is a skill developed from working on various film sets, where every job is like being the new girl at school, even if everyone is primed to like you.

When we walk through the door to her hotel room, it's like entering Wonderland. It's very modern and clean, an understated luxury of beige and cream furnishings and upholstery. Through the doorway on the left-hand side, I can't help but notice the sheer size of the bath in the marble-clad bathroom. It looks like it's been imported straight from ancient Rome.

She motions for me to sit down in a leather armchair in front of the large leather-inlaid desk, then saunters over with a bottle of champagne.

'My God, I've drunk so much I feel like I'm turning into Withnail – I'll be on the antifreeze soon,' I joke as she pours me a glass.

'That's, like, my favourite film,' she exclaims, laughing. '"You're drunk,"' she says challengingly, quoting from *Withnail and I* and squinting in a comedy fashion.

'"I assure you I'm not, Officer. I've only had a few ales,"' I counter, doing my best Richard E. Grant impression, then adding, '"But we are indeed drifting into the arena of the unwell."'

'"I must have some booze. I *demand* to have some

booze,'" she slurs jokingly, waving the champagne bottle around and giggling. "'I mean to have you even if it must be burglary,'" she says suddenly, leaning forward and stroking my hand while doing a disturbingly accurate impression of Uncle Monty from the film.

Quoting another of Uncle Monty's lines, I reply suggestively, "'There is, you'll agree, a certain *je ne sais quoi*, oh, so very special about a firm, young carrot.'"

At this she falls about laughing and I start giggling too.

'That's so funny,' she says to me. 'I love that film so much I think I've seen it, like, fifty times. And I love that *you* love that film too.'

I smile at her and the atmosphere aches with sexual tension.

'Go and get some more champagne from the bathroom. It's in an ice bucket in the bath,' she tells me, crossing her legs so I notice her ultra-slim ankles. She's wearing a short black cocktail dress, having changed since the show.

I stroll into the bathroom, and when I walk back into the bedroom, champagne bottle in hand, she's moved from the desk and is sitting on the bed with an inscrutable look on her face. I refill our glasses, but then, not wanting to rush things, sit back in my chair.

'So you're a musician?' she asks.

'A pianist,' I reply, wondering where she's going with the conversation. I already told her I studied music, but she didn't pursue the subject earlier.

'You must have very dexterous fingers,' she tells me flirtatiously. 'They must get quite a workout.'

'They get very stiff when I've played for a long time,' I tell her, sipping my champagne and tapping my finger on the side of the glass.

'I studied massage. I know all the acupressure points. Come here, I'll see if I can make your fingers better.'

I take off my jacket and walk over to the bed. She looks incredibly elegant, lounging on the bed, and she grabs my hand as I reach out to her, pulling herself up. She puts her hands on my shoulders and gently pushes me down so I'm sitting in the same spot she occupied previously.

'Pass me your hand,' she tells me, and takes my left hand between her dainty fingers.

She obviously wasn't lying about studying massage. I start to feel slightly dizzy and then incredibly relaxed. I close my eyes and let out an involuntary deep sigh.

'Does that feel good?' she asks.

'Incredible,' I tell her. 'You must have healing hands.'

'Take your shirt off and lie down,' she orders me. 'I'll give you a back massage.'

I slowly unbutton my shirt as she looks at me with an unwavering gaze. The role reversal is extraordinary. She is seducing me with all the favourite tricks men usually employ.

As I lie down, face first, she straddles my lower back, and when I turn my head to the side I notice in the large mirror opposite the bed that her dress has ridden up to her waist. After ten minutes of pure bliss, she instructs me to turn over and then grabs my belt buckle and proceeds to unfasten it with a wicked gleam in her eye.

I gasp as she starts to give me oral sex, looking up at me with her big, brown eyes. A few minutes later she changes her technique, swapping soft, delicate strokes with her tongue for more aggressive sucking. 'Do you prefer it this way?' she asks, and then swaps back to the first method, saying, 'Or this way?'

'Both ways are good,' I say – my voice comes out as a squeak. I can't quite believe what is happening and am overcome with a mixture of shock and pleasure. It's not very often you get a movie star checking the state of her oral technique with you. I say a silent prayer to God that if He has planned an early exit for me, this is the perfect way to go.

Beautiful as the moment is, I feel I need to give something back. I gently turn her so she's resting on the bed and start to road-test my oral techniques on her. 'Which way do *you* prefer it?' I say, looking up.

'Oh, God, every way. It feels *so* good,' she moans.

After five minutes she begs me to enter her. We begin to have the most frenzied, noisy sex I've ever had. Her performance in the bedroom is just as mesmerising as her performance onscreen – she really gives it her all, writhing around, arching her back and begging for more at the top of her voice. As she comes, she shrieks so loudly I fear we'll get kicked out of the hotel for creating a disturbance – until I remember who she is.

Afterwards, we fall asleep in each other's arms. I smile to myself as I realise that I never did get to sleep alone in a big hotel bed, which, after all, is the gigolo equivalent of being redundant.

The phone wakes me and for a second I feel disorientated and wonder where I am. Then I turn my head and see the beautiful, almost angelic face of a movie star resting on the pillow beside me. Far better than a dream, I think to myself.

Celebrity X sleepily answers the phone, then smiles at me. 'My limo is picking us up in twenty minutes. I have to go to a meeting, but my driver can drop you off at your hotel,' she tells me, stroking my leg.

We kiss and then head for the shower together.

'I'd love to stay here all day,' she whispers to me as things heat up, 'but you know, my work comes first.'

As a gigolo, I understand. I'm not here to create *more* obligations; I'm here to alleviate the pressure.

Back in the bedroom, my phone goes and Celebrity X snatches it and answers with a cheeky smile on her face, clearly used to getting away with anything. 'Hello, princess,' she laughs.

I sit bolt upright, trying to get it straight in my mind. She's answered *my* phone but appears to know the caller.

'Of course. I'll have my driver drop him off,' she says, then passes the phone to me.

'Hello, darling. Did you have fun?' It's Aunt.

I laugh and affirm that I did. 'Do you two know each other?' I ask incredulously.

'Of course. I know *everyone*,' Aunt replies. 'Anyway, I have to leave this afternoon: some business has come up. Let's have lunch before I go.'

Obviously the A-list believes in sharing the wealth, and Celebrity X just smiles at me enigmatically as I finish the call and sit on the bed like a modern-day geisha passed between businessmen.

'Let's go out tonight,' Celebrity X tells me. 'I have a movie producer friend and his girlfriend I need to meet. We can double-date.' She scribbles her number in pencil on a Mercer Hotel notepad and hands it to me.

★

Ten hours later I'm standing in the hallway of her apartment being eyed suspiciously by the concierge. I adjust the collar of my green tweed hunting jacket and tell him the number of the apartment I'm visiting. His whole demeanor changes as he says the name of Celebrity X and smiles warmly.

As he takes me up in the lift, I laugh to myself that Celebrity X stayed at the Mercer last night when her own luxury apartment is just a few blocks down the road. Even the super-rich like a freebie, it turns out. I knew that she got paid to sit prettily on the front rows at fashion shoots to guarantee press coverage, but I didn't think a free hotel room would lure her away from her own bed.

Her front door is open, so I stroll in and mentally drop my jaw at her home. It's vastly spacious, with deep-brown wooden floors and lots of expensive-looking curios and antiques. I see an acoustic guitar propped up against the wall, pick it up and start to strum a serenade.

'Who's there?' Celebrity X calls from another room in a sexy, breathy voice.

I'm confused – she asked me to meet her here. I carry on playing and she walks through. There's a look of surprise on her face.

'You asked me to come here to pick you up,' I remind her.

'Oh, yes, of course,' she says, smiling, but there's a strangely vacant look in her eyes. Then, as if someone has flicked on a light switch, she's back to her normal self, the beautiful, funny woman I spent the previous night with. She walks up and gives me a slow, lingering kiss, then starts to unbutton my shirt. 'Take all your clothes off,' she tells me, before asking me to wait in bed for her.

I wonder if we are going out at all or if it was just a ruse to get me round. Not that she needed one, of course. I would be more than happy to courier myself over as a male delivery. I wait in the bed as she disappears into the bathroom for what seems like an eternity.

When she emerges, I'm surprised to see that she's fully dressed for the evening. 'Oh, we're late,' she says absent-mindedly, and then, without undressing, gets in bed with me and strokes my chest. 'You'd better get your clothes on. I said we'd be there half an hour ago.'

Getting dressed, I try not to feel like another beautiful accessory for her to play with and wink flirtatiously as she pulls on a huge woolly hat and shades so she can be incognito when we're out and about.

She seems a little downcast when we get into her car. The driver holds the door open and she slides in with a faraway look in her eyes.

'You're very beautiful,' she suddenly tells me. 'I love your style too,' she adds, looking out of the window wistfully.

I say thank you and tell her I think *she* is the beautiful one with incredible style. She smiles wanly, with the kind of look that has garnered a million compliments and believed none.

'It's very difficult for me to have relationships, you know, with my celebrity status,' she confesses with an air of conspiratorial camaraderie. 'I suppose it's hard for someone like you too, for different reasons of course. I once had a boyfriend, a musician. I thought he really loved me,' she continues, playing with a ring on her finger in an agitated manner. 'We lived together, did everything as a couple – all the ordinary stuff like making each other breakfast, shopping in the supermarket to get food for dinner, watching DVDs in our pyjamas on the sofa at night. Then one day I overheard him talking to his friend on the phone. He was basically laughing and gloating that he was on to a good thing, talking like I was just a meal ticket. You can't imagine how much that hurt.' Her expression is full of sadness.

'That's awful,' I tell her with concern. I truly am shocked. I despise deceit. When I hear stories like this, I feel that at least my profession is honourable – both parties' intentions are clear from the outset.

'At least I know where I am with you,' she says, echoing my thoughts. She leans her head on my shoulder so her soft black hair tickles my neck.

In the restaurant, a waitress comes over and gushes how much she loves Celebrity X's movies. 'Oh, thanks, that's really sweet,' Celebrity X says graciously, then orders a Martini sour, telling the girl, 'The sourer the better.'

The movie producer arrives and gives me a strong handshake, tactfully avoiding the question of who I am and what I'm doing with Celebrity X. The night passes pleasantly with idle banter about films, anecdotes from sets and gossip about other stars. Eventually the movie producer ventures to ask if I'm an actor. When I reply no, he is visibly relieved. I imagine the most dangerous species for a famous thirtysomething actress is a handsome twentysomething wannabe actor looking to advance his career by any means necessary.

After the bill is paid – discreetly by Celebrity X – the producer invites us to an industry party.

'Oh, no, I hate those things,' moans Celebrity X, turning to me and saying, 'Come back to mine and watch DVDs.

I used to be on the Oscar committee, so I've got a copy of every film ever released.'

'But most importantly *Withnail and I*,' I laugh, putting my arm round her slight waist. I can't help thinking to myself how surreal it is that rather than have her DVDs delivered by Amazon, she gets them directly from the Oscar committee.

I hail a cab and we jump in, waving goodbye to the movie producer and his date. By now Celebrity X's entire mood has changed. She is happy, giddy and excited. As soon as the taxi door closes, she almost pins me against my seat and gives me a deep, intense kiss.

'Talk to me in English,' she pleads with me.

'I am talking in English,' I say, puzzled.

'No! That quaint British way of talking, with all those funny phrases.'

'Well, I think you're rather splendid,' I whisper in her ear in a silly, exaggerated British accent. 'I really rather fancy shagging you.'

She shrieks with laughter and collapses her head into my knee, her shoulders shaking. 'So funny. You sound just like Dick van Dyke,' she laughs, looking up.

I'm glad to have amused her and taken her out of her previous melancholy mood, but I'm starting to feel worried about her erratic temperament. The one rule of gigolodom is never to engage with anyone who isn't mentally stable enough to handle it – celebrity or no celebrity. I get the feeling she is confused and looking for love, not for uncomplicated pleasure on the side.

We get back to her apartment and have another energetic sex session. Once again, as soon as I am naked she is extremely bossy – which I love in a woman – and I start to feel like my misgivings were unfounded. Just as

I'm about to approach my denouement, however, she whispers in my ear and begs, 'Come inside me.'

The fact that safe sex is a must for a gigolo goes without saying, and a 'baby gigolo' is beyond thinking about. I get the strange sense that this isn't a kamikaze attitude to safe sex, but a reckless turn on the wheel of fertility roulette. Luckily for Celebrity X, I'm not interested in having a meal ticket – even if it does have half of my DNA imprinted on it. I politely decline.

Afterwards, this refusal seems to elicit a meltdown. 'I'm just a girl who's good at her job,' she sobs, lamenting the horrors of being famous. 'I can't trust anyone. I'm not married, I don't have children, I can't even go to the shops without being accosted by the paparazzi.' She wipes her eyes and smears black mascara all over her face. I gently cuddle her and rock her in my arms until she stops crying.

'You should go to bed and get some sleep,' I tell her softly. She nods, with tearstains all down her face. I carry her over to the king-size bed and tuck her in, saying, 'I think I should leave.'

Once again she nods, snuffling into her pillow. It feels terrible to witness her pain and see her mask slip. I know she won't thank me for it in the morning.

I leave the apartment and walk down the road, worrying what will become of her, but knowing there is nothing I can do to help. My mobile rings. 'I'm in bed. Come and give me cuddles,' she says in a muffled voice down the phone.

'If you *really* want me to, I will,' I tell her, 'but I think it's much better that you get a good night's sleep.'

'You're right. I have work in the morning. I *always* have work in the morning.'

I go to say something soothing but the line has gone dead.

It turns out I will be spending a night alone in a hotel bed after all, I think to myself, pondering on what has just happened. The thought of Hollywood superstars may be enticing, I muse, but I miss my usual clientele, who can shamelessly use me for sex, safe in the knowledge their story will eventually end in a happy ever after. The fish bowl of fame is a prison for some, it turns out.

The next morning I get a rambling ten-minute message on my answer phone from Celebrity X, starting with, 'I'm sorry. I know I'm difficult, but I *really* want to see you again . . . '

Tempted as I am to call back, I know that a gigolo isn't the person to untie her messy emotional hang-ups, so I head to one of my favourite New York florists, where I pick out a pretty bunch of daffodils, after remembering her telling me she prefers simple flowers to the expensive bouquets she usually receives. Once again quoting from *Withnail and I*, on the card I write, 'Even a stopped clock tells the right time twice a day.'

I know she'll understand what I mean. As with *Withnail and I*, there are always moments of perfection, even in the most unlikely pairings. They just can't last for ever.

Chapter 7

The Dandy Trade Union Meeting

Back in England, news of my liaison has already got out. Honestly, gossip travels faster than the speed of light on the gigolo grapevine. My voicemail is clogged up with messages from various friends wanting to know if the rumours are true. If I were a company floating on the stock exchange, everyone would be screaming, 'Buy,' and rushing to grab a piece of equity in me. But just one message sticks in my mind: the small, forlorn voice of Charlotte saying that she would wait ten more minutes for me at the Literary Café. We'd arranged to meet, but caught up in the drama of my celebrity engagement, it had totally slipped my mind.

I feel like I've been a real bastard and suddenly I'm worried I've lost her friendship for good. I've left numerous messages apologising, but she hasn't returned any of my calls. Charlotte is not the kind of woman who takes well to being slighted. What feels most odd is that there appear to be indefinable boundaries between us, one of which I have inadvertently crossed, without quite knowing why or how. This is, I imagine, how a real relationship is conducted. Often I think to myself that people seem to overcomplicate their relationships, and I can never understand how there is room for such a margin of error and miscommunication. Now, though, I think I understand. You see, in my professional life, I would never let a client down. There is total clarity in the arrangement. But personal relationships, even the friendship between Charlotte and me, are so much more opaque. Although I know I was an idiot to let her down, I have apologised profusely and, being a man, my instant reaction is, can't I be forgiven and can't the meeting be rearranged? It's only looking at it from my gigolo perspective that I understand the scale of the offence I have committed.

My little apartment seems unusually lonely after the drama and excitement of the weekend, and even more so because of the situation I've created with Charlotte. All I want is to pop over to the Literary Café and say hello, rather than sit here in solitude, but I don't want to impose myself where I'm not wanted.

Luckily, I don't have to sit here and dwell on things all evening, as the Dandy Trade Union meeting is scheduled for tonight. The meeting, which on this occasion I am hosting, is a get-together of all the London dandies, and it's a night out I always look forward to – it's good to hear everyone else's stories and let off some steam. Our lives are a social whirl, filled with glamour and intrigue, but

I'm increasingly aware that gigolodom can also be very lonely. Usually when our paths cross, we are out on the town entertaining our ladies, so there's no chance for a proper chat. Then, like today, I finally get some time off and find there's no one to share it with.

Tonight is going to be very special, though – and not just because I am virtually the homecoming hero. We have a guest of honour flying over from America: the irrepressible Miami gigolo ZZ (pronounced 'Zee Zee'). Just the thought of him brings a broad smile to my face. ZZ is one of the most successful gigolos I know, and also one of the most unconventional. For the most part, a prerequisite of being a gigolo is to be tall and handsome. It's what women want when they're indulging in short-term fun. However, ZZ, at five foot two, is more Ben Stiller than Ben Affleck. What he lacks in classical good looks, however, he more than makes up for in personality. He has so much charisma he could give half of it away to charity and still be the funniest man you've ever met. Now, we're not talking witty or humorous here. As I've mentioned before, all gigolos are expected to make their ladies laugh. Dour does not go down well. But ZZ is in another league – crazy, zany, high-octane, off-the-wall fun. He likes to dress up in silly costumes, and he does more than laugh women into bed; he laughs them into the silliest, craziest, most exhilarating, liberating sex of their lives. Sometimes it's easy to suspect a lie when women say they would rather have a man with a sense of humour than a handsome face, but ZZ is a testament to its truth.

He is a *big* hit with career girls. The more high-powered the woman, the more addicted to ZZ they get. They have to present a serious persona to get ahead at work and survive the stress of office life, so ZZ is a refreshing change. Also, the main ingredient of hot sex is the ability to relax. This can be difficult when you've just spent the last week working ten hours a day in a tense environment, so often just being in the company of a gigolo, with no pressures or commitments, can press the release valve. But sometimes, if you're truly wound up, only a touch of the ZZ magic can unlock your inner calm and reduce you to the sex-crazed, reckless level of a happy, horny teenager. Really, women should be allowed to claim his services back as a business expense.

His personality is so infectious it doesn't just work on women. Everyone is buzzing with news of his arrival, and I genuinely feel he is just the tonic I need.

Every month when the Dandy Trade Union meets up, the host gets to choose the venue. Of course, the brief is to pick a place that befits our profession, but it also has to serve premium chilled beer. Without any well-heeled women to take care of the bill, champagne is off the menu. The rule is that no one can bring a lady or procure one on the night. It is a gigolo-only zone. It's our opportunity to be in our natural state of manhood (less impressive than it sounds!), without the need to seduce women.

I've picked the opulent Grill Room at Café Royal, situated in the heart of Piccadilly, a hang-out of dilettantes since the seventeenth century. I thought its history gave it suitable credentials to host an evening for modern dandies. Oscar Wilde used to dine there, and although it no longer attracts that kind of rarefied company, the baroque gold and blood-red décor, elegantly lit by Venetian glass chandeliers, makes it the perfect setting for our soirée. As luck would have it, Rochester has informed me that the venue is holding a 1920s night this evening, so all the ladies and gentlemen must dress up in suitable attire. I'm quite looking forward to seeing everyone turned out in their finest.

With my sense of responsibility as the host, I arrive first. I have reserved a booth in the furthest corner from the entrance, which gives a view of the entire floor. Reclining into the wine-red velvet seats and surveying the extravagantly decorated surroundings, I congratulate myself on my choice. Popular with models, celebrities and the world of fashion, it's like a scene from a faded postcard a decadent aristocrat might send. Beautiful women are fluttering about in vintage silk dresses, trimmed with fur and finished with jewels. Looking across the room, there is a sea of feathered hairpieces and net-adorned pill-box hats in rich reds, greens and midnight blues. Whalebone corsets and sheer stockings abound, and the tinkling sounds of 1920s tunes seem to follow the tapping of hundreds of fine-pointed stilettos, as the women dance following old-time steps or simply do a turn of the room to talk.

Looking up, I see Johan, my good friend the Swedish supermodel, arrive. He explained his strange behaviour of late over lunch a few weeks back, when I discovered he has started a relationship with a beautiful, wealthy divorcee. I know his baby face and beta-male personality make him the perfect kept man, but I worry for him. While he's been a player in the past, this time he seems to be enthralled. He's in a constant state of anxiety that she'll get bored of him and move on, or that she'll decide to marry a rich man again. I'm even starting to suspect that he's developed a borderline eating disorder to keep the Dior model looks that attracted her in the first place.

He is well over six foot, with chiselled cheekbones, sparkling blue eyes and soft, honey-toned skin that compliments his dark-blond hair. His serene, angelic demeanour feels like a soothing sea breeze just blew in. The diversity of gigolos makes me smile. He and ZZ are so different it's like they come from a different species.

'Hey, Golden,' Johan says, shaking my hand with his long fingers. His voice is soft and melodic. 'So what you been up to, you dirty dog?' He gives me a naughty grin that belies his sophisticated attire. His outfit brings to mind a beautiful, spoiled prince regent who is the apple of his mother's eye. The white shirt, kindly donated by Hedi Slimane, is worn with a casually loosened cravat and vintage fitted black suit, topped off with a trilby. Being a relaxed Scandinavian, he is also wearing well-worn black Converse trainers.

The combination of his laidback demeanour, formed by an idyllic childhood in rural Sweden, surrounded by untouched woodlands and ice-blue seashores, and an almost inhuman beauty make him appear like someone not quite of this world – and by all accounts his chief trouser attraction is so sizeable it could be classed as extraterrestrial.

'Do you want a beer?' he asks me with a quirky little smile on his lips. Then, without waiting for an answer, he walks off to the bar, unconsciously strutting like he's on a Parisian catwalk.

Next, in walks Rochester, looking dishevelled and Byronic. He has on an extremely fitted black suit with a slight sheen to it, very tapered towards the ankle, and pointed black winkle-pickers. His black shirt is also fitted, and tucked in, highlighted with a pencil-thin white tie. To finish off the look, he has a white handkerchief carefully displayed in the upper pocket of his suit jacket. His jet-black hair skims his shoulders, like a gothic hero who has stepped out of an Emily Brontë novel, and his startling aqua eyes are enhanced with smudged black eyeliner.

He strides up, casually drapes his arm round my back and surveys the scene like he owns the place. 'Good choice,' he affirms, before high-fiving me with a knowing twinkle in his eye. 'So you've joined the A-list club.' He winks.

I laugh and say, 'Johan is at the bar,' before he forces me to spill all the dirty details.

Without a word he weaves his way through the crowd to join Johan, and I see him laughing and joking with the barman, whom he knows, no doubt trying to get our drinks for free.

Heathcliff and Valentino come in together, looking like perfect dandies. Valentino, who models himself on silent film stars, sports a pencil moustache and has perfect bone structure. His dark-blue almond-shaped eyes are framed by long, black eyelashes, which are so striking you could mistake them for being false. I don't think they are, but who knows with a gigolo. He is the type of man who employs all the romantic clichés to sweep a woman off her feet, but somehow manages to breathe new life into them. He creates a world of continuous movie scenes for his dates and casts them as his leading lady. Women like nothing better than a dramatic love affair, in which they are allowed to discover their inner Gilda and become the sharp-talking bombshell they always wanted to be. Valentino even lives in a disused film studio, where he uses old props and sets to transport ladies to another time, when men were dashing and chivalrous and women were worth dying for.

As the two gigolos walk over, I notice ladies glancing at them, but having a night off, Heathcliff and Valentino leave it at a flirtatious smile and make their way over to us. Heathcliff is in a different mould to most dandies. He has a swarthy, manly allure that hints at a wild, romantic gypsy spirit. He has a larger frame than most of us, and a deep, sonorous voice. His persona is that of the strong, silent type. He has a very powerful aura, masterful but gentle – very much of the 'please don't – oh, go on then' school of seduction! He is also a brilliant chef and wins over women with his kitchen skills. Tonight he is wearing generously cut black trousers and a white shirt, open at the collar and cuffs, with flamboyant ruffles. He looks like a dangerous circus master who'll take you on an X-rated adventure. What woman could say no to that?

By the time Heathcliff and Valentino make it to me, Rochester and Johan are back with the drinks. Rochester has somehow negotiated a supply of free drinks for the evening, probably because the staff know that on other occasions we facilitate the flow of champagne. Of course, this time we still have to settle for beer.

With everyone sitting down, Rochester raises his eyebrows in a suggestive, quizzical manner. 'So?' he asks, his voice loaded with expectation. 'What happened with you and Celebrity X? *Everyone* is talking about it. Don't even think about being discreet – it's a union meeting and we're allowed to divulge trade secrets.'

'Dudes!' I'm interrupted by the hysterical, high-pitched

voice of ZZ, who appears in front of us with a flourish just as I'm about to launch into my tale.

I had sent a message to him saying to come in dandy costume. Being from Miami, and with no inkling of what the word means here, he's interpreted my instructions in his own inimitable way. I see Heathcliff and Valentino's jaws drop, and Rochester nearly falls off the side of the banquette laughing. ZZ looks like a helicopter has just dropped him off for a guest-star appearance in *Miami Vice*. His super-tight white trousers could just about work on Johan's model frame, but on a five foot two, cuddly love machine, the effect is purely comical. The pink shirt is unbuttoned shamelessly low and teamed with a pale-lemon jacket with rolled-up sleeves.

He removes his gold-trim aviator shades with a theatrical gesture and beams. 'Good to see you guys,' he yells, throwing himself at us, one by one, for a big bear hug.

'What are you wearing?' I exclaim, laughing.

'Whaddya mean?' he replies with mock offence. He turns to survey the club. Against the elegant scene, he looks incongruous in his flashy pastel garb. A beautiful girl swishes by, looks at him and giggles. 'Oops,' he says, turning back to us and squeezing in between Rochester and myself. 'Oh, well, all these fancy-pants would look stupid if they turned up in Miami looking like they were old dudes from the British aristocracy,' he continues, shrugging his shoulderpads and crinkling his face into a silly grin. 'So what's new?' he asks, placing a clumsy hand on my knee.

'Good question,' butts in Rochester. 'That's what we were getting to before you arrived.'

'I just came back from a liaison with Celebrity X in

New York,' I say, trying not to look too pleased with myself
as ZZ's brown eyes widen comically. 'But what we discuss
during a trade union meeting goes no further, right?'

Everyone nods solemnly.

'Oh, gee, I better get myself a beer – this is gonna be
a big one,' ZZ says, excitedly taking off his jacket and
adjusting his tight trousers with a grimace.

Everyone turns to me expectantly and I start to reveal
the ins and outs of my time with Celebrity X, from the
hot sex to the neurotic meltdown.

'Wow,' says Rochester, leaning back in his seat. 'Did
you get her to autograph your dick? I would have!'

Everyone cracks up laughing.

'You're so gross,' I tell him good-humouredly, and add
teasingly, 'No wonder Celebrity Z ditched you.'

Rochester's botch-up of his liaison with Celebrity Z
has become notorious in gigolo-land, but he thinks his
outrageous behaviour with her is downright funny. 'Yeah,
well, you know what? She still texts me, so she can't have
been that pissed off with me,' says Rochester, smiling.
'She'll come back to the good stuff – when she's next
drunk and horny at least! No one can resist a gigolo for
long.'

He's probably right. His A-list conquest is a party girl,
so she'll use him for sex whenever she feels like it, or is
too wasted to resist. Celebrity X is in a different league,
though. Her life and relationship with fame is far too
complicated to come back for more, or for me to allow
it. Tempting as it might be.

'You know what?' I confess to the boys. 'I've never felt
"bought" as a gigolo before, but Celebrity X made me
feel like I was just another hired help on the payroll. I

guess fame is a currency that buys people – time, opin-
ions, affection – so that's how these celebs relate to
everyone.'

'Shit, I wouldn't mind if a celebrity bought me. She
could even stick me in her handbag as long as she gave
me the opportunity to wag my tail,' remarks ZZ, lolling
his tongue stupidly, in an impression of an eager puppy.

'Yeah, she might have had the spending power, but you
were giving her something priceless,' adds Rochester,
resting his chin in his hands and leaning on the tabletop
with a knowing expression. 'OK, so she might have been
as neurotic as hell, but at least you gave her a good time.
Most men aren't successful with women – especially good-
looking, independent ones – because they're so pleased
with themselves for getting laid they never think about
what the woman wants. They approach sex from a purely
selfish angle. But any gigolo knows you get out what you
put in – turning a woman on is the catalyst for me getting
off. Otherwise you might as well just have a wank, right?'

I open a bottle of beer and pass it to Rochester, nodding
in agreement with what he is saying before commenting,
'With Celebrity X there was no chance of putting myself
first – with someone like her, you're only allowed to say
what she wants to hear. Actually, thinking about it, a gigolo
is her perfect man!'

'All women would secretly prefer a gigolo, wouldn't
they?' butts in Heathcliff, his deep voice stating the
obvious. 'They say they want this alpha male who's in
control, but the truth is, they prefer being boss. Their ideal
situation is ordering their man to be in charge.'

We all laugh in agreement, and ZZ stalks off the bar
to refresh the supplies, saying over his shoulder, 'You

wait until a woman orders you to wear a furry Tigger suit.'

'What is he going on about?' says Rochester with a filthy grin. 'Anyway, I'm happy for women to pay to have power over me – it's a win-win situation, isn't it? Unless you did something stupid like fall in love, of course. And what kind of idiot gigolo would do that?' he jokes without thinking, accidentally putting his foot in it.

'I might.' Johan looks down at his trainers and scuffs one foot with the other.

All eyes are trained on him. The sound of 1920s music drifts across the room, filling the expectant silence. ZZ comes back from the bar balancing a host of beers on a black tray.

'I think I'm in love,' Johan mumbles, still shuffling his feet and looking at the floor.

'Jeez, did I hear that right?' exclaims ZZ as he sits down. 'I haven't heard that word since 1982.'

'You *think*, or you *are*?' Rochester asks Johan sharply.

'I am,' he says firmly, suddenly looking up with a defiant glint in his eye.

'You've got to be careful, really careful,' says Rochester with a concerned look. 'Love can destroy a gigolo, you know that. It's easy when there are boundaries, but take them away and it's carnage. I don't want you to get hurt.'

'Look, I know what I'm doing. Besides, she loves me too.' He looks at us sheepishly.

ZZ claps him on the back and grins. 'Well, good luck to you. If you think you've found love, hold on to it. Or at least enjoy the ride.'

'I agree,' I chip in cautiously, thinking for some reason of Charlotte. I've checked my mobile continuously all night, but still no message. 'Be careful of course, but why not go for it? After all, we can't all live the gigolo dream for ever.'

Johan nods. 'Look, I never expected this; it just happened. But she's amazing.' A huge grin spreads across his face, and he taps his finger on the table like an excited schoolboy.

'Go on, then, tell us about her,' Valentino says, always ready to hear a good love story.

'We met a few months ago. She'd just flown back from Los Angeles, fresh to London, almost fresh to life, following her divorce. That's when I first saw her. It was like someone pressed "play" on an old romantic movie. Everyone else in the room just melted away and I was stuck there, staring into her brown eyes, completely mesmerised. Everything went still for a moment. It sounds like a cliché, but we gave each other the look of love right there on the spot.' Johan looks up shyly, worried we'll tease his newfound romantic streak, but everyone is just listening intently, following his story.

'Carry on,' says ZZ, leaning forward excitedly. 'So what does she look like?'

'Oh, man,' replies Johan, leaning back and grinning wider. 'She's so beautiful. Beyond sexy, beyond hot – like a movie queen brought to life. My first thought was of a modern-day Ava Gardner. But her smile, that's what killed me – all soft and teasing.'

'Sounds like my perfect woman,' says Valentino, a look of rapture crossing his face.

'I walked over and we just hit it off,' Johan explains. 'We spent hours talking. She told me all about her divorce and her nightmare ex-husband. God, he sounds like such a shit. I could see that she was all wound up over it. Even though she was laughing and trying to be carefree, there was something sad in her eyes. It broke me. We went back to her penthouse at the Covent Garden Hotel and had this wild, crazy, intimate sex. At first I thought it was a regular gig, but then I knew there was something different, like we had a real connection. I just knew we were soul mates. We saw each other every day for three weeks, until she had to go back to LA. Then I *did* worry it was over. You know how it is: you're a fun diversion when they've got a gap in their schedule, then they go back to their real life and leave you behind.'

I nod knowingly and ask, 'So what happened? How did you break the pattern?'

'I didn't do anything, it was her. She came back and called me. Then I knew for sure there wasn't going to be a sell-by date on our affair. Yeah, sometimes I stress out – like when she flicks through my model book and jokes that I'm her "boy toy" – but every day our relationship gets deeper, and every day I feel less and less like a gigolo.'

'So how does it work between you, then?' asks Rochester, struggling to get his head round a relationship in which meetings aren't made by appointment only.

'We don't "see" each other; we just "be" with each other. We do regular things that couples do – go to the cinema, shop at the supermarket. You should see her house. It cost millions, courtesy of the divorce settlement obviously. She's asked me to move in.' Johan looks down nervously, then quickly looks back up, wanting our approval.

'OK, now you're on dangerous ground,' I jump in. 'A love affair is one thing, but this is dangerous. If you move in with her, you'll lose all your power as a gigolo. Then what if she kicks you out? Shiva is always telling me you can never come back from true love – not to the land of gigolos, anyway. I don't want to be harsh, and I can see you're really into her, but she's probably just playing with you. She's a lonely divorcee looking to pass the time until she meets her next husband. Look, Johan, women love to play with men like us, but they don't marry us. She'll meet a rich, successful man, settle down and have babies. How can you provide for her? Not to be funny, but everyone knows that male models don't earn anything like the girls do.'

'I don't have to provide for her,' Johan argues back indignantly. 'She has *millions*. She doesn't need a man to look after her. She's free. Now she can choose love, not security.'

'Do you know this for sure?' I ask, getting anxious about how deep into this Johan is.

'I promise you. I'm not just a stupid, pretty face. Don't you think I've had all these doubts? We had a big heart-to-heart when she got back from Los Angeles. She told me that being over there, seeing all the rich guys who were after her, gave her new resolve. Her ex was a domineering, controlling bully who thought his money could buy her. He didn't love her for *her*. She was just a trophy that he kept to himself, only parading her when it suited him, with no thought about what she wanted. He demanded gratitude for every scrap he gave her, and never made her feel like she belonged or that she owned anything for herself. That's not life; it's a prison. I know she never wants to go back to that with any man, however rich.'

'I understand what you're saying,' I soothe him. 'But it's almost like the ultimate gigolo treat for her. Why would she hook up for an affair when she's got the money and can have you for keeps? But doesn't that mean she's got power over you, just like her ex-husband had over her? It's the same situation in reverse, except this time you're the trophy.'

'Look, I can see what you're getting at. But what you're forgetting is the basic difference between men and women. Men want to control, but women want to *nurture*. Of course she has the upper hand in one sense, but she'd never use it against me – it's just not her style. Yeah, she could be a bitch, but she's too sweet, and I could be a bastard, but I haven't got enough power – it's the perfect balance. I promise you, it's the way of the future.' With a hint of triumph, he takes a swig of beer and looks around the table, almost daring us to beat his argument.

We can't. His theory does seem to make sense, but then theories often make sense – it's whether they work when put into action. So we'll see.

'Well, I'll drink to that future,' says ZZ, giving Johan a big hug.

'So will I,' laughs Rochester, chinking his bottle against ZZ's.

I smile and to lighten the mood ask ZZ what his gigolo news is.

'I have a new string to my bow, boys. The girls *love* it. Recently I had a lady who was a real big shot at work. Could she relax in bed? No way. So one night – in a stroke of genius – I turned up at her hotel room wearing . . . Wait for it . . .' We all lean towards him expectantly. 'A Tigger suit!'

'What?' Rochester explodes with laughter. 'So that's what he was going on about.'

'I'm talking a full-on furry Tigger suit, paws and all. I cut a hole for the necessaries.'

'You are something else,' I say, laughing so hard it hurts.

'You may laugh, but it worked. She *loved* the Tigger suit. I chased her round the bed like a naughty, hyper cartoon character, pounced and gave her the best, silliest sex she's had in her life. She came *so* many times. After all, how can you take life seriously when you've got five foot two of orange fur on top of you?'

We all fall about giggling, and Johan pats him on the back, joking, 'And you're worried about me?'

My mobile beeps and I hurriedly get it out of my pocket. My heart sinks when I see it isn't from Charlotte. It's a message from Miss Alpha's PA. Miss Alpha is a top lawyer I met a few months back. The text simply reads, 'Booking imminent.'

'A new appointment?' asks Valentino.

'Hopefully,' I mutter without my usual enthusiasm, and then change the subject.

A few hours later the night winds up. As I make my way home, I feel strangely unsettled. Johan's speech about love, and the idea that something transitory can become permanent, is disturbing. The truth is, it scares me and appeals to me in equal measure.

I call Trustfundista.

'Hey, gorgeous,' she purrs down the phone. 'Come over. I was just thinking about you. I'll put some champagne on ice. Jump in a cab and I'll pay him at this end.'

With the sour taste of beer in my mouth, I agree, happy to be back in my familiar world.

Later, lying in bed after an incredible sex session, the

strangest feeling overwhelms me: a real need for us to fall asleep in each other's arms. I am consumed with the sense of longing.

'Daddy's picking me up early in the morning,' Trustfundista tells me. 'He's got some finance person he wants me to meet.' She gets up and wraps her silk dressing gown around her. 'I'll get my driver to whizz you home,' she adds with a smile, kissing me fondly on the head.

'No problem,' I tell her, climbing out of bed and returning her kiss.

I walk into the bathroom, get dressed and, without thinking, pull my mobile out of my pocket and reread the message from Charlotte. I wish I could have seen her when she was eighteen, when *I* was eighteen. You could have the romantic ideal back then – pure thoughts trapped in a glass jar. Now, I feel like an animal trapped in a human body. That's what a sex drive does to all those good intentions.

Chapter 8

Male Equivalent of a Trophy Wife

I've decided to do something I know could be construed as romantic, but I feel that desperate measures are needed to get Charlotte to return my calls. I'm working on an original composition to play to her, a musical gift you might say. I have a battered old piano in the corner of my apartment. It faces the window that looks on to the street. As I sit at it, tapping out notes and imagining Charlotte sitting with me, playing the melody with her right hand, while I play the accompanying bass notes with my left hand, a memory drifts through my mind. Instantly I abandon the piano and walk to the window, where I look out pensively. I'm not sure what triggered the memory, probably the message I received last night from Miss Alpha's PA. The memory is so distinct I can close my eyes and imagine myself back there. It makes a mockery of my current endeavour.

I'm at the counter at Harvey Nics and Miss Alpha is handing her black titanium Amex card over to a young assistant, who is barely concealing her shock. She's just about to spend £3,000 on me, like I'm a spoiled trophy wife. Minutes before, she'd made me say 'please' nicely so I could have some Marc Jacobs sunglasses I wanted. Did I feel ashamed? Not really. Of course I felt slightly patronised when she laughingly referred to me as her 'boy toy', but the truth is, I felt aroused. I had a hard-on. I must be a gigolo to the core. After all, who else would get an erection when a woman spends money on them like a pampered pet?

This memory makes me feel my friendship with Charlotte is futile. The reality is, Miss Alpha is the kind of woman I work with best.

I met her at a party in London a while ago and was instantly struck, as any man would be, by her huge, blatantly fake breasts. She has long, glossy brunette hair and a tanned body, with a curvy bum and big boobs, and looks like a classic example of someone with glamour-girl aspirations. As my friend introduced us, my eyes couldn't help but linger, for a moment, on Miss Alpha's chest.

'Honey, you're looking at ten thousand dollars of prime investment there,' she laughed with a Southern drawl.

I'm ashamed to say that I pegged her as an American stripper over here to work. But her outfit didn't make sense. She had on a black cashmere polo-neck, jeans, black high-heeled boots and a woollen coat. Her clothes looked very expensive and understated for someone of that profession. Also, her confidence was verging on brash. I felt as though I'd been scolded like a schoolchild for sneaking a peek.

As I tried to get her measure, I batted back, 'Well, it looks like you got a good return.'

She threw back her coiffed hair and roared with laughter, putting her arm round my shoulder and saying, 'You seem like my kinda guy.'

At this point, my friend whispered something in my ear. His revelation stunned me. 'She's a partner in a top New York law firm and she's worth about twenty million,' he informed me.

'I heard ya,' she drawled suddenly. 'Just cos I got fake boobs doesn't mean I'm deaf. But he's right – I *am* a successful businesswoman. And you know what that means? I can buy myself a new pair of breasts if I want, or a hot boy for that matter. What else should us ladies spend our bonuses on?' With that she let out another throaty laugh, then fixed me with a suggestive stare. 'Let me tell you something, in case you're wondering,' she continued to us both. 'I might only be two generations away from poor Southern white trash, but I was the youngest person ever to make partner at our firm at twenty-two and I'd made twenty million dollars by the time I was thirty, so don't let the double Ds dazzle ya, cos I could beat your asses in a second.'

I was so taken aback by her speech I was stunned into silence.

'Cat got ya tongue?' she said, looking at me provocatively.

Just at that moment another friend brought over a celebrity singer to meet me, hoping, in light of my success with Celebrity X, to hook us up. I politely shook her hand and said hello, then carried on my conversation with Miss Alpha. Now *this* was an interesting woman.

'You're very intriguing. I'd love to find out more

about you,' I told Miss Alpha, leaning in to whisper in her ear.

'Now you're talking. Let's get to the bar,' she replied, slapping my behind.

Later she admitted that she had been impressed I'd turned down the advances of a celebrity to talk to her. This had won me infinite brownie points in her book.

We spent the rest of the night drinking champagne and talking. Then we headed back to her room at the Mandarin Oriental in Knightsbridge, where she gave the cab driver a £30 tip for an £8 journey.

In bed, she was boss. She stripped off as soon as we walked through the door, almost pinned me against the wall and tugged off my clothes.

'Is your dick hard?' she demanded, thrusting her hand down there to check. 'Good boy,' she told me, after confirming that it was indeed *very* hard. 'Lie on the bed. I wanna go on top,' she instructed me. Then she proceeded to straddle me and play with her huge breasts as she found a rhythm she liked. We had barely kissed at this point, and my usual gigolo charm didn't seem to interest her one bit. She just wanted my body.

After ten minutes, and with no orgasm in sight, her mood turned aggressive. 'Go harder,' she panted, riding herself into a frenzy on top of me.

I did what I could, but suddenly she stopped, mid-thrust. 'Honey, this just ain't working for me,' she chastised, pulling herself off me.

My heart sank. In all my years as a gigolo, I had never failed to please a woman. I thought she was going to throw me out, along with my previously untarnished record. But within minutes I discovered this was just her way of getting what she wanted. Other women might make the best of something, but not Miss Alpha. She was proactive at work, and, God, was she proactive in bed.

She lay down, opened her legs and ordered me to get on top. I assumed she wanted to start again, but this time with me on top. As I attempted to enter her, she yelled, 'No,' then instructed, 'Masturbate hard against my pussy instead.'

Within seconds she was writhing under me, moaning and virtually purring as I played with her breasts. 'Honey, this *is* working,' she drawled excitedly in my ear, then orgasmed loudly with an abandon I rarely see.

For once in my career I didn't quite know what to do with myself afterwards. Did she want me to stay? After all, she didn't appear interested in seductive chat.

'We should get some sleep,' she said, smiling and almost reading my thoughts. 'I'm taking you shopping tomorrow as a reward for that performance.'

I smiled to myself. She was a total one-off, and I *loved* it.

The next day when I woke up, Miss Alpha kissed me and asked me to call the kitchen and order a champagne breakfast. As I made the call, she yelled, 'Tell them to bring that vintage Dom Pérignon, not the usual crap,' in my ear.

After our room-service order was delivered – then sent back twice because it wasn't to her liking – we finally started to have a proper conversation.

Strangely enough, her situation wasn't that dissimilar to the story Johan would later tell us at the Dandy Trade Union meeting. Despite her money, she'd been married to a controlling bully of a husband who had drained her of all energy and desire. On divorcing, she'd vowed to have some fun at last. She told me I was the 'perfect post-divorce treat'. I started to think that maybe divorce lawyers should discreetly start to recommend a gigolo in case of a favourable outcome with the settlement. A bad marriage, it seemed, left women desperately craving good sex. And who better to provide it?

I tuned the stereo into a jazz station I knew and she looked at me quizzically. 'Ya like jazz?' she asked, as if it had just registered I might have another life beyond that which occurred below my belt.

'I'm a musician,' I told her, smiling at her obvious surprise. 'I studied music, and it's my one great love – apart from women of course.'

I wondered if I'd veered too far off safe territory, but I knew if our affair was to proceed she had to see me as more than merely a sex object who could be tossed away. Her whole demeanour changed instantly, and she curled up next to me and questioned me about the music I played. It turned out that she was an amateur painter and had a lot of respect for the artistic process and for creative people.

'So you're more than just a pretty face,' she told me, dragging a frosted-pink talon across my cheek and leaving a mark. 'You should come over to New York for the opening night of my exhibition.'

I kissed her and agreed, but never thought anything would come of it. That was three months ago – and then came the message from her PA. So here I am, simultan-eously involved in some futile romantic gesture for Charlotte, a woman I haven't even slept with, while waiting to hear if I'm about to be flown to New York as a 'boy toy' for a woman who could make a nuclear physicist feel like an air-head sex object. Surely nothing is crazier, or more complicated, than the life of a gigolo?

I'm flying to New York today for the exhibition. Even though the Literary Café is only a five-minute walk away, I get the taxi to take me there and wait outside – after all, it is paid for by Miss Alpha. I've handwritten, with a vintage fountain pen, a musical score of the composition I've created for Charlotte, so she can play it on the piano in the café. I scribble a note on the back, saying it would sound better with me accompanying her. I hope this will soften her resolve against me.

I slip the music in an envelope and drop it behind the counter. My taxi drives me to the airport, where I board a first-class American Airlines flight to New York. The airline staff treat me like a total VIP, rushing me straight through to board and settling me into my seat. I'm wearing the dark Miu Miu shirt Miss Alpha bought me in Harvey Nics. As a pretty air hostess pours me a glass of champagne, I smile to myself at the incongruity of it all.

When we touch down, a large black limo is waiting to pick me up. I sit in the back, once again saying a silent hello to the city that never lets me sleep, and sip on the bottled water provided, gearing myself to meet up again with the lovely, incorrigible man-eater that is Miss Alpha.

We reach our destination and pull up outside a skyscraper that looks like it might pierce the clouds. The driver informs me conspiratorially that a mega-famous, rich hip-hop star lives there, then eyes me suspiciously. I laugh to myself, knowing what the driver is thinking. The famously macho hip-hop star is rumoured to be gay. The driver obviously suspects I'm a home delivery. He couldn't be more wrong. Men might order a sexual snack on room service but women want a banquet with silver service. I'm a high-class tryst, not a hired hand.

I ride up in the elevator and knock on the door, getting ready for the whirlwind.

'Glad ya made it, honey,' Miss Alpha purrs, opening the door and virtually pulling me inside by my belt, while kissing me aggressively. 'Nice shirt.' She smiles, looking approvingly at the outfit she hand-chose, then orders, 'Now get your trousers off.'

As I start to unbutton my trousers, I scan the apartment. My jaw drops to about fifty feet below sea level. Never in all my life have I seen such an incredible place. It is wall-to-wall glass, which gives a stunning bird's-eye view of uptown New York. I see Central Park in the distance, a tiny green speck. We're almost above cloud level and you can see people scurrying about below – little, tiny, insignificant crumbs, smaller than ants. No wonder the rich have such a superiority complex.

As I'm dragged into the bedroom, I notice a beautiful grand piano in the centre of the lounge, which then disappears out of view as I'm almost flung on the bed, by now trouserless.

'I woulda paid American Airlines to fly ya here faster, but even money can't buy time,' she says laughingly, placing my hands on her breasts and sighing as I start to fondle them. 'Husbands suck – you boys are where the party's at,' she exclaims as I gently pull off her knickers and start to touch her. 'Yeah, that's good – but just to the left a little,' she tells me. 'Yeah, now go faster . . . Now a little slower . . . No, to the right . . . *Softer* . . . Not that soft . . . Yeah, that's it.' Her arousal is punctuated by a continuous stream of instructions, which could no doubt guide a missile precisely to its target. I love her dedication to her own pleasure. For a gigolo, it makes your job far easier if someone is giving you clear and constructive feedback. Women may have to bear the bungling hands of a boyfriend, but they should never have to endure the same treatment from a trained expert.

Suddenly she grabs a remote control and flicks a button. I'm wondering if she's putting on music to set the mood, though admittedly that isn't much like her, when the largest TV screen I've ever seen emerges from the bottom of the four-poster bed we're reclined on. This, I have *never* seen before – a wide-screen plasma TV actually built into the framework of the bed. When fully risen, it obscures the view of New York and creates an instantly more intimate atmosphere. I presume she wants us to watch porn together, to heighten her pleasure, but I am again mistaken. The darkened screen has a mirror effect, and she makes me kneel, straddles me backwards so we are both facing the TV and slides herself on to me, using her hands to guide me. She gasps as I enter her, then starts rocking backwards and forwards. I don't know what they teach them in Texas, but it feels mind-blowing.

She moves my left hand to touch her clitoris and tells me to be firm, then places the other on her breasts for me to massage them. She's resting back into my chest like I'm a chair, with my arms strapping her in and simultaneously stimulating her. Pinned down, other than the work my hands can do, I am unable to control the rhythm or pace we're going at. She is fucking *me*. I am beside myself with pleasure, as, it seems, is she, judging by the loud, gasping tone of her increasingly frequent moans.

With my head resting in the curve of the back of her neck, the scent of her perfume arousing me even more, I manage to look over her shoulder and glimpse our reflection in the makeshift mirror. The obscured image of Miss Alpha's sexy dream body is displayed – legs wide and breasts shuddering at every thrust – like a flickering picture on the television screen. It's as if we have mistakenly picked up the frequency of an otherworldly porn channel. Only a dark shadow hints at the object behind her – me – which she is pushing against to create such pleasure. With the highlighted curves of her body shimmering on the screen like candlelight, she is the star of the show.

'Now ya see why those breasts were worth it,' she says teasingly afterwards. 'They sure as hell look good on screen, don't they?'

I nod an enthusiastic affirmative. The TV screen slides back down and all of New York is once more laid out literally at my feet.

'You see, in my trade it ain't worth getting caught out with any home-movie shit. But like everything, I find ways to get round it.'

'Very sexy, very smart and *very* rich – I'm not sure if you're just a figment of my wishful imagination,' I laugh, bringing her robe over to her and helping her on with it like a modern handmaid.

'Ya didn't dream me up, darlin' – I'm living large here in the flesh. Now grab a shower – we're going shopping. Ya need a new outfit for the exhibition. Don't want ya showin' me up, now do we?'

'Any excuse for a New York shopping trip is fine by me,' I reply, smiling.

*

Within an hour a stretch limo is driving us through the hectic streets to Saks Fifth Avenue.

'Hello, ma'am.' The female assistant greets us (well, Miss Alpha) with a familiar friendliness I imagine means she spends a *lot* of money here on a regular basis.

'I'm shopping for my gentleman friend here – or should I say my "toy boy"?' she says almost gleefully, with a wide Texan twang, almost missing off the 'y's.

I stand a few paces behind with a fixed expression, like a male doll.

'Whaddya reckon would look good on him?' She addresses the assistant, not even looking at me, let alone seeking my opinion.

'I know just the thing, ma'am. I think I've come to know your taste by now,' says the assistant, walking off into another room and then coming back moments later with a silver Hugo Boss suit that looks like it's stepped straight off the *Zoolander* set. I inwardly groan. It's flashy and loud – not at all my style. Nevertheless, I smilingly head to the changing room to try it on. If only my fellow dandies could see me now, I think to myself, as I slip it on, feeling like I've been wrapped in a giant piece of tinfoil. I walk out, to appraising looks from both Miss Alpha and the assistant.

'I don't know if it's tight enough around the crotch,' muses Miss Alpha, walking up to me and grabbing the aforementioned area. 'Whaddya think?'

I go to open my mouth, until I realise she's addressing the assistant, not me. Like a redundant fish, my mouth flaps shut as the assistant's gaze falls to my crotch. I even feel I may blush.

'I see what you mean,' the assistant says after some consideration.

'No point in nice packaging if the goods ain't on display,' cackles Miss Alpha, and I can see by the gleam in her eye that she's enjoying this little scene.

The assistant smirks and walks off to get the trousers in a smaller size.

'Why don't we just get the male equivalent of a Wonderbra down there?' I laugh, trying to ease my discomfort and assert some kind of presence again.

'Honey, I would, but I don't want to damage anything with underwiring.'

'There is actually a human being inside this body,' I jokingly chide her.

'Look, when I've got time to hear men moan about being objectified, I'll call you. Until then, you're my pretty plaything.' And with that she gives me a lingering kiss on the lips.

I really like her, but much as I admire her bold, empowered attitude, there are boundaries that can be crossed – even with gigolos.

My discomfort is only momentarily alleviated when we come to pay. The assistant smiles broadly as she rings through $20,000 – all spent on me. I have shirts, ties, suits, even pants – none of them particularly to my taste. It feels churlish to complain, but being on the receiving end of the medicine that women have tasted for years isn't quite the experience I'd imagined it to be. My grin certainly isn't as broad as Julia Roberts's during her *Pretty Woman* moment, but thinking again, maybe it's something that us postmodern men might have to get used to. I'm sure a wealthy businessman might like to splash his money on a cleavage-enhancing outfit for his amour, so why should it be any different for women? Even if the area of enhancement is slightly lower down.

With the exhibition due to take place in two hours, the dilemma facing Miss Alpha is not what artistic school to claim her influences come from, but what clothes to dress me up in.

'No, not that – it ain't quite right,' she says, wrinkling up her nose as I parade up and down the bedroom in the silver suit. I sigh with relief as it is discounted.

Eventually she settles on a cream Brioni jacket with pale-lilac pinstripe and cream nubuck brogues – the look is English dandy mixed with more than a dash of *Miami Vice*. ZZ would love this look on me, I think to myself, smiling.

As the limo drives through the fashionable Meatpacking district, I squeeze Miss Alpha's hand. 'Are you nervous?' I ask comfortingly.

'Hell, no,' she answers, snorting with laughter. 'I'm way too rich for anyone to give me an honest opinion. Whichever way, this show will be a success – well, that's what people will tell me. And hey, that's all that counts.'

I laugh at her honesty. It's refreshing to see someone so at ease with their wealth. Thinking back to Celebrity X and her misery about her fame and fortune, it seems such a shame that she couldn't accept her situation for what it was and make the most of it.

'Anyhow, I don't know if I'm more excited about showing off my art, or showing off *you*,' she says teasingly, stroking my knee and then suggestively tracing her hand higher.

We get out of the limo and walk up the winding white

stairs. Inside is an ultra-modern white loft space, with people mingling, drinking cocktails and making polite conversation. The whole atmosphere exudes money. What strikes me is how grown-up it all is. Unlike celebrity or fashion parties, where decorum is often abandoned for debauchery, most people here seem to be using the exhibition as an opportunity to network. In fact, it is such a vanity project that I notice the paintings aren't even for sale.

After a few muted conversations about the obvious influence of Cézanne on the brightly coloured still lives hanging on the walls, talk gets round to the favourite topic of conversation in these circles: money – how to make it, and how to spend it.

I smile nicely, trying to look pretty and make the odd witty, charming observation, but ultimately I'm a show pony.

'Whaddya think of my new *friend*?' drawls Miss Alpha, putting comic emphasis on the word 'friend' when she introduces me to her financial law partner.

The prim-looking woman smiles at me wanly, then pulls Miss Alpha to one side and mutters, 'I'm sure he's good for you, but it doesn't look good for business.'

'Bullshit,' I hear Miss Alpha retort fiercely. 'He looks good on my arm and in my bed. And ya know what? If I can afford a trophy toy boy, I think that says more about the size of my bank balance than any polite chit-chat about bonuses could.' Then she storms off, squeezing my arm affectionately as she passes me and whispering loudly, 'Wait till I get you home, boy,' so her partner, who instantly blushes, can hear. 'She's just jealous,' she continues in mock secrecy, giving a glare in the uptight woman's direction.

A few hours later the party is over. Financiers and legal

high-flyers don't do all-nighters. Who wants to have a bad hangover when you're playing roulette with millions?

As we drive back home in the limo, I gauge that success evidently is an aphrodisiac, as Miss Alpha unzips my trousers and starts to suck me very hard. The driver looks impassively ahead. After a few moments she stops, saying she just wanted to warm me up so it would be more fun for me when I pleasure her, then uses her right hand to move my head downwards. By the time we make it back to her apartment, we have both been pleasured to within an inch of our lives. After viewing far more than his job calls for, the driver's retinas must be burning.

At home, her mood turns whimsical. 'Play me a tune,' she tells me, nodding in the direction of the grand piano.

I walk over, open it up and sit down. With the backdrop of a lit-up New York skyline, it feels surreal and enchanting. I think about playing a beautiful piece by Bill Evans. Instead, Miss Alpha, Texan to the core, asks me to play 'Free Bird' by Lynyrd Skynyrd. Not quite the atmosphere I had planned on creating, but she who pays the piper calls the tune. As I start playing, she comes and rests by the side of the piano, closing her eyes and mouthing the words.

'You playing like that is getting me all hot again,' she says, smirking.

I smile and carry on playing, enjoying entertaining her. She walks behind me and starts to unbutton my shirt, stroking her talon-nailed hand across my chest. I try and keep my concentration, but it's very tough.

'I wanna spank ya,' she says suddenly.

I don't know quite how the thought popped into her mind, but hesitantly I agree. I don't mind a little light S&M, but I prefer sexual seduction to fetish.

'Strip off and lean over the piano,' she commands me.

I slowly remove my clothes, feeling strangely uncomfortable. Somehow, there is nothing playful in Miss Alpha's demands. I get the sense there are darker forces at work. She is on a power trip, and I have been singled out as the victim.

Uneasily, I obey and lean across the piano. New York doesn't seem quite so charming from this angle. Miss Alpha goes into the bedroom. I was expecting a flirty little hand spank, so I doubtless look surprised as she departs to fetch her 'instrument'. She walks back in, naked apart from high Versace black heels and the largest bull whip I have ever seen in my life.

'Even if you're a good boy, I'll still punish ya,' she laughs, a little too vindictively for my taste, as she struts over and starts to prowl around, brandishing the whip.

'Look, I'm not going to be the whipping boy for your ex-husband,' I exclaim, leaping up and grabbing my trousers.

Her face is like thunder. 'If you won't do as I say, you're no use to me,' she says bluntly. 'Pack your things. I'll get ya a flight home in the morning. Is that what ya want?'

'In the circumstances, yes,' I reply, hastily getting dressed. I don't mind atoning for other men's sins in the bedroom, but I won't be punished for them.

I sleep on the sofa that night, and by the time I wake up Miss Alpha has already left for work, so there are no awkward goodbyes, just an American Airlines ticket left on the table. The limo arrives to drop me off at the airport and I pick up the ticket and look at it closely. My heart sinks: economy. Such is the fate of a gigolo who won't do as he's told, I sigh to myself.

Chapter 9

She's Behind You!

After a cramped journey in the sardine tin of economy, I'm in no mood to rush back to my equally space-challenged apartment. Catching a ride on other people's premium lives when your own is much lower rent creates some terrible chasms.

Luckily, like a guardian angel, Trustfundista messages me just after my plane lands. 'I want wild, crazy adventures, Golden. I'm bored of City guys who sound like talking bank statements. I'll throw myself off the Gherkin if you don't save me from these dullards. I need YOU' are her exact words. I instantly reply to let her know I've just landed at Heathrow but am still on the plane. She texts back to tell me her driver will be at the airport to pick me up by the time I've cleared customs. Perfect, I think: a knight in shining armour who is missing a white charger,

which the damsel in distress can provide. I barely have
enough money for a cab journey, and taking the Tube in
my illicitly gained finery would feel too tragic. As I wait
for the car to arrive, I dwell on the crazy experiences of
the last few days.

I think about the hot sex, and also how, despite the
unsavoury ending, I have a great respect and admiration
for Miss Alpha. She's a woman of incredible spirit and
energy. Spending time with women such as her is like
taking a peek into the future and seeing a sell-by date
stamped on men's foreheads. She has such determination,
ambition and strength it is almost scary.

But I had also seen a different side to this powerful
lady, and this is what plays on my mind. More haunting
even than the harrowing sight of a hyper-empowered
woman bearing a grudge and wielding a bull whip was a
phone call that had taken place last night, just after my
argument with Miss Alpha, and before my unceremonious
exit from her world.

Miss Alpha was taking a bath and was seemingly
unconcerned about our little spat, just as if I were a court
case that hadn't gone her way. I was sitting on the plush
leather sofa, looking out of the window and trying to iden-
tify the famous New York landmarks to pass the time, when
the phone started to ring insistently. It would ring off and
then start again. After a while I started to worry someone
may be trying to get through with urgent news. I shouted
to Miss Alpha in the bathroom, but she either couldn't hear
or was ignoring me. Being a hired hand, rather than a
boyfriend, I felt I couldn't invade her privacy by walking
into the bathroom without an invite. After much delibera-
tion, I picked up the phone.

'Mommy, is that you?' the sweet voice of a little girl asked me chirpily. She sounded about five years old.

'No, it's Mommy's friend,' I replied cautiously, regretting picking up the phone.

'Where's Mommy? I want to speak to her – I painted her a picture of a cat,' the little voice told me excitedly.

'She's popped out to the shops,' I told the girl, thinking that saying her mum was taking a bath was somehow inappropriate.

'Who is that?' An adult female voice came on the line, and when I stated again that I was a friend, the person revealed she was the nanny and was looking after Miss Alpha's three children at her home in the Hamptons. Miss Alpha was due to come home the next day, and they needed to know what time she would arrive. I told her that I'd pass on the message. I hadn't even been aware Miss Alpha had kids.

Miss Alpha's face was like thunder when I told her later that evening, after we'd curtly agreed my travel arrangements home.

'Don't *ever* discuss my children,' she had warned me, like a protective lioness.

Once again, a reminder: a gigolo's sphere is the bedroom; our permit does not allow us entry into other areas of our clients' lives.

Now, standing on the tarmac pavement of terminal three, with thick English cloud hanging overhead, I feel strangely saddened that I will never get to see the warm, maternal side of a woman like Miss Alpha. And thinking about it, I will never get to see this side of *any* of the women I frequent. I cannot help but think this is my loss, not theirs.

As the limo pulls up, I see Trustfundista looking through

the window, waving and smiling prettily. 'I decided to come along for the ride,' she tells me excitedly, as I get in the car. 'We stopped off at Bond Street to go shopping, and then I thought I might as well come along, as I've not really got anything better to do,' she carries on, laughing at how little she does with her life.

'So lovely to see you,' I say, smiling broadly, then kissing her on the lips.

Both of us tactfully avoid discussing where I'm flying home from, and who I have been visiting. Like a cocooned little princess, there is something reassuringly uncomplicated about Trustfundista – she's like a daddy's girl who never really grew up. Buy her a nice pony, throw a fun party and she's happy. This is one arrangement I'll miss when it inevitably comes to an end, I think to myself.

'Daddy is virtually trying to set me up with an arranged marriage,' she says to me, as if reading my mind. She pouts sulkily and carries on, 'I've met so many boring men over the last few weeks I feel like my brain cells have gone into early retirement. Daddy thinks I'm wasting my life away shopping and running around. You know what he said?' She doesn't wait for me to answer, but continues her rant: 'He said I'm turning into an "air-head heiress". Can you believe that? I know my life is vacant, but I'm not an air-head, am I?'

'Of course not,' I reassure her, putting my arm round her and squeezing her shoulder.

'But I realised that in one way Daddy's right. I can't carry on like this. So you know what I told him?'

'What?' I answer, looking at her beautifully shaped tawny eyes.

'I've told him I want to work in the family business.' She looks at me triumphantly, waiting to see my reaction.

I smile and try to conceal my astonishment.

'You're surprised! Let me tell you, not as surprised as Daddy was. I thought he was going to fall off his chair. The thing is, I know I will marry one of these men he's trying to set me up with – a "prudent match", as he calls them. But when I thought about it, I realised that although I *am* ready to move my life on, I need to do it in my own way. If I got married tomorrow, what would really change about my life? I'd be like a piece of property being passed from one man to the other. The only difference is, the payments on my American Express bill would stop being made by Daddy and start being made by my new husband. I'd still be idling my time away, shopping in Selfridges and going to lunch – just financed by my new daddy. And it would be much harder to have someone like you along to keep me company and make things fun. So it's the perfect solution – I'll have a job myself!'

'Good for you,' I tell her, thinking about Miss Alpha and how she made millions as a hot-shot lawyer.

'I'll miss you, Golden,' she says softly, stroking my cheek thoughtfully. 'I love your world, it's just so much fun. But I won't be able to have a full-time gigolo when I'm a proper career girl with marriage prospects to consider . . .' She tails off and looks down, like she is about to pack away her favourite childhood toy.

'You don't have to say anything. This is the gigolo way,' I tell her gallantly. 'When I stop getting your messages, I'll just presume our arrangement is terminated – until then, let's have fun while you're still free.'

'You're right,' she squeals. 'I've been so wrapped up in all these serious decisions over the last few weeks that I hadn't thought of how important it is to make the most of the little time I have left. I start work at Daddy's bank next month. I'm keeping my London flat, but I'll spend a lot of time based in Monaco. Let's go out and party tonight. I want to go out in style!'

'You're on,' I tell her. 'Let's go back to yours and choose the sexiest, coolest, most un-banker-friendly dress for you to wear tonight, then go out and get up to all sorts of mischief.' I lean over and kiss her, stroking her leg teasingly.

I could do with a fun night out, and strangely I don't feel like sex. Obviously, I can't tell Trustfundista this. Firstly, because you can never tell *any* woman you don't feel like having sex with her, and secondly, because when you're a gigolo, it's tantamount to heresy. With Trustfundista, because she's not the sexual predator most of my ladies are and doesn't get her kicks from initiating sex, it's easier to avoid sexual engagement.

Although it's rare, to the point of utterly exceptional, for me not to feel like performing, these last few weeks have left me feeling unsettled. I'm sure after a night out and a few glasses of champagne my libido will be revved up again, but at the moment the perils of my trade have left me feeling a little hollow.

'There are *so* many parties happening tonight it's hard to choose.'

I can barely hear Rochester as he tries to speak over the loud music pumping in the background. I've called him for a heads-up on the social itinerary for the night as I'm temporarily out of the loop after being out of town.

Always reliable, Rochester knows exactly what's going on. He reels off a few parties, and I shout to Trustfundista, who's in her bedroom getting ready, 'Do you want to start at the PPQ party?' knowing that the first place we head to might help with her choice of outfit.

'Sounds perfect,' she shouts back.

When I've finished speaking with Rochester, I poke my head round the bedroom door. Trustfundista's wearing only some very skimpy, sheer, black silk underwear and is looking appraisingly in the mirror at different dresses. She holds a black sequinned shift dress, which is slashed to the waist at the back, against her. 'What about this?' she asks, biting her lower lip thoughtfully.

'Perfect,' I reply. 'It's probably going to be quite "fashion" there tonight.'

'OK. Maybe I'll wear it with black tights and boots, then,' she says, slipping it over her head and revealing just how thigh-skimmingly short it is.

When we're both ready, the driver whisks us into central London for our night of debauchery. The queue outside the club is already trailing down the street, and the entrance is a bottleneck of fashionistas scrumming to get inside. The bouncer is pushing people away, making anyone who is rude in their endeavours to gain entry go to the back of the queue. As we walk towards the entrance, fragments of conversation drift towards us, and I smile to myself as I hear a young girl almost swoon and repeat to her friend, 'Apparently Kate Moss is in there.'

Trying to protect Trustfundista, I place one arm round her waist and use the other to bat off revellers as we make our way through the bottleneck to the front. I hear one of the door staff shout, 'Let Golden through,' and feel a hundred pairs of eyes train on us curiously, trying to figure out if we're famous and why we should be so privileged to be let through automatically. Trustfundista tries to retain an equanimous look, but I know she secretly loves this kind of treatment, and that it makes it worthwhile to have a gigolo on her arm, as well as in her bed. Her expensive hair swishes behind her, framed beautifully by her bare back, as we walk down the stairs, hearing the music get louder with every step we take. The energy of the party is like an aphrodisiac, enticing us onwards.

As we walk into the main room, the black walls seem to swallow us up. In the centre the DJ's white Perspex booth is raised above ground level. Like a dark angel, Rochester is standing on top of it, with his shirt off, flaunting his tattoos and raising his arms as if the dancing crowd is there to worship him. We head over to him, saying hello to passing acquaintances who jostle past with drinks balanced precariously in their hands, and climb up on to the DJ booth.

'Golden!' yells Rochester, pulling me into a bare-chested embrace, then following suit with Trustfundista, who laughs loudly and kisses him on both cheeks. 'You have to have some pussy,' Rochester says conspiratorially, leaning towards us.

'What?' I reply, slightly aghast at what he's just said.

Trustfundista blushes, then throws her head backwards and roars with laughter, saying, 'I'm not even going to comment.'

Rochester rolls his eyes theatrically and wags his finger at us. 'You and your dirty little minds. No, it's this totally cool cocktail they're serving at the bar, which has a mystery energy ingredient aptly called pussy. Honestly, I've had so much of the stuff I'm flying,' he tells us, shrieking with laughter and turning back to face the crowd, raising his arms imperiously again.

'I *love* Rochester,' giggles Trustfundista. 'He's absolutely crazy.'

'I don't think you're going to meet many men like him in your new banking job,' I joke, tracing my finger down her back.

'Can you imagine Rochester as a bank manager?' she yelps with laughter. 'There would be anarchy within minutes.'

'He'd just withdraw all the money, buy an island, fly there in a private jet filled with champagne and then party until the investors tracked him down and lynched him,' I jokingly reply.

'Don't give me any ideas,' says Trustfundista, winking at me. 'If you hear of an heiress who just fleeced her father's bank, you'll know exactly where I've gone and what I'm doing with the money.'

'I won't need to hear – I trust I'll be there with you, as your number-one concubine,' I say teasingly, kissing her before she has a chance to reply.

After a few minutes of passionate kissing, high up in the DJ booth, on display, she looks into my eyes and says, 'Naughty, you've made me into a total exhibitionist. Daddy would kill me if he saw this,' and with that she pulls me even closer, hitches up her dress dangerously high, leans against the side of the booth and kisses me harder. 'You're worth robbing a bank for. Maybe I'll have to do a heist to have you,' she whispers softly, nibbling my ear.

'Now that's the kind of talk I like,' I say, placing my hands on her petite waist and pulling her even closer to me. 'Although I'd hate you to mess up your hair wearing a balaclava, or break your nails brandishing a gun.'

'Don't worry – I could afford to have a stylist and a manicurist in the getaway car,' she laughs, with a fantastically self-aware twinkle in her eyes. 'Anyway, let's be serious, as if I'd need to hold up my father's bank – I'd do it as an inside job.'

'We could be an upmarket Bonnie and Clyde – hijack your driver and hit the road,' I say, continuing the fantasy.

'What are you two giggling about so secretively?' says Rochester, coming up behind us and putting an arm round each of our shoulders.

'Oh, just nonsense,' I say, rapping his knuckles playfully, 'so never you mind.'

'It's such fun to talk nonsense. I wish I could talk it for the rest of my life,' says Trustfundista whimsically. 'You can't be sensible and talk nonsense, that just wouldn't make sense.'

'Have you had too much pussy?' teases Rochester, as she finishes her little speech.

'No, but I'm heading straight to the bar to get some. Right, Golden?'

'Walk this way, madam,' I say guiding her towards the bar, which is lit up with white neon, contrasting sharply with the black interior.

After both knocking back a shot of pussy, my phone rings.

'It's Johan,' I mouth to Trustfundista as I answer.

'Where are you?' he shouts down the phone.

'I'm at the PPQ party.'

'Come over to Bungalow 8,' he says. 'It's all happening here. Supermodels, film directors – you name them, they're here.'

The star-struck girl outside must have got her information wrong, I smile to myself.

'OK, we're heading over now. We've just had some pussy,' I tell him.

'What?' he screeches down the line.

'Don't worry – it's a drink,' I laugh. 'See you in a minute.' And with that I guide a bemused Trustfundista, still reeling from the shot we've just downed, outside into the chaos of the street.

'Where are we going?' she asks, lacing her arm through mine.

'Bungalow Eight – that's where Johan is,' I reply. 'I know it's a chore, but can you endure hanging out with male supermodels for one night?'

'I think I might just manage it.' She smiles, snuggling closer to me.

We arrive just in time to see the paparazzi go into meltdown over an A-lister who is arriving at the party.

'I'm already liking the look of this place,' comments Trustfundista, walking confidently down the stairs into the monochrome interior.

I look at my mobile to check the time and notice a text message I must have missed. Casually, I scroll down, not expecting it to be anyone of any importance. Then my eyes widen. It's Charlotte. 'OK, you're forgiven. Why don't you meet me after work tonight?' I look at the clock on my phone again. It's almost half eleven. She finishes in half an hour. My stomach muscles instantly tense. I realise I have a terrible dilemma on my hands.

Trustfundista smiles warmly at me, squeezes my hand and leads me to the bar.

'No pussy this time,' she jokes. 'Let's stick to champagne.'

Johan strolls over, looking casually cool, as if he just

wakes up looking like he's on a fashion shoot. 'Hey, you made it. Good to see you both.'

Time is almost standing still in my mind, but I smile to hide my turmoil.

You're on an engagement, there's nothing you can do, I tell myself. But I know that I can't explain this to Charlotte and I will have blown my last chance.

'Have you met Sky?' Johan says, introducing a fellow model, who looks like God was on the happy pills when He made him. Trustfundista looks mesmerised.

'Have I met you before?' she asks flirtatiously.

'I don't think so. Maybe you just recognise me from the Dior adverts,' he replies, with a transatlantic twang, then reaches out and kisses her hand, like a modern-day Prince Charming.

I see my moment and pull Trustfundista to one side. 'That weird cocktail has made me feel ill – I'm almost feverish,' I tell her in a subdued voice. 'If I go home, will you be OK to stay with Johan and Sky? I'll make sure they look after you.'

Her eyes light up. Then she looks concerned. 'Are you OK? Yes, you must go home if you feel sick. I'll be fine staying here with Sky . . . and Johan,' she adds quickly.

'You're a darling,' I say, kissing her cheek. Then I lower my voice and whisper, 'And you know I don't mind if you dip your hand in the Dior-model cookie jar. After all, you only have a few weeks of freedom left.' I sound like her indulgent daddy treating her to a gift.

'Golden, you're incorrigible,' she says with a smirk. 'That thought hadn't even crossed my mind. But now you mention it . . . would it be rude not to, in my circumstances?'

'*Very* rude,' I tell her, laughing, before saying farewell and walking towards the exit.

Just before I leave, I look back over my shoulder and see Trustfundista handing her credit card over for a magnum of champagne, and Sky's arm round her waist.

This is what I love about my world: there is no jealousy or possessiveness – just sexual communism, a veritable free-for-all. But here I am heading off into a far, far more complicated world, where this kind of behaviour wouldn't be tolerated, which I find very disconcerting. Nevertheless, something I can't put my finger on draws me towards it.

Walking through the door of the Literary Café is like passing through a portal to another world. The hazy atmosphere, flickering with candlelight, seems to be suspended in time, as if from another era, preserved for posterity. I can see Charlotte behind the counter, her auburn hair tied back, closing all the tills down, whistling to herself. The place is empty, way past its closing time. I walk from table to table blowing out each candle, so only the dimmed chandeliers cast light across the room.

'Thanks, Golden,' says Charlotte, still with her back to me, not even checking if I'm someone else – a stray customer or even an intruder.

As I reach the counter, she turns round and we face each other. Only the wood surface separates us. Her features seem illuminated in the half-light.

'Nice to see you again,' I say hesitantly, then lean over to kiss her on both cheeks. My easy gigolo charm seems to have deserted me for a moment.

She walks round and hugs me, saying, 'I love the music you wrote for me. Thank you.'

'So I'm forgiven, then?' I ask, smiling sheepishly.

She play-punches me, not that softly either, on the arm and says, 'Almost.'

'Almost?' I laugh, 'Why? What else do I have to do? You drive a hard bargain.'

'Buy me a few drinks and you might be fully forgiven,' she jokes, walking to the coat-stand and wrapping up in her jacket.

'Where would you like me to buy you these all-redeeming drinks?' I ask, following her out and watching as she carefully locks the front door and slides the keys into her bag. The café, empty and dark, seems to be impassively watching our conversation in the background. I feel on entirely unfamiliar territory: even the prospect of buying her a drink is a total role reversal of the terms under which I usually operate.

'Let's go to a jazz bar,' she says impetuously. 'Let's have a proper night out.'

'You're on,' I reply, linking my arm with hers and hailing a passing taxi, mentally calculating how much money I have on me. Usually such things aren't a consideration. 'Let's go to the 606. It's a fantastic hard-bop place just off the King's Road. Have you been?' I ask.

'Yes, but not for ages – I love it there, though,' she replies, sitting snugly next to me in the cab.

When we reach our destination, I try and pay for the taxi, but Charlotte insists on going halves. 'You're buying the drinks, after all,' she laughs.

We walk down the steps into the dark, decadent interior, and I head for the bar, while Charlotte finds us a table. I buy a beer for myself and a glass of wine for Charlotte. It feels freakishly normal, and I consider maxing my credit card out on champagne just to make things more familiar.

We talk about the Literary Café for a while, the gossip from the regulars and the antics of the eccentric boss. Then the conversation turns more intimate.

'I've known you for so long now, but I still hardly seem to know anything about you,' she says, lightly touching my arm. 'Tell me something about yourself. You know all about my father and why I love jazz so much, but how about you? How did you get hooked?'

'I grew up on the Isle of Wight,' I say, as she smiles at me encouragingly. 'As a teenager, I wasn't really interested in girls – well, they weren't really interested in me,' I laugh, as she feigns mock astonishment. 'I know, hard to believe now,' I joke. 'So I guess instead I fell in love with music. I took piano lessons at home and mainly listened to my father's old rhythm and blues records for inspiration. One day, when I was about sixteen, a group of jazz musicians came from London to give a workshop in our school auditorium. These old guys in their fifties and sixties blew my mind. Suddenly I heard all these new sounds, rather than just the twelve-bar blues I'd been used to. The drummer took a shine to me and gave me lots of encouragement. Afterwards, I gave him my address, thinking I'd never hear from him when he got back to London. But a few weeks later a parcel came through the post from him. It was a cassette of jazz piano he'd recorded from his own vinyl collection – you could even hear him putting down the stylus. Count Basie, Duke Ellington, Red Garland, Oscar Peterson, hearing the way they all played gave me a rush inside my chest. From that moment I spent all my time practising and playing jazz piano. At that point, playing a

piano solo was better than sex for me. Improvising made
me feel like I was channelling God, it had such depth. It
was like a whole new world of possibilities had opened
up.' I stop, embarrassed that I've revealed too much and
gone on for so long. 'I'm sorry, how boring of me,' I say,
suddenly thinking I would never inflict a speech like this
on one of my clients. 'I've ranted on for ages.'

She reaches forward and puts her hand on mine, saying,
'Carry on, I love hearing all about it. My father used to
talk like this and it makes me remember what got me so
passionate about music in the first place. He was a massive
champion of British jazz music, which he thought was
really underappreciated.'

'I know – I feel the same,' I say excitedly. 'There are
too many British musicians who don't get the recognition
they deserve. They get overshadowed by the Americans.'

'That's so true,' says Charlotte, nodding her head vigorously in agreement. 'So many of our jazz legends are still
struggling to make ends meet. They could have made a
fortune if they'd sold out but they've kept their integrity
instead.'

'God, I have so much admiration for those men who
dedicate their lives to music,' I say a little sadly, thinking
of my own circumstances.

'Go on – tell me more about how you got into music,'
Charlotte urges me.

'Well, after the workshop I started taking a bus to the
other side of the island on Tuesday nights for the live jazz
recitals at a hotel in Ventnor. These old guys, retired cabaret
musicians who used to play in ship orchestras on the cruises,
would gather together to play all the jazz standards. I always
remember the bass player had these big banana fingers, and

he would pluck the bass and get the most beautiful sounds from it. They took me under their wing and during the intervals I'd sit chatting to them, me clutching a soft drink, and them nursing their bitters.

'After a while I'd sit in and play piano with them on one tune, then the next week I'd sit in for two, until eventually I played with them all night. You could see the beach from the windows, and we'd play "Take the 'A' Train" as the sun set over the sea. Those nights were so magical, and so emotional. We'd play "Quiet Nights" by Antonio Carlos Jobim, a love song about two people spending their last days together, then I'd watch the old couples spending *their* last days together and listening to us playing about the very same thing . . .' I trail off, touched by the memory.

'That's the sweetest thing I've ever heard,' says Charlotte softly, bringing me round from my reverie. She almost has tears in her eyes, and her hand is resting in mine.

I hadn't thought of that memory for years, and now, with all the turmoil in my head, the thought of love lasting a lifetime, and lovers spending their last days together, seems especially poignant. With perfect synergy, Charlotte and I look up at each other and something passes between us that feels powerful, loaded with electricity and emotion. I think we're about to kiss, which terrifies and tantalises me, but suddenly Charlotte pulls back and breaks the moment.

'We should really call a cab,' she says briskly. 'I'm tired and I need to get some sleep.'

My mind can barely process what has happened between us, but I feel glad just to have her in my life, someone real in the madness of my existence.

I arrive back home still a gigolo, but only just.

Chapter 10

Men Can Lap-Dance Too

After a particularly wild spell at college, a very perceptive tutor of mine wrote in my report that I 'chose hedonism over study and would always be better at fucking women than playing the piano'. At the time, of course, I was outraged at the accusation (OK, and slightly amused), but now I realise how spot on he was.

Following the emotional and intellectual high of my evening with Charlotte, discussing music and bonding romantically, my week gets hijacked by gigolodom – and I have to admit, I love it!

It all starts off innocently enough when I decide to call up one of the jazz musicians I used to play with, for old times' sake. Inspired by my conversation with Charlotte, I feel reconnected with the dreams and aspirations of my youth, so I call my saxophonist chum, Eddie. There I am daydreaming about melodies and improvisations, but it turns out that the old boy has got something much less cerebral in mind. He wants to go to a strip club. Not that I'm complaining, of course. Few things are as sexy as seeing a beautiful woman dancing with barely any clothes on.

In my experience, many lap dancers are savvy businesswomen who enjoy the power over their audience, and the lucrative wages. They don't moralise about what they do – or what I do for that matter – and are far more pragmatic about the role sex and titillation plays in our lives. On account of this, I count many strippers, lap dancers and indeed porn stars as good friends of mine – and quite a few as clients. They don't judge me about my lifestyle, and love to amuse themselves with me, much as other men use them for amusement.

For most men, walking into a strip club is like a Viagra shot to the backside. And I'm no different. All my whimsical imaginings about Charlotte disappear as soon as I step through the pink neon-lit door, and my libido does a celebratory lap dance of its own round the stage. It's an upmarket, stylish place, without being a magnet for City boys, who in my experience are the worst behaved. This place is full of men who just want to worship at the altar of the female form. Including me.

'Let's get a seat close to the stage,' says Eddie, his eyes boggling at the sight of the scantily clad girl writhing in front of us.

'Calm down,' I joke. 'I don't want to have to call the paramedics – your heart can't cope with too clear a view!'

We choose a seat in the middle with a good view of the stage, but still close enough to the bar. A beautiful brunette in a short red skirt, cheerleader-style, brushes past carrying a tray. The tops of her thighs press against my arm and she looks back over her shoulder and gives me a saucy smile. I fear I might need to call the paramedics for myself. These girls are professionals; they can arouse a man with ruthless efficiency.

For a gigolo, there is endless inspiration in a place like this, seeing these masters at work. In turn, though, I know I can titillate the girls back. Looking around, I notice how different I look from the other men, who are slurping down their beers, slack-jawed with lust, looking like punters to the core. I, on the other hand, look like I could give the girls a fantasy fuck of their very own, using my charm, good looks and secret weapons of seduction. I can sense an air of anticipation around me as the strippers and waitresses – who are used to seeing bald men with beer bellies – rev themselves up for full-on sexual warfare over a man they might genuinely want to get into bed. I almost feel dizzy with the heady atmosphere of sexual tension.

'Look at this girl,' says Eddie, in wonder, as a gorgeous blonde takes to the stage.

She has the most beautiful body I have ever seen. Curvy, but toned – like a Renaissance painting that has a gym membership. Her breasts are voluptuous without being comically large, and her bum juts out from the inward curve of the small of her back like a seductive ski slope. She doesn't seem to walk across the stage; she undulates, as if a complex mechanism of circular movements, which hold her curves together, are dancing in unison. It is mesmerising to watch, and she hasn't even begun her act yet.

Ironically, the music starts up with a sleazy saxophone solo, which drips with sexual longing. Eddie's tongue is virtually lolling out – his two favourite loves, women and the saxophone, entwined in such a seductive manner has blown more than a fuse in his gasket.

I inch my chair closer to the stage and sip on my beer, my mouth suddenly parched. The stripper moves across the stage, her pelvis making an inward figure of eight, creating utterly sexy shapes. The effect is like a tidal wave of seductiveness rippling through her body as she dances. She slowly unzips the back of her silky black French knickers to reveal a tiny G-string made out of flesh-coloured fabric and decorated with oyster and blush sequins, a dazzling radar attracting the widened eyes of every man in the room. I realise I am actually holding my breath, and try to relax and breathe normally. This woman is amazing.

She moves towards the pole in the middle of the stage, wraps her legs round it, tips herself upside down and slithers down with serpent-like agility. I can't help but admire her acrobatic grace, as well as her fantastic body. After a few dizzying twirls round the pole, she moves across the stage and unhooks her bra, a glittering shimmer of flesh-toned fabric. I'm not the only one holding my breath, the whole place is. The saxophone-punctuated music is like a siren call egging her on to greater debauchery. Only the wait-resses, who carry on bringing drinks, are unconcerned by the magic unfolding on the stage.

The stripper embraces the pole. This time her naked breasts, pertly tear-shaped, are pushed apart by the metal rod. She suggestively slides down, opening her legs wide, thrusting her bottom out as she sexily squats, and, clasping the phallic pole, pushes herself back up along it, as if she's pleasuring herself. As she drops down again, I get the feeling she is playing the pole like a musical instrument, making filthily potent notes with the power of her movements.

For her finale, she walks to the front of the stage and turns her back, so our view is of her sexy, curved bottom. She crosses her legs and with balletic grace bends over while sliding her tiny G-string down her sleek thighs. For a split second we get a glimpse of her beautiful waxed pussy, then she twirls round to face the audience, snatching the view away from us before our retinas have adjusted to the shock of what we are seeing. She is naked bar a small, cerise heart made of sequins, which is pasted over her absent pubic hair. Flirtatiously, she flicks her G-string in my direction, where, embarrassingly, it lands, slightly lopsided, on my head. She winks and walks off stage as the crowd breaks into uproarious appreciation, clapping wildly and laughing in my direction.

I remove the knickers from my head with as much dignity as it's possible to muster in these situations and smile to myself. This is one souvenir I'd love to keep.

'You lucky bastard,' says Eddie, in awe, grasping to touch the G-string.

'Keep your filthy paws off,' I tell him, laughing. 'The lady might want them back.'

A few minutes later I see Miss Stripper, now dressed in a tight black dress, walking towards our table. Full of confidence, she pulls a chair over and sits down, proffering her hand in my direction, which I duly kiss.

'I hope you're not holding my G-string hostage,' she says teasingly with a middle-class Home Counties accent, leaning forward across the table and looking directly in my eyes.

'It depends what the ransom is,' I laugh, handing them back over. 'At least you know I'm not just trying to get your knickers off,' I joke, as she cheekily slides her hands under the table and pulls them back on.

Close up, I can see she's in her thirties. She is not aged in any way – far from it, she looks amazing – but there is a confidence, a knowing look in her eyes that only time bestows. There is also a slight edge of steel flickering in there.

'Let me get you a drink. What would you like?' she asks, with a direct gaze.

Her radar must be spot on. Protocol in these places is always that the man buys the woman a drink. Strippers don't spend their hard-earned cash on punters. It's just unheard of. Unless some wily woman, with more than a smattering of worldly knowledge under her belt, can spot a gigolo from a mile off and wants to have herself some fun.

Bingo, I think, and reply, 'I'd love a glass of white wine, please.'

I go for wine because I fear if the owner sees one of his girls buying a man champagne, he'll not only think the world has gone mad, but no doubt eject me from the premises within seconds. And I get the feeling that Miss Stripper and I are going to have a lot of fun together. It is a particular point of pride for me to pleasure a professional girl – they know what money can buy and they demand exceptional value.

As she slinks back over from the bar, two glasses of wine in hand, Eddie wanders to the bar to buy himself a beer, muttering that I have the golden touch and shaking his head in awe. As Miss Stripper sits down next to me, I notice a few of the other girls' heads turning. They pout jealously and walk past me with increasingly sultry wiggles.

'I think some of my co-workers are jealous that we're chatting,' she coos seductively in my ear. 'We don't get many men like you in here.'

'Well, after your performance, rest assured I don't have eyes for anyone else,' I whisper back, desperate to touch her skin but not wanting to land us in trouble.

'Wait and see what the other girls get up to before you make up your mind,' she smiles, shrugging her bare shoulders with a knowing look in her eyes, confident she is the best.

The brunette with the cheerleader skirt prowls around our table and tries to sit on my lap, turning her big, brown eyes towards me. 'I'd love a drink,' she tells me in a breathy voice, twirling my Prada tie with her moon-manicured nails.

Miss Stripper laughs, then shoos her away. 'I've got a feeling your biggest bulge isn't in your wallet,' she teases, sipping her wine, briefly brushing her hand on my knee, then looking towards the stage as the next girl takes to the pole.

Over the next few hours I am treated to what can only be described as a catfight of erotic dancing. Each girl in turn tries to outperform the others. I'm surprised the pole doesn't have to be taken for emergency resuscitation, such is the extreme grinding it receives. Miss Stripper sits by my side, plying me with drinks and taking to the stage when it is her turn. Her final performance is the *pièce de résistance.* The stage is showered with money at the climax, like an apocalypse raining down £50 notes, provoked by Salome's final debauched dance. A seductively slow sideways splits, *sans* the G-string, is the final straw. The pink glitter heart on her pubis glides down as her legs slide further and further apart until her bottom touches the floor and her stiletto-clad feet are eye-wateringly far apart. She then leans slowly forward until the tips of her nipples touch the floor and squeezes her breasts up to allow her stomach to lie flat, her blonde hair fanning out on either side. I can see a few girls gathered in the wings, and my heart misses a beat thinking of the rear view they must be seeing. Simply stunning, I bet.

Afterwards, Miss Stripper saunters towards me and asks if I still only have eyes for her.

'I think you know the answer to that,' I reply. 'I really think you should give me your number,' I say, staring into her sea-green eyes.

She leans towards me and whispers, 'I can't be seen to give you my number. Wait five minutes and I'll slip it to you as I walk out. A driver from the club is taking me home, so I can't have you in the car with me, but I'll call a taxi and you can follow behind.'

The need for secrecy makes the frisson even stronger, and I can barely wait to be alone with her and pay her back with pleasure for the entertainment she has already given me.

Five minutes later she walks back over and makes a big show of saying goodbye to Eddie and me. First, she shakes Eddie's hand, at which he looks like he's going to faint. Then she takes my hand and presses a tiny slip of paper into my palm. I casually put my hand in my pocket and safely deposit her number there. Even my drinking companion is unaware of what has just occurred, and I leave it that way. Secrets like this aren't for sharing. I bid Eddie farewell and wait outside. Lit up in hazy neon, I lean against the wall, feeling every inch the dirty gigolo I am.

'It's Kali, the goddess of creation and destruction,' says Miss Stripper, lounging back in a black silk kimono, which is slashed to the waist, revealing her nakedness underneath.

My eyes move from the scary-looking statue of the terrifying deity, her tongue pressed out aggressively, with four arms and a garland of skulls round her neck, to a more pleasing-to-the-eye representation of a beautiful woman with hour-glass curves, her hands entwined above her head.

'That's Tara, the Bodhisattva of compassion,' she advises, smiling at my curiosity. 'I'm a bit of an expert on Hindu and Buddhist mythology. It's my little hobby.'

Her house, in the leafy, middle-class suburbs, is beautifully decorated with an eclectic mix of modern and exotic pieces. It feels like a cross between a Himalayan hill station and a bohemian retreat for a professor of the arts. Not at all what you would expect from someone who took her clothes off for a living. There is a genteel atmosphere, very calming and spiritual. Shiva would be in his element here, I think to myself.

'Let me fix you a drink,' I tell her, moving towards the drinks cabinet to pour us both a neat brandy. 'You must be exhausted after tonight.'

'You'll have to revive me,' she says, leaning back into her chair, so her robe slips open even further.

The room is half-lit by candlelight and is hazy with musky incense. Through a gap in the curtain, I can see the starlit sky beyond the deserted streets and grey rooftops. I walk slowly over and hand her a drink, which she knocks back, then closes her eyes in satisfaction. I swig mine down too, then lean over her and give her a deep brandy-heated kiss, tasting it back on her tongue. As I'm kissing her, I use my right hand to slowly tease open the satin belt on her robe. I pull backwards and see that the kimono has fallen to either side, revealing her breasts and what the pink heart previously concealed. The music playing in the background is a lazy sitar sound, creating a provocative atmosphere, akin to a harem. I feel like I have found my perfect dragon lady.

I take the black satin belt that I have removed and use it to blindfold her, making sure I tie it tightly, so she has total visual deprivation. As I secure it with my hands, I use my knee to gently part her legs as wide as they will go. Then I walk back to the drinks cabinet and pour myself a large brandy.

She remains silent as I do this, but on my return I can see that her legs are trembling with anticipation. I dip my thumb into the brandy and then push it into her mouth, at which she starts to lick the hot liquid slowly and sensually. As I push my thumb into her mouth again, a drop of brandy falls on her pouting lower lip and I teasingly lick it off, my tongue instantly heated by the alcohol.

I slowly move down to her breasts. She lets out a low moan as I once more dip my thumb into the brandy, touching both her nipples in turn until they become erect. I drip the brandy carefully over her right breast and lick it off, feeling intoxicated by both alcohol and arousal.

As I move lower, she places her hands on my shoulders. The sound of the sitar playing in the background is accompanied by her increasingly heavy, irregular breathing. This time I dip my tongue into the brandy until it is coated in fiery liquid and then begin teasing her clitoris with it, the heat of the brandy and the slow circular movements of my tongue forcing her to writhe with pleasure as I hold her legs down. The magic she can perform onstage with her circle-of-eight pelvic movements is equally seductive when used at home with my tongue. Using more brandy, and my patented oral technique, I fire her up so she is so hot I can't tell if my tongue is burning from the brandy or her desire.

Within minutes she comes, gasping for me not to stop until the very final second of her orgasm. I remove her blindfold, and she sits there, stunned, with her legs still carelessly parted, trying to get herself together.

'Wow,' she finally manages to say, still breathless. 'I'd pay you good money for that kind of performance. It was incredible.'

'Well, I'm very expensive – at least fifty pounds for five minutes,' I joke.

She leans over to her handbag, slowly removes her purse and gives me £300 in rolled-up fifties – the very same ones that showered her with gratitude on the stage earlier.

'I never overcharge,' I say in a serious tone, holding the money in my left hand. 'I was only on the job for about fifteen minutes.'

'The other half is payment in advance,' she laughs. 'You don't think I'm going to let you get away without a repeat performance, do you?'

I smile broadly and shake my head. 'I've used brandy to heat you up – next time I'll use honey to calm you down,' I say, reclining back on the burgundy vintage sofa.

'Aren't you just the perfect plaything,' she teases, slipping the robe off her shoulders and walking over to pour us some more drinks, stark naked. As a stripper, she has zero insecurities about her body and no inhibitions about walking around with her clothes off. It is a pleasure to see. Most women, even those blessed with perfect bodies, don't have the confidence to subject themselves to total scrutiny. After a session, they'll slip into something or head straight for the shower. But for men, just seeing a woman undressed and unselfconscious in her natural state is a beautiful sight, no matter if she has lumps or bumps. Women never seem to realise that they are their harshest critics, not men.

She uncorks a bottle of expensive French white wine and pours us both a glass. 'I think I've had my fill of brandy for one evening,' she laughs, her gorgeous breasts at my eye level as she hands over my drink.

'So you enjoyed my performance tonight?' she asks, once more sitting down in the French-style, blood-red velvet armchair she was previously pleasured in. She hooks both legs over one arm of the chair and looks at me provocatively.

'I loved it,' I answer eagerly, thinking how she looks like an out-take from a beautiful 1970s *Playboy* shoot. 'You were very sexy – you looked like you were enjoying it up there. I know I certainly enjoyed watching you.'

'You're right – I do enjoy it,' she replies, switching her long legs slowly to the other side, one by one, giving me a centrefold shot along the way. 'It feels good to have a captive audience hanging off every flick of your G-string . . .' She trails off and a sly smile starts to spread across her face. 'Do you think you'd be any good on the stage?' she asks.

'I've never thought about it,' I say with a surprised look. As a man, it never crosses your mind that anyone would want to see you prance about. Of course, women on hen nights go mad for Chippendale types, but I've always thought there was something fun and tongue in cheek, not erotic, about lusting after an oiled-up beefcake in a loincloth. 'I've never imagined anyone would want to see me doing a striptease,' I say.

'I'd like to see you strip,' she says, smirking. 'I bet you'd be a natural.'

I start laughing and then stop when I realise she's being serious. 'I'll strip for you,' I say with a shrug. 'You might have to give me some pointers, though – and I don't think that G-string will fit.' We both start to giggle.

'Come with me,' she says, nodding for me to follow her. 'Let's get you a costume. You see, to strip properly you have to get into character.'

'Well, I had wondered how sexy removing my tweed jacket would be,' I tell her, as I trail behind her into the bedroom.

She rifles through her drawers and pulls out a theatrical-looking top hat. 'You can be the circus master,' she laughs, 'and his glamorous assistant,' she adds, pulling out an opulent red feather boa.

'I'm loving the boa,' I say, draping it seductively round my shoulders and dancing about with an exaggerated Jaggeresque pout.

'See, I knew you'd be a natural,' she shrieks, trying to tug my shirt off.

'No,' I tell her off in a strict voice. 'Rules are rules. If the boss sees you touching me, I'll be in big trouble. You can look, but you can't touch. Now get back to your seat, young lady, and wait for the performance to begin.'

She skips back into the living room, still laughing, telling me that she can't wait to watch. 'Any music or lighting requests?' she shouts, as I rummage through her make-up bag and apply some dramatic-looking black eyeliner. I want to look sexy and a bit Weimar Germany, without looking like I'm in drag. I take my shirt off and put some black braces on I find in the drawer the top hat appeared from. I look in the mirror. With my slim-fit black trousers, naked chest, top hat and feather boa, I look every inch the sleazy, slightly perverted circus ringmaster.

'Could you red out the lights?' I shout back. 'Don't worry about the music. I'll sort that out myself.' I practise a few moves to myself in the mirror and crack up laughing. 'Close your eyes,' I tell Miss Stripper as I walk into the room. She has draped red chiffon fabric over the lamps, creating a wanton sex-show vibe.

I flick through the CDs, skipping past the obvious stripping-friendly ones. I need something amusing and entertaining, rather than titillating. After all, I don't flatter myself that a man taking off his clothes is going to have the same allure as a woman doing the same. I need to throw in some light relief. Perfect! I laugh to myself as I cue up the CDs.

'When the music starts to play, you can open your eyes,' I inform Miss Stripper teasingly.

The music begins and when she blinks her eyes open, I strut to the centre of the living room and strike a pose as the opening bars of Phil Collins's 'Easy Lover' kick in. I start to twirl round, lacing my feather boa round my neck, across my shoulders and then in between my legs, pouting seriously as I do so. Miss Stripper shrieks so loudly with laughter I fear she might injure herself. I strut right up to her, place one leg on the arm of the chair and start to gyrate wildly in front of her face.

'Stop, stop, it's too much,' she screams, tears of laughter streaming down her face.

I have no mercy and proceed to turn my back on her

and shimmy my behind in front of her face to the strains of 'Young and free, only seventeen . . .' I pirouette back towards the stereo and flick on the next track. Justin Timberlake's 'SexyBack' starts to play loudly and I slowly, teasingly, pull down one side of my braces, followed by the other. I then start to unzip my trousers with a mock tantalising expression on my face. She stands on the chair and starts clapping wildly, her breasts bouncing beautifully as she does. I slowly slide my trousers off until I am left in my tight Calvin Klein shorts, my boa, top hat and nothing else. (I had the foresight to remove my socks and shoes before my striptease began. I don't want to look like a plumber who has disrobed in the house.) I stride towards her, push her back on the seat and give her an up-close and personal lap dance she won't forget in a hurry. By this time she is sobbing with laughter.

I remove my hat and place it on her head, take the feather boa and lash her hands behind her back with it. 'The management rules are you can't touch me but I can touch you,' I advise her as the atmosphere turns from comical to sexually charged in an instant.

'I've never taken advantage of a lap dancer before,' she tells me, smiling.

'Don't worry, I'll be the one taking advantage of you,' I tell her, moving her so she is bent over the side of the armchair, her arms strapped behind, tickled by the red feather boa with which she's tied up. Like a good boy scout, I already have a jar of organic honey placed nearby (sourced during an innocent trip to the kitchen for a glass of water) and I begin to perform gigolo-speciality oral sex, this time with the cooling, soothing honey. Her orgasm is lower and softer.

Afterwards, I untie her, sit on the chair myself and start smearing the honey all over her amazing breasts. She straddles me, her blonde hair falling over her shoulders, and begins to ride me slowly as I gently lick the honey off with smooth strokes of my tongue.

To finish, she treats me to a special little technique of her own. As I take her from behind, she laces her feet round my ankles to pull me in deeper than I realised was physically possible. So perfect is our mutual intuition for rhythm, we come together, then collapse in a heap on the floor, twining our arms round each other.

I pick her up and carry her into the bathroom, shower her off from all the sticky substances we have been playing with and then lead her into bed.

'I've got a job on tomorrow,' she says, resting her head on my shoulder. 'I want you here waiting for me when I get back – you're the perfect way to unwind.'

'At your service,' I reply, stroking her hair.

I don't ask her where she is going – I'm imagining the last thing she wants to do is talk shop, but she starts to confide in me. 'Guess how much I earn a night just for taking my clothes off?' Before I can hazard an estimate, she says, 'A thousand pounds,' and shakes her head in disbelief.

'Is it worth it?' I ask curiously.

'Of course,' she replies nonchalantly. 'But you have to use the money wisely if you want to succeed in this game.'

'What do you mean?' I say, leaning on one elbow to look at her.

'Well, take me. I love stripping, I don't feel demeaned, and I'm not exploited, but still, night after night, month after month, year after year, even if it doesn't damage you,' she says thoughtfully, trying to choose her words carefully, 'it can *harden* you. You need to find a way to decompress.'

'And how do you do that?'

'I spend six months of the year in India,' she informs me. 'That's why I know so much about Hindu and Buddhist philosophy. I strip for six months, so I can afford to spend six months in a house on the beach, meditating, doing yoga and generally repairing my soul. When I'm sipping on a mango lassi and writing in my journal, I'm a million miles away from this life in every way. It's the perfect compromise.'

I kiss her and think to myself how prophetic Shiva's advice has been. I've found my very own dragon lady to practise on.

'I've got a few tantric sex tricks up my sleeve,' I tell her conspiratorially, kissing her.

'I'm a bit of an expert myself,' she replies, returning my kiss. 'Tomorrow night looks set to be *very* interesting.'

It's the perfect contradiction of modern life that the woman I'm about to have spiritual sex with is a stripper. No doubt if I ever managed to find myself in a convent (OK, it's a stretch), the nuns would probably demand to be spanked, then kidnap me as a sex slave. Whatever we repress – be it our spiritual side or our sexual fantasies – always pops up somewhere else, demanding satisfaction, so it seems only fitting that two sex-seekers like Miss Stripper and me should end up getting off on soul-searching together.

Chapter 11

It Really Is Miami Vice

'Never burn your bridges' is a good motto to live by –
even if there is a whip-wielding woman with issues at the
other end of the aforementioned bridge. For a gigolo,
forgiveness isn't so much a luxury as a necessity, so when
Miss Alpha's PA puts in an apologetic call, who am I to
hold a grudge? Note: Miss Alpha's *PA* phones to make
amends. I love that – it just about sums up the mad world
of a wealthy female law partner. The to-do list she prepared
for her PA probably read something like this: arrange
dinner, pick up laundry, call nanny, smooth things over
with my hired-to-hump gigolo. Like I said, though, I admire
Miss Alpha, and if I'm needed back in the saddle, I am
more than willing to ride to her rescue.

So once again with Air Miles measuring my sexual
prowess, I find my British wares imported over the Atlantic

by plane. Abusing the privileges of first-class flying, I indulge myself in a little champagne-fuelled philosophising. Attending to so many women's different needs in such a short space of time not only creates a form of sexual vertigo, it also gives some rare insights. To pass the time, I imagine what would happen if all my women were in the same room at once. I realise that Celebrity X and Trustfundista would be instant friends, united by a sense that money or fame can't buy what they're looking for, but too jaded to see beyond what they can purchase. Miss Alpha and Miss Stripper would hit it off too. They're both strong women with a soft core who made it in a hard world by toughening themselves up. Ms Antoinette, the feisty estate agent, would probably enjoy a few drinks with my Essex assailants, women who enjoy the joy ride through hedonism, knowing their final destination is safely in suburbia. I feel like an X-rated anthropologist.

After clearing customs, I find myself sliding into the black leather seat of a luxury limousine and sighing with satisfaction. This is the problem – I'm getting too accustomed to this life to truly consider anything as pedestrian as settling down.

'Hey, babe, ya still got it,' drawls Miss Alpha, looking me up and down appraisingly as I walk through the door into her apartment. The sunshine streaming through the windows is lighting up the room like a film set, and Miss Alpha looks just as gorgeous as I remember.

'Honey, I'm home,' I joke, throwing my bag down and sweeping her up in an embrace.

As I kiss her, I expertly reach inside her black satin shirt and unhook her bra. The feel of her breasts under the material is amazing and she murmurs, 'I missed you,' under her breath as I stroke her nipples through her top.

'I got ya a present.' She pulls back and walks over to the bureau at the other end of the room. 'Well, really it's a present for me,' she laughs, unbuttoning her shirt as she talks.

'What is it? Or shouldn't I ask?' I laugh.

'There ya go.' She winks, throwing a packet of Viagra at me, then brandishing a spanking paddle from behind her back. 'This not quite as scary?' At which she throws her highlighted hair back, laughing naughtily. She passes me a glass of champagne.

'As long as it's a two-way treat,' I reply, smiling and washing down a couple of Viagra with my champagne.

'It's diamond-encrusted, darlin' – ya won't see that in your normal Hustler store. I got it specially made.'

'They say diamond spanking paddles are a gigolo's best friend, and I'm inclined to agree,' I say, playfully rapping her on the bum with it. Somehow I sense she won't be quite as gentle when it comes to my turn.

'I've got a big case that's going my way,' Miss Alpha tells me, sitting down, her shirt still hanging open to half reveal her breasts, 'so I fancy doing some celebrating. Let's have a champagne bath. By the time we're done, those pills ya popped should've kicked in. Fill that baby up – and only use the best vintage champagne,' she instructs me.

Ten minutes later I'm half submerged in a luxury bath filled with Dom Pérignon and have a massive hard-on, courtesy of the Viagra.

'Come and join me,' I shout through to Miss Alpha, who had to take an urgent call just as she was about to slip in the bath with me.

There is no reply, so I dunk my crystal champagne flute in the bath and start sipping, laughing to myself at the indulgence but feeling slightly chilly. Suddenly Miss Alpha appears at the door with a pensive look on her face I'm not used to seeing. All her playfulness of moments ago has evaporated.

'Jeez, is everyone else in this world a frickin' idiot?' she rants in no particular direction. 'I've got to go away on an urgent business trip,' she tells me, handing me a robe.

I step out of the bath, dripping with the sweet smell of champagne, a quizzical look on my face and an artificial erection that just won't go down, even with the dampening of the mood.

'The case I was telling ya about . . . there's a problem I need to fix. My flight leaves in two hours. Dammit, just as we were gonna get frisky,' she says impatiently, flicking her hair with annoyance. 'Never mind. Business comes first, doll – those are the rules.' She laughs ironically. 'Well, this *is* business to you, ain't it, babe?'

'We'll have fun another time,' I tell her, shrugging and wishing that I hadn't taken *two* Viagra. 'I'm always at your service,' I add, kissing her softly on the lips.

A smile starts to cross her face at last. 'You're right, honey. I'm just disappointed, that's all . . . but you'll keep till next time.'

'When are you back?' I ask, pulling my trousers back on, then sitting on the side of the bath and scooping my glass in again. No point being wasteful, I figure to myself.

'Who knows?' she replies. 'My PA will book you on the first flight back to England in the morning.' Then she strides off to her study to make arrangements, while I flop on the bed and flick between TV channels on the plasma screen that has emerged from the bed at my command. Not quite as interesting viewing as the last time I was here, but that's the way it goes.

'Fuck, fuck, fuck!' I sink back into the bed and curse my own ineptitude. The clock sits impassively on the bedside table, still saying 10.30 a.m. My plane flew at nine o'clock. I look at my phone and see seven missed calls from Miss Alpha's driver. I must have slept like the dead. I knew tucking into the champagne bath was a mistake, but this is too much. I reach over the bed and pull my wallet out of my jacket pocket. I see that £30, a dry-cleaning ticket and Celebrity X's handwritten number are all that remains. I can't call Miss Alpha on her important business trip. I'm only here as light relief for her, not to make her life more complicated. I pull a pillow over my head, a hangover just starting to fray the edges of my mind, and hope that the situation will go away. It doesn't. I get out of bed and open the black slatted blinds. The crisp New York sunshine cuts through my haze. I need a plan. Who do I know in New York? Celebrity X. That's not really an option. Then it hits me that I don't know anyone here. Another thought occurs to me: ZZ is back home in Miami by now. I'll call him.

'Dude, you are one dumb fuck!' He screeches with laughter down the phone as I tell him my predicament.

'Thanks for the sympathy,' I laugh. 'It was a heady mixture of jet lag, a champagne cocktail in a bath-sized glass and an attention-seeking Viagra hard-on that got me in this mess. But seriously, what am I going to do? I have zero money, and I don't think American Airlines accepts rapid tongue movements as payment.'

'Give it a go, you never know – one of those steward-esses might sneak you on if you work the Golden magic.' He giggles with laughter down the other end of the phone.

'Glad that I'm fodder for your amusement,' I say, real-ising how funny the situation is, and trying not to feel sulky.

'Look, I don't think I can get you all the way back to London, but I can get you on a flight out to Miami. Stay with me until we work out how to ship you back home.'

'Really? Is that OK?' I say, oozing gratitude.

'Not a problem. I'll get my keeper to whack it on her card. She likes treating me, and no doubt she'll make you hand over some payment in kind.'

In a stroke of extraordinary luck, ZZ has a beautiful porn-star patron who is just as liberal with her purse as she is with her principles. He can indulge in whatever sexual shenanigans he likes and still have a home to go to. In exchange, his big personality and good heart give her a welcome respite from an industry in which both those traits can be hard to come by.

Within hours I find myself on an economy flight (beggars can't be choosers) to Miami – the city that never sleeps with the same person twice.

I hear ZZ before I see him. The loud growling of his car, the Red Dragon – a pimped-up scarlet BMW with low profile tyres and a lot of attitude – announces his arrival to everyone in the immediate vicinity. 'Art for Art's Sake' by 10cc is pumping out, and ZZ pulls up, his arm resting on the open window, smiling insanely. 'Get in, you hobo gigolo,' he yells over the noise of the engine.

I jump in, suddenly feeling in a great mood. I just know

we're going to have a *lot* of fun. 'I never thought I'd be
so glad to see your chubby face,' I tease him, turning the
music up louder and taking in the blue skies and white-
washed scenery.

'Boy, is it your lucky day,' ZZ informs me. 'My patron
has got her porn-star and pole-dancing friends over.
There's virtually a sexual apocalypse happening at my
house and that's straight where we're heading.'

'Never a moment's rest for the wicked.' I grin back,
amazed at how my earlier bad fortune is turning into pure
gold. It seems, as always, I have the Midas touch.

'Actually, I have a better plan,' says ZZ, swerving off
the main road that goes to South Beach and instead
heading to the poorer suburbs.

'Where are we going?' I ask him, desperate to get to the
awaiting erotic Armageddon and perturbed by our sudden
off-roading as we drive deeper into the downtown ghetto.

'Look, what's the competition like here in Miami?' ZZ
asks me, somewhat randomly.

'I don't know.' I shrug, wondering where this is leading.

'OK, either it's your super-cool, handsome model types
or flamboyant, party-crazed queens, so we need a strategy
to stand out. We need to ramp up the volume.'

'And your point is?' I ask, as we hit the freeway, listening
to a classic rock station. Lulu's 'To Sir With Love' comes
on, and I loudly sing along to the words 'taking me from
crayons to perfume'.

ZZ laughs and tells me, 'We're going to the craziest
costume and vintage shop this side of the hemisphere.
Tonight we're playing dress-up – the ladies won't know
what's hit them.'

★

Within minutes of arriving in the shop we are beside ourselves with laughter. ZZ pulls out a jewel-encrusted, tight black sweater; I turn to him and comically pose in a white batwing shellsuit jacket embroidered with gold anchors – so Versace gone wrong.

'Perfect!' yells ZZ, strutting around like he's just walked off the set of *Dynasty*.

'I look like Alan Partridge doing *Miami Vice*,' I laugh, pulling some tight white trousers off the rack and eyeing up some matching white golf shoes. 'Are you sure this will be a hit with the women?'

'Trust me,' replies ZZ, draping his arm round my shoulder. 'This is Miami – anything goes. The wilder the better.'

'I'm still not sure,' I tell him, doing a comedy twirl in my new, very un-me ensemble. 'But to hell with it – why not? It obviously works for you.'

'We'll keep it all on,' says ZZ to the bemused shop assistant, as he peels two $10 bills from his wallet and pays for our wares. A far cry from my shopping extravaganza with Miss Alpha, I think to myself.

We get back in the car, looking like we've stepped out of a low-budget 1980s film, and roar off in the Red Dragon. I wind down the window and look out at the passing scenery, pondering on this new adventure.

As we head back into South Beach, the cars whizzing past us get gradually more and more flash. Lamborghinis and Porsche Boxsters race us at the traffic lights, and on the sidewalk beautiful women strut along in heels, short skirts and nothing more than a bikini top. The atmosphere in Miami is exhilarating and so different to London and New York, which while both being very cool, don't have the same air of liberation and pure, unadulterated fun. It feels like a holiday destination where everybody forgot to go home. The crazy mix of people makes for a strange, intensely upbeat city: the rich families on vacation from New York, with their holiday tans; the local bohemian crowd of writers and artists; the rock 'n' roll stars here to retox; the Cubans and Haitians over from Latin America looking for a slice of success; the Eurotrash party people making the most of sunny days and debauched nights; and the glam holidaymakers from random parts of the world just kicking back and hanging out.

Also, being a big centre for swimwear modelling, the place is like a magnet for beautiful women too curvy for the catwalk but the perfect accessory on the beach or in beach attire. Couple this with all the millionaires floating around, with their expensive yachts moored up in nearby Fort Lauderdale, and you have a heady cocktail of sexual tension just waiting to combust when the sun sets and the bars start serving.

I have to admit I feel quite intoxicated myself. OK, so being a gigolo isn't hard work as most people would know it – I don't ride the Tube into work every morning or have an appraisal to assess my performance – but there is still a hell of a lot of pressure. Like most 'creative' industries, I'm only as good as my last job, and if I don't work, I don't get paid. The future floats ahead of me under one big question mark, and now I have these untenable feelings for Charlotte threatening to knock me off course. It strikes me that *I* need a vacation too. Fate has conspired to land me here, with ZZ as host, to enjoy the spoils of Miami's easygoing hedonism, so I decide to put all thoughts of my gigolo life behind me for a few days and make like a tourist – albeit a badly dressed one.

As we pull up into the driveway of ZZ's – or rather his patron's – beautiful art deco apartment, a sense of anticipation creeps up my spine. Before I can even gather my thoughts, a gorgeous girl waves out of the window, shouting ZZ's name.

'Hello, boys,' she yells, then on seeing our outfits, peals with laughter and starts humming the *Miami Vice* theme tune.

ZZ pirouettes through the front door in perfect time to the improvised music.

Compared with Miss Alpha's pad, the apartment isn't half as jaw-dropping, but it's still very impressive – more elegant charm than bling opulence. It has the feel of a lovely villa. Sitting on one of the large sofas are four gorgeous girls who look like they've stepped off the pages of a glossy magazine. I almost pinch myself to check I'm not dreaming. They say hi to ZZ, then look in my direction with wide, friendly smiles.

A bouncy brunette walks through the door, precariously balancing cocktails in her hands. I step forward and help her out, taking them from her and placing them on the glass table in the centre of the room. She gives me a megawatt smile and says thank you.

'Anyone for a pina colada?' she shouts out, starting to hand out the drinks.

I help myself to one and take a sip. It tastes like summer and I almost imagine George Michael and Andrew Ridgeley will come prancing through the door singing 'Club Tropicana'.

'This is Golden,' says ZZ, introducing me to the girls

and whoever else is floating around the room. 'He's another good-time boy like myself.'

Their smiles get broader on hearing I'm in the trade too.

'Hello, Golden babe.' ZZ's patron walks in and gives me an affectionate hug. 'I can see you two have been up to mischief already.' She grins, looking at our incongruous outfits.

Miss Patron, as I shall refer to her, is a curious mix of pure sex appeal and steely determination. Working as a porn star in LA's San Fernando Valley is one thing, but becoming one of the most successful X-rated DVD stars takes quite a lot of strength, business sense and self-promotion. If you've got issues, then the industry will destroy you, but if you've got a sex drive that bypasses your emotions, it can be lucrative. Miss Patron has obviously made it and recently retired on the proceeds.

I don't want to trivialise the realities of her chosen profession: like mine, they are not without serious pitfalls. Women like Miss Stripper and Miss Patron, who make it through to the other side, self-esteem intact, with enough money tucked into their G-strings to buy nice houses to live in and gigolos to hang out with, are not the norm. You have to hand it to them for succeeding in a notoriously tough environment. That takes guts.

'Me and the girls have just been talking shop,' says Miss Patron to me, sipping on her cocktail and lounging on a large easychair, her stilettos hanging casually off her toes. 'Women need a PhD in strategic thinking just to strip these days. See, it's different for you boys – you just create one persona and then spend your lives fine-tuning it. We have to be different things to different men.'

'In what way?' I ask, interested to know the tricks of her trade.

'Well—' Before Miss Patron can finish her sentence, one of the girls, a confident-looking brunette, laughs and says, 'Let's show him!'

'Sounds good to me,' I reply with a cheeky smile. 'I've always preferred practice to theory.'

They make their way into the bedroom, walking with sexy struts that would set a catwalk on fire, as Miss Patron looks on, smiling. 'These girls are some of Miami's hottest pole dancers,' she tells me. 'I can't believe they're going to let you in on their inside secrets.'

'See, what other men pay for, us gigolos get for free,' I joke, turning my head towards the door in time to see one of the girls shimmy back in wearing nothing but a gold lamé fishnet body stocking. I almost choke on my pina colada, so stunning is the sight.

'OK, Golden, this is the hot-sexpot look,' she tells me with a provocative pout, as she starts to wind her body round me like an X-rated Bond girl. 'What do you think?'

'I'm all for it,' I tell her. 'Which men do you roll this one out for?'

'This is for the rich businessmen who want full-on titillation without being intimidated,' she tells me. 'It's very sexy without being overtly sleazy.'

Just as she finishes her performance, another girl twirls in wearing a white basque with matching stockings and suspenders. She coyly smooches in front of me with a naughty twinkle in her eye.

'I like this look,' I say with approval. 'Let me guess – this is for the married middle-aged men?'

'You got it,' she says, laughing as she puts her leg up

on the side of my chair and sensually starts to roll down her white, lace-topped stocking with the sultry finesse of a nympho on her wedding night. 'They want to imagine sharing their marital bed with a siren who turns slut for them – rather than the wife they already have, who gets into bed with a face pack and a good book.'

A blonde then struts in with 100 per cent sexual velocity, modelling a criminally small red G-string and a peep-hole bra with matching red nipple tassels. She simultaneously sips on her cocktail, dragging her heavily pencilled lips along the straw, and twirls her tassels round with delirious abandon. 'I'm the vamp,' she winks, narrowing her eyes sexily and bending over, with her legs straight, to demonstrate her eye-watering flexibility. 'The younger ones go for this,' she tells me. 'Especially the frat boys out on the town with their friends. They like their sex appeal to be laced with danger. Fast cars, fast girls – you know the kind of thing they're after.'

'Wow,' I say, impressed by the level of thought that goes into their manipulation of the male fantasy. Then I lean over to ZZ and add, 'If us gigolos suddenly morphed into Miami pole dancers, I bet I'd be the unthreatening sexpot, Johan would be the debauched, blushing bride, and Rochester would be the dangerous vamp.'

'That's so true,' agrees ZZ, trying to waft air underneath his thick black jumper. His comedy attire has not only ramped up the volume, it seems to have ramped up his temperature. 'Much as we appreciate the tutorial, we need to make a move – we're meeting Sharky at Rok Bar in half an hour. We need to parade around and show off our own outfits. The whole of Miami needs to enjoy these babies.'

Sharky is a friend of ours, but not one of our kind – he

doesn't have that special gigolo chromosome, and he doesn't want to develop it. He's happy to hang out and watch the magic in action, knowing he can go back to his regular life. Of course he likes to party, and he loves women; he's just never wanted to take it a step further.

We say goodbye to Miss Patron and the girls, who are now sitting around, still dressed in their outfits, talking about shopping and shoes, and sipping on cocktails. They wave us off casually and turn back to their conversation, concerned with the latest bargain now they've finished entertaining us.

ZZ and I dash out to the car, like a latter-day Crockett and Tubbs, and roar off towards the night's adventures, arriving fifteen minutes later outside Rok Bar, one of Miami's coolest haunts.

As we walk inside, I once again get the feeling we're stepping on to a movie set – especially in our comical costumes. The décor is very late 1980s. The back wall is decorated with mirrored tiles with circles cut out. Overhead are red lights with mirror bulbs, which flash in different sequences, and three chandeliers are suspended in red Perspex cubes. Another wall is decorated with pictures of girls wearing hotpants and fishnet tights, playing electric guitars and drums. It's all extremely rock 'n' roll, and a refreshing change to the rarefied dandy world I usually inhabit. Legend has it that Rochester caught the eye of Donatella Versace in this very bar, and I can understand why. It's very much his kind of lair.

We stride up to the bar (me slightly gingerly, thanks to the tightness of my white trousers) and order a bottle of champagne on Miss Patron's tab. Cleared by her first, of course. ZZ jokes, 'Gigolos are players, not payers.'

A pretty, toned girl walks past and pinches my bum, winking as she says, 'I love your style.' I do a turn for her benefit and she stops and breaks into a white-toothed smile.

'I'd attempt to moonwalk,' I tell her, 'but I don't think the cut of my trousers would permit it. And I do like to stay just on the right side of decency.'

'Nice accent too,' she tells me. 'Where are you from?'

'London,' I reply, conscious of how very proper my pronunciation sounds compared with her warm drawl.

The barmaid interrupts us to hand me a champagne glass and says conspiratorially to the girl, 'Honey, I'd fuck him for his shoes alone.'

We all crack up laughing, and ZZ declares that it's the best compliment he's ever heard. 'I can't believe girls are getting hot over your "fuck me" shoes – you're like the male Carrie Bradshaw!'

'Ha ha,' I answer sarcastically. 'Just because you're jealous that my shoes are more pimp than yours.'

'Girls, girls, let's not catfight over who's got the sexier shoes,' jokes the girl, inviting us over to her table, where she's sitting with five girlfriends.

Her group of friends are typical Miami girls, with pretty smiles, nice tans and killer abs under their cropped white vest tops and low-slung hipster jeans.

Sharky suddenly appears in front of us with a wide grin on his face and shakes my hand vigorously, saying, 'Nice to see you again, man,' then leans in closer and whispers, 'With a bunch of pretty girls – no change there, then!'

A cheesy tune comes on and ZZ leaps up, grabs two of the girls' hands and pulls them on to the dance floor, clearing a path with his over-the-top moves.

'I've never met anyone like you two before,' laughs one of the girls. 'You're not scared to be silly – I love that. Most of the men here are so uptight.'

'Well, it's hard to be up yourself when you're wearing a batwing jacket,' I comment, knocking back my glass of champagne and dragging her on to the dance floor to join ZZ and the others.

I pirouette her round in time to the music and pull a pretty nifty impersonation of Michael Jackson's dance moves to amuse her.

After a few hours of crazy dancing and far too many cocktails, ZZ gets a call from Miss Patron requesting our company back at the house. The girls look stricken that we'll be leaving them as we've had so much fun together. Sharky is nonchalant about our departure and says, 'Why don't we stay for, like, half an hour more?' He's laidback and doesn't understand the need to jump when a lady who pays for the pleasure calls.

'We've been called back to party – everyone's invited,' reassures ZZ, throwing a random shape and getting some of his diamanté appliqué caught on one of my gold anchors. 'Oops,' he giggles, as one of the girls tries to detach us, shaking her head and laughing at the ridiculousness of the situation.

Back at Miss Patron's, the party is raging hard. As we walk through the door, a wall of sound and heat hits us, followed closely by the realisation that many of the partygoers are either naked or in a state of partial undress. The Miami girls looked awestruck. 'ZZ's patron is a porn star,' I explain, at which they nod as if that makes perfect sense.

Just as I mention her name, Miss Patron breezes through.

'My little get-together for the girls seems to have got out
of hand,' she tells us with a casually dismissive flick of her
hand as we walk through. 'I thought I better have you boys
back here – I didn't want you missing out on all the fun.'

I weave my way through the throng of bodies, who are
kissing, dancing, embracing and *much* more. The girls all
file into the kitchen chattering excitedly and I fix them a
cocktail.

'Didn't I say it would be wild!' I laugh. 'But don't worry,
you don't have to join in – just get drunk and have a
dance if that's all you feel like doing.'

They look happy to embrace the adventure of the
evening on their own terms. We stand around chatting
and knocking back cocktails in the kitchen, and I make
them take it in turns to try on my comedy jacket and do
a *Miami Vice* twirl in it.

After ten minutes the mood is so relaxed they decide
to go and mingle. 'I've never been to a party like this
before,' one of them comments as we make our way back
into the lounge. 'I kinda like being a voyeur,' she adds in
a confessional tone.

As they disappear into the crowd, I make my way into
ZZ's bedroom to change. Fun as my outfit is, I'm craving
something a bit more stylish now. It's never good to wear
a joke too thin, I reason to myself. This might be ZZ's
persona, but it was just a passing visit for me.

'So sorry,' I exclaim, as I walk through the bedroom
door to see ZZ and Miss Patron *in flagrante*. Miss Patron
is on all fours, her magnificent fake breasts hanging down,
and ZZ, now dressed as an Egyptian pharaoh, is taking
her from behind. 'Sorry,' I mutter again, backing out and
politely looking away.

'Honey, you owe me a flight. Get the hell back in here!' Miss Patron yells.

I get the feeling that my company's required for more than a chat, which is fine by me, and ZZ doesn't look bothered about my arrival either. That's Miami for you – San Francisco might have been the birthplace of free love, but Miami is its final destination. Sometimes I wonder if they accidentally added Viagra to the water supply instead of fluoride. Relaxing, I grin, throw my batwing jacket on the bed and loosen my shirt.

'Thank God you asked,' I reply. 'I don't believe in debt – I'd much rather have the opportunity to pay back in full.' I walk over and gently push Miss Patron's shoulders back, so now, rather than being on all fours, she is sitting on ZZ's lap, giving me much easier access to perform oral sex as my repayment.

'She's the boss,' says ZZ with a shrug, as I get down to my duties and he carries on with his. My final sight as I head downwards is of his Egyptian headdress bobbing in time to the rhythm. As Miss Patron's moans build up, and I quicken my pace to satisfy her, the image of the headdress is ingrained in my mind, giving a light-hearted edge to the proceedings. At the finish, I look up and see that the headdress has slipped under ZZ's chin in the final moments of frenzy, creating a comedy beard.

'Remind me to have you owe me more often,' says Miss Patron with a satisfied smile, as she reclines on the bed.

I slide in on one side of her and ZZ slides in on the other. Just at that moment the Miami girls stumble in by mistake and, like myself previously, exclaim their apologies, looking mortified that they've barged in on a clearly debauched moment.

'Don't worry, girls. Come and sit on the bed,' says Miss Patron, patting the duvet for them to sit down.

They hesitantly walk over and perch on the edge, two of them either side of the bed.

After a few moments of awkward chat one of the girls finally pipes up, 'Is it true you're a porn star?' to Miss Patron.

'Well, I retired recently,' she tells them, 'but before that I was ten years in the business.'

'Wow,' says one of the Miami girls, 'I've never met a porn star before . . .' She trails off, obviously wanting to ask more questions but afraid to appear rude.

'Look, honey, ask me anything you want.' Miss Patron smiles warmly, seeing her hesitation. 'When you've had sex on set, you lose your inhibitions about this kind of thing.'

'What was it like, you know, having sex in front of all those people?' Miami girl asks curiously.

'How do you feel when you eat your breakfast in a café?' she responds. 'You're just eating, you're not worried about who's watching.'

'Did you specialise in anything?' asks another of the girls. 'You know, like . . .'

'Don't be too shy to spit it out,' laughs Miss Patron. 'Literally, in fact! Yeah, my speciality is deep throat. I'm the queen of pro blows.'

'Cool,' all the girls chime at once. 'Any tricks of the trade you can let us in on?' they ask eagerly.

Miss Patron pauses for a minute, thinking, then says, 'Talk is cheap. A practical demonstration is way better.' She looks in my direction mischievously, then tells me to undo my trousers.

Of course I gladly oblige, not quite believing what I think is about to happen, but liking the direction the proceedings are taking. As Miss Patron positions me on the bed, and the girls gather round to watch, resting their heads on their hands like industrious students, keen to learn, I realise I really am about to be the oral-sex equivalent of a demonstration dummy.

As Miss Patron gets to work, with a frankly mind-blowing combination of butterfly strokes and obscenely accommodating deep throat, I look at the audience of beautiful Miami girls and realise that I have an exhibitionist streak a mile wide.

Just at that moment Sharky bursts into the room and starts laughing as he sees what's going on.

'Don't worry,' shouts ZZ. 'Golden is just playing guinea pig for today's lesson.'

Sharky looks over at me and shakes his head with a smile. 'It could only happen to a gigolo,' he remarks. 'You crack me up. Anyway, I just came in to see if anyone wants to come to another party. There's a hot fashion launch going on across town.'

The Miami girls jump up and say they're on for it. They enjoyed the demonstration, but like Sharky, they're happy to get back to a more familiar world. I tell him I'm going to stay behind and take care of business. I might have taken a vacation from my gigolo life, but I still feel obliged to fulfil my contractual obligations. I can see that Miss Patron and her friends definitely need my services on standby.

'Well, let's meet up for beers tomorrow, then,' says Sharky as he leaves, surrounded by the Miami girls. I almost envy the simplicity of his life – until the confident brunette from earlier walks in and asks if I want a private viewing of her previous performance.

Chapter 12

When a Man Becomes a Mistress

Much as I'm enjoying my well-earned rest, I have a niggling sense that the real world is waiting for my return. Miami feels like a wonderful hologram that could disappear at any moment. I appreciate Miss Patron's kindness in extending her hospitality to me, but I feel in need of my own patron, or at least to be back in my own place, with Charlotte across the road. Being in this crazy, amazing city, surrounded by beautiful, liberated women but still thinking about Charlotte makes me realise the depth of my feelings for her. When you've been entertained by gorgeous strippers wearing gold lamé but you're still pining for someone whom you usually see in a ponytail and a coffee-stained apron, you know something serious is going on. Thinking about my predicament back home feels like a British cloud appearing in the blue Miami sky and raining on my parade. Over a breakfast of orange juice and bagels, I fall into a slump thinking about how I'll get back home – and what will happen when I do.

'Dude, this city is on Prozac – you can't be on a downer,' chides ZZ, drumming his fingers on the table and trying to come up with a solution. 'You'll get back to London somehow, so just enjoy the party until then.'

'I suppose you're right,' I say, perking up. 'What's on the menu of adventures for today? I don't think anything can quite top last night.'

'I know – let's go to the Delano Hotel and hang by the pool,' suggests ZZ enthusiastically, jumping up from his seat like an eager jack-in-a-box.

I could do with a spot of sunshine and relaxation, so it sounds perfect. That's the appeal of a place like Miami: it's hard to be miserable against a backdrop of blue skies. You can just idle your life, and your worries, away – until the bailiffs turn up, of course, and you're homeless. That said, even the tramps seem happy here. The streets are sunny, there are free showers on the beach – what more could a hobo ask for?

We head out in the Red Dragon, cruising past the cafés and crowds. There's an early afternoon sense of anticipation tingling in the air. I look over at ZZ, who's humming along to the radio and looking at life through his rose-tinted shades. He doesn't analyse situations; he just enjoys them. You wouldn't find him getting into complications over a cerebral connection with a girl like Charlotte, but then again he's not me. The fact that I'm not some instinctual ditz is part of my appeal – I just wish I could take my thoughts off the hook sometimes. I also realise that if I'm not entertaining a client, I feel redundant. Once again, my work ethic will not let me have a moment's rest.

'Nooooooooo!' squeals ZZ as we approach the pink-fronted Delano. 'I've forgotten my swim shorts.'

'You idiot,' I laugh, as he flaps about searching futilely for his trunks on the floor of the car.

'I remembered mine,' I say with a teasing gloat. 'You'll just have to go naked,' I add, jokingly.

'No I won't,' he says, pointing his finger in the air with a manic look on his face.

It's an expression that amuses me and scares me in equal measure. I get the feeling his madcap idea will mean a fast track to mortification, with me forced to share in his shame.

'OK, what's your plan?' I ask him uneasily. I can't see anything that vaguely resembles a pair of swimming trunks in the vicinity. I can only pray he isn't planning on paying tribute to naturism at one of Miami's swankiest, hippest hotels.

'Wait and see,' he tells me gleefully. 'You are *so* gonna love this. If you didn't have a smile on your face before, you certainly will after.'

We pull up outside the Delano, and a friendly valet takes the keys and drives the car off to park it. Part of me suspects the entire staff might have been micro-chipped to give service with enthusiastic sincerity and a smile. It's a million miles away from the surly sneers one usually receives in London.

A few minutes later I head out of the changing rooms first, wearing a pair of slim-fitting, red Armani trunks, which are flattering without being toe-curlingly tight. My upper body and arms are toned and muscular but not overtly worked out. A good physique should always appear effortless – not like it's been sweating in a gym for hours a day. That isn't sexy, either on a man or a woman. Though better than a beer belly, I imagine!

Rather than heading out to the pool, I lean against a chair, waiting for ZZ's grand entrance and getting quite a bit of attention from the ladies in the meantime. Lots of beautiful women are hurriedly whisked past me by men with paunches and grey chest wigs who don't want their high-maintenance women ogling what they can have on the side. I can sense the women's wandering eyes looking longingly back in my direction, while their pragmatism is pointed towards the no-expense bar tab. I'd be exactly the same in their situation.

My thoughts are rudely interrupted by what I can only describe as the most incredible sight I have *ever* seen. And I mean *ever.* I observe passing hotel guests' looks of sheer incredulity before I have the pleasure of witnessing the sight myself.

ZZ, with an admirable ingeniousness, has fashioned a bathing costume out of a Wal-Mart carrier bag. He seems to have punctured two holes in the bottom of the carrier, through which he has stuck his thick-set legs, then hoisted a handle over each of his arms, making a virtue of his compact body. I have genuinely never in my life believed it is possible to wear a carrier bag in such a manner, but ZZ has managed it and, along with everyone else in the vicinity, I crease up laughing, tears streaming down my face.

ZZ struts over and, with mock haughty grandeur, beckons me to follow him. Together we stroll out through the glass door and into full sight of the crowded pool, which is full of Miami's most beautiful, successful and eligible society. As jaws drop, ZZ performs a comedy bow – a risk, I feel, considering the precariousness of having only a Wal-Mart carrier bag to preserve his dignity. If that's a word that can be used in such a circumstance as this.

We find some sun loungers and claim them as our own. ZZ finally gives in to a giggling fit he has suppressed since his unveiling. 'What did I tell you,' he says with a juvenile grin, and adjusts the carrier bag, which has ridden up a very delicate area. 'Didn't that put a smile on your face?'

'It certainly did,' I reply, looking around in amazement when I see lots of hot women are checking us out.

ZZ catches my gaze and informs me, 'These girls want some of the Wal-Mart action! They're stuck with their boring rich dudes having to smile nicely, look pretty and say nothing. I bet they'd rather be over here with us having some good old-fashioned stupid fun.'

'You're so right. I don't know what I've been worrying about. This is the perfect scenario for my services – women with their husbands' money to spend and an unfulfilled sex drive that needs servicing.'

'That's it,' ZZ exclaims, as if he's in the grip of a painful brainwave. 'I can't believe I didn't think of it before. I know the *perfect* woman for you. Her number's in my little black book – well, little mobile book – from way back. I'll give her a call and see if her husband is out of town.' He dials, stands up and postures as he talks to the mystery lady, looking like a bargain-basement lifeguard in his swimwear.

'She's coming over,' he tells me triumphantly, as he

hangs up. 'Hubby is indeed out of town, and she says a diversion is exactly what she needs. She's on her way here. Just one word of warning . . . Oh, no, maybe I won't tell you,' ZZ dithers.

'Tell me,' I demand, starting to fear for what is on its way over. 'Is she weird?'

'No way,' he reassures me. 'She's a beautiful swimwear model with an absolutely sweet personality. It's not her that's the problem; it's the psychotic millionaire husband she hooked that's the cause for concern.'

'Oh, I don't care about him,' I tell ZZ dismissively. Possessive husbands are part of the package for a gigolo. We get danger money for that kind of thing. Usually the more jealous the husband, the less he's delivering the goods in bed, so you just get used to it.

Naturally, women want security in a man, but if the hot sex isn't there too, they aren't afraid to set some up for themselves as their own dirty little secret. Sometimes I actually think the illicit nature of these types of rendezvous is part of the attraction, and therefore something even the most attentive husband could never provide. Skullduggery is like rocket fuel to a sexual charge. A gigolo is the ultimate naughty treat.

'Well, this one's a real live one,' continues ZZ. 'Let's just say, you have been warned.'

I'm prepared to deal with an axe-wielding spouse if I have to. I ask ZZ to tell me more about Miss Married Model so I can be prepared, and I like what he tells me.

'Oh, you'll *love* her. She's like the all-American dream girl – slim and blonde with big boobs. But she's got a lovely nature too. She's from Ohio and has a soft voice and really gentle mannerisms. But don't let that fool you

– she's a pretty determined lady. She's the classic kind of girl who wanted to escape from Hicksville and managed it, making it big in Miami and marrying well. She really is an iron fist in a velvet glove. She's a different breed to Miss Patron, though. She's not hard-nosed or tough, she's just smart. She knows she's got the looks and she worked it, but underneath she's still this sweet, sensitive girl from the sticks. It's quite a combination. You'll be perfect for her. I'm too nuts, and Rochester would be too scary. She'll love your British charm and gentlemanly manners – it'll be the ultimate seduction for her. Especially as, by all accounts, her husband is a bullish moneyman who thinks charming a woman means barking orders to get the bill.'

'She sounds absolutely perfect,' I say, reclining on my lounger, sipping my cocktail and allowing a broad smile to spread across my face. 'Now this is what I came to Miami for.'

'Hi, ZZ.' A pretty, leggy girl walks breezily towards us. She's wearing a simple sundress and a large brimmed hat.

I stand up and greet her. 'I'm Golden. Lovely to meet you,' I say, taking Miss Married Model's hand in mine and using the other to guide her over to where we're sitting. I pull her up a seat and adjust the umbrella so she can remove her hat – models often can't afford to catch the sun, even swimwear ones.

As she takes off her hat, I catch my breath – she is like a beautiful, delicate Bambi. When she speaks, it's slightly throaty with a soft intonation. She's confident without being pushy and is happy to let me assume the role of leader, which is often not the case nowadays. There's a femininity about her that is ephemeral and very appealing. I can see why she's done well, when lots of other equally pretty girls have failed. She is exactly as ZZ described her.

I start to make idle chit-chat with her about Miami, especially the beautiful art deco buildings.

'Oh, I love the architecture here,' she says, looking at me with a truly lovely smile. 'It's what attracted me to this place. I love driving along and seeing all these crazy pastel-coloured buildings. It's so unique. You know the first art deco buildings here were made in the 1920s during prohibition?' she tells me, dipping her straw into her pina colada. 'Al Capone used to hang out here, and the whole area was famous for drinking and gambling.'

'Hey, nothing changes there, then,' I laugh, looking attentively into her eyes.

'Sometimes I just walk along Ocean Drive soaking it all in, watching the crazy people – it makes me smile,' she continues, looking whimsically at the pool.

I stretch my hand over and push a strand of hair from her face. She gazes into my eyes with a deep stare, then looks back into her cocktail, like she's searching for something.

I notice that she hasn't commented on ZZ's Wal-Mart costume, despite the fact that he's now showing off in front of a crowd of girls, playing the entertainer. I beckon for her to come and join me on my lounger, and she does, folding her legs like a newborn colt and nestling her head into my shoulder as I put my arm round her.

'What do you think to ZZ's outfit?' I finally ask.

Miss Married Model looks like she thought it would be too rude to mention it – something that hasn't occurred to the gaggle of women teasing him good-humouredly about his costume. Then she breaks into an even grin and says, 'Yeah, I did think it was kinda strange, but I didn't want to mention anything – I mean, it's so shameful to be seen wearing a Wal-Mart carrier and not a Wholefoods one.'

I crack up laughing and reply, 'I know. I told him to at least go for a better class of bag, but he'll do anything to get some attention.'

'I can imagine,' she agrees, laughing and glancing over in ZZ's direction.

On seeing her look, ZZ starts waving his arms about comically and dive-bombs into the pool, closely followed by his entourage of admiring ladies – despite the fact his carrier bag has comically filled with water in a very unflattering way.

The afternoon drifts on in a haze of summer alcohol, idle chatter, silly jokes at ZZ's expense and stolen caresses, like we're lovers who are flirting with discovery.

'If my husband saw you with your arm round me, he'd kill us both,' Miss Married Model confesses, snuggling in closer and clearly enjoying the frisson of the situation.

'What car do you drive?' I ask.

'A black Mercedes,' she replies, looking puzzled. 'Why?'

'Just wanted to check we've got a fast getaway car,' I joke, stroking her shoulder.

Eventually the sun sets and the skies turn satsuma orange through the leaves of the palm trees. The cocktails we've consumed blur the edges of the night into something soft and warm.

'We should take this party somewhere private,' I murmur into Miss Married Model's ear, the tension building as the slow sensuality of night sets in.

'Let's go back to my place,' she whispers back. 'But we have to take a crowd of people with us.'

'That's not quite what I had in mind,' I say softly, stroking the inside of her leg.

'I know, it's a nightmare. My husband pays the concierge to spy on me, so I can't smuggle you back alone – we have to go under the cover of a crowd.'

'A party back at yours it is, then,' I laugh. 'Your husband must be very jealous – not that I blame him.'

'You can't even imagine what he's like. He's obsessed. He's goes away on business a lot, so he can't keep his eye on me all the time – that's why he gets the concierge to spy on me instead.'

'You still manage to sneak a few treats on the side, though,' I laugh, as she hands her platinum American Express card to the waitress to settle our tab.

'Of course.' She smiles naughtily. 'I have to have *some* time off from being the perfect high-maintenance wife.'

ZZ walks over and I explain to him that Miss Married Model will be throwing a party at her house as a ruse to smuggle me in and that we have to round up a crowd to come along with us. 'We need to make it look like a few of us are just casually going back to hang out and party. We can't draw too much attention to ourselves,' I tell him. 'And somehow I'm thinking your attire will have the concierge not only notifying the husband, but putting a call in to the police and mental health authorities!'

ZZ assures me it isn't a problem and promises he will change out of the Wal-Mart carrier bag before we leave the hotel. The girls who've been hanging out with ZZ in the pool decide to carry the party on with us, and I call Shark to come over with a few of his friends.

As Miss Married Model and I walk through the hotel lobby, Donatella Versace passes to our right, and I see a host of cars, including a brand-new white Porsche and a red convertible Porsche Carrera, queuing up to be collected from the valet. ZZ waits for the Red Dragon with the girls, while Miss Married Model's car, a sleek black Mercedes, the auto equivalent of a black panther, slides up. I open the passenger door for my lady before the valet can even get to her. As I do, a beautiful woman walks past and nearly trips over staring at me.

Miss Married Model looks over at me in a winning fashion and says, 'It's nice to *have* arm candy, not *be* arm candy for once.'

'Look, and I even talk if you pull these strings at the back of my neck,' I joke, as I climb into the driver's seat.

I press hard on the accelerator. It feels amazing to drive such a beautiful car, and Miss Married Model stares happily out of the window as I take corners like the car is on smooth rails.

'I Miss You' by the Rolling Stones comes on and she turns it up, singing sweetly along. 'I'll think of you when I hear this song from now on,' she tells me fondly.

She tells me to stop about a hundred yards away from the apartment so that she can drive there on her own to avoid suspicion.

I stroll along the sidewalk, looking up as I approach the block of luxury high-rise apartments she calls home. They're ultra-modern in style, and I think sadly of Miss Married Model's predilection for the faded elegance of Ocean Drive's art deco buildings and their sense of time and history. Marriage, like gigolodom, rarely involves compromise when one half holds the purse strings.

I reach the glass-fronted door just as ZZ pulls up in the Red Dragon, leaping out with the girls. He is thankfully in normal attire. Miss Married Model is already chatting amiably with the concierge and looking every inch relaxed and guilt-free. What a great actress, I think to myself. No doubt she's done this before. Only a slight tenseness to the clasp of her fingers on her purse gives anything away, but the spy is too busy chatting to notice such details. He is totally fooled. Especially as one of the girls, primed by ZZ probably, drapes her arm round Miss Married Model's shoulder and joins in with some inane chit-chat of her own. It looks for all the world like an innocent soirée for some girly friends and a few male hangers-on.

Once past the concierge, we race upstairs giggling like naughty children who are up to mischief and burst through the front door of the apartment. Like most of these American new-build apartments, there is wall-to-wall glass throughout. Money, it seems, does not buy imagination, but the décor is plush and the views are astounding. High up on the thirtieth floor, we can see downtown Miami twinkling in the distance and there's a lit-up pool and parking lot beneath us, with only the gently swaying palm trees for company.

I've already hatched a plan for how we can be alone together. 'Have you got a hot tub?' I ask Miss Married Model, as the others start pouring drinks, putting the stereo on and dancing.

'Of course. Let's go there, that's a good idea,' says Miss Married Model, with a breathy intonation suggestive of a little girl about to unwrap her favourite present.

We slip into robes and head for the hot tub. I whisper

to ZZ on my way there, telling him to discreetly take the party somewhere else as soon as possible, without the concierge realising that everyone is leaving apart from me. I'm banking on the fact that if they leave quietly, he won't realise that I'm not in the departing head count.

In the dimly lit sauna room I slowly peel off Miss Married Model's robe and carry her into the tub. We kiss and touch each other underwater. The swirling bubbles create the perfect sensuous backdrop. I move her legs apart and the combination of my fingers and the pulsing water brings her to an intense climax.

'These are the moments that make three years of marriage worthwhile,' she whispers in my ear afterwards, still breathing heavily.

'Well, we'll have to make sure you have something to get you through the next three years,' I tell her, leading her by the hand into the bedroom. The house is quiet and empty now. All the revellers have been led away by Miami's Pied Piper, ZZ.

With a new client, the first few moments of sexual engagement are always key to unlocking the lady's sexual signature. With Miss Married Model, despite the fact that she appears to be a rare, delicate flower, a few initial investigations show that she likes things to be more passionate and animalistic than most. Eventually I hit on just the right position for her: from behind, with me pulling her hair just enough to be felt, but in no way painful. Rather than seductive words, she responds best to a fast and furious rhythm and caveman grunts. In turn, she pushes herself violently back on to me and lets herself go with wild, guttural moans. At the point of climax, she almost growls at me to come over her back, so I withdraw, slip

off my condom and champagne-spray all over her beautiful back, which is arched in ecstasy.

Being the picture of discretion, as always, I don't
mention her preference for things being on the rougher
side of sexy, but with slight embarrassment, she brings it
up afterwards as we lie together in bed.

'Sorry if I got a little wild there,' she says, her voice
back to its hushed, gentle tones. 'You see, my husband
treats me like this little princess he has to wrap up in
cotton wool. I knew I was a trophy wife when I married
him, but it seemed like the best thing for me to do – so
many girls were getting back on the bus home after modelling didn't work out here, and I didn't want to become
one of them. Believe me, there's nothing to go back home
to where I'm from, 'cept a fat husband, a few kids and a
part-time job in a diner.

'I thought I could handle it, but he treats me like his
favourite doll. We don't even have sex that often, and when
we do, he acts like I'm gonna snap in two. You know,
sometimes I just want someone to give it to me hard and
make me feel like a woman, not a precious little girl.'
Ironically, with that statement she starts giggling and buries
her head under the duvet. I marvel to myself how uniquely
we develop our sexual preferences.

We fall asleep in each other's arms. I can see how difficult it is for her boorish husband to see her as a real
person, not a figment of his idealised imagination, but it
is an unforgivable mistake. I almost think that for girls
like Miss Married Model, the strength of their character
will only be allowed to shine through when their delicate
looks have faded.

★

The next day we decide to head to the Ritz for lunch. 'What are we going to do about the concierge?' I ask Miss Married Model.

She frowns and then goes to a locked drawer. 'I only usually take this measure in emergencies, but I guess this counts as one,' she says, removing a bundle of $50 notes. 'I'll be back in a few minutes.'

When she returns, I ask her what she's up to.

'Bribing the concierge,' she tells me with a knowing smile. 'If I outbid my husband, I can get away with whatever I want. The concierge doesn't have any special loyalty to my husband – just to his wallet.'

I kiss her and laugh. 'What a strange life you lead,' I comment.

Getting into the black Mercedes on our way to the Ritz seems like the most natural thing. Now I'm back at work, I feel totally in my element in Miami, like I've been infected by the pastel-coloured mood.

Over lunch, we hold hands under the table, and generally make out like I'm the fantasy romantic partner Miss Married Model wishes she had, rather than the controlling cager she's got. The surroundings are ostentatious in a good way, with elaborate chandeliers, but we decide to take a table under the porch in the sprawling gardens and sit on the veranda, which looks out at the palm trees and the sandy lemon-coloured beach in the distance.

Sadly, our beautiful affair is not destined to last. After a week of floating around together, spending our days on the beach and our nights fuelled by champagne and raging pheromones in the hot tub, our party is abruptly brought to a close.

'Did you hear something?' I whisper to Miss Married Model, from the comfort of the marital bed we have just desecrated with fast and furious sex.

'Oh, my God! Oh, my God! It's *him*. Why's he back? He must know! Shit, he must have outbid the concierge.'

She carries on with this frenzied dialogue until I put my hand over her mouth and say, 'Is there any escape route out of here?'

'Yes,' she exclaims. 'There's a fire exit over there. Quick, run now!'

I grab my clothes and sprint out just as the bedroom door is opening.

Outside the apartment, the concierge, now apparently full of remorse, calls me a cab and I head back to ZZ's.

'Dude, you're lucky to be alive,' ZZ tells me with a laugh, as I recount the story on arriving at his place.

'I just hope she's OK,' I say, feeling worried as I remember ZZ saying what a jealous psycho this guy was. I'd left in the heat of the moment because I didn't want to land her in it, but now, on reflection, I wish I'd stayed around to protect her from her crazy husband.

'She'll be fine. He'd never touch his princess,' ZZ reassures me. 'But he'd sure as hell rip you to pieces!'

The next morning a note arrives from Miss Married Model, who knows about my predicament regarding returning to England. 'Click your heels three times, Dorothy, or just use this plane ticket,' reads the note. 'You deserve it. I had such good fun, and "I'll Miss You". xxx.'

Homeward bound at last, I sigh. Now that I know Miss Married Model is fine and that she doesn't regret our time together, I can relax. I've had my fun, but London beckons.

Chapter 13

Gigolos Go Domestic

As the cab nears my home, I'm surprised at how happy I feel to see all the old, familiar sights. The elegant architecture of the area is strangely suited to the fading days of summer, and white stucco buildings are framed beautifully against crisp, cold, blue skies.

Walking towards my front door, I notice curled leaves crunching underfoot, and an exquisite sense of changing seasons hangs in the air.

Released from the bubble of Miami, my thoughts go straight to Charlotte. This time of year is particularly magical at the Literary Café, sitting at the front window, watching people walk past through shafts of autumn light. There's no better time to feel the warmth of the fire, pour a nice red wine and play a few old tunes on the piano. I promise myself that as soon as I'm unpacked I'll pop round there, catch up with Charlotte, play the piano and earn my supper. After all, there'll be no food in my apartment. A gigolo pad operates with the barest nod to domesticity.

A message beeps through from Rochester. He's hosting a rakes and dandies party tonight. Perfect, just the right reintroduction into society.

I turn up the collar of my jacket and smile to myself, thinking about the crazy times I've just had, but also of how I'm looking forward to the decadent edge that London gives to its own debauched proceedings.

Within half an hour of throwing my bags in my bedroom I'm heading over the road to the Literary Café. As always, Charlotte is behind the counter, her hair pulled back and a black apron tied round her waist.

'Hello, stranger.' She smiles warmly and gives me a hug. I squeeze her back tightly and find it strangely difficult to pull away, which of course I manage to do after a moment or so, not wanting to set off any freak alarms. 'Where have you been?' she asks, without a hint of suspicion – just an innocent, friendly enquiry.

I blanch inwardly and reply, 'I had a few gigs away, nothing special.'

'No, that sounds exciting,' she says eagerly, opening the Bordeaux she knows I like and pouring me a glass. 'Tell me about it.'

Moments like these make me despair of our friendship, with all its implicit deceit. What can I say? 'Oh, you know, I've been off abroad in my capacity as an international ambassador of pleasure, having orgies with top American porn stars and sexual arrangements with married women.' I can imagine that would be a conversation-stopper, if not a friendship-terminator. I hate lying to her as a friend, and my worst fear is something *will* happen between us – not because I don't want to be with her, but because I don't want to have to lie to her, and I don't know if I've got the courage to tell her the truth about me. Of course my intention would be to be honest, but I know how life has a way of railroading good intentions.

'Oh, it was quite boring really,' I reply. 'Anyway, have you been practising our song?' I ask in order to divert the conversation to safer territory, trying not to tap my wineglass nervously.

'Of course. It's such a beautiful piece. It was really easy to learn, too.'

'Shall we play it?' I ask, feeling warmed by the wine. 'I'm sure the customers won't mind,' I laugh, nodding towards an old gent who looks like he's about to nod off in the comforting ambience of the café.

'Sure, why not. The boss won't be back for a while,' says Charlotte, taking off her apron and heading towards the piano.

We sit together, our shoulders touching, and our outer thighs brushing as we reach towards the keys closest to each other. Neither of us says anything, but I can sense that she feels the electricity too. So far in our friendship we've haven't had much physical contact, but now, feeling her leg against mine, suddenly the atmosphere is charged. What surprises me is that it feels more intimate than the most explicit sex acts I have indulged in.

The sound of the piano drifts through the café, and I feel utterly relaxed by the way our fingers are moving in harmony and intuitively sensing the music. I glance at Charlotte's face and see her eyes are closed. She looks almost angelic, I think to myself. Then, as if sensing I'm watching her, she opens her eyes and looks at me. We are staring straight into each other's eyes while playing. An intense look passes between us that seems to last for ever, until finally she turns away. I honestly believe that if we'd held each other's gaze for just a second longer, the magnetic forces of chemistry would have made us kiss, without either of us making a conscious decision to do so.

Afterwards, I drink my wine as she puts her apron back on and wipes down the bar with studied intent. I know this is a moment ripe for the picking, but I just can't bring myself to do it. My life is too complicated, and I don't want to hurt her.

'I'd better get off,' I say with a tone of resignation. 'My friend's throwing a party and I said I'd go along.'

A silence stretches out between us, and I wonder if I should invite her after work. Then a vision of Rochester drifts into my mind. Not such a good idea, I think. Reluctantly I get up, peck her on the cheek, almost tenderly, and walk out into the cold, foggy street.

To clear my head, I decide to walk to the club where Rochester is hosting his party. The memory of sitting side by side with Charlotte just won't shift. What's going on? Walking briskly, I eventually succeed in pushing it to the back of my mind – but not without a struggle.

Half an hour later I hit the West End feeling pretty chilly, but ready for the night ahead. Crazy as Rochester is, I'm actually looking forward to seeing him and being around his uncomplicated outlook on life. Some people medicate themselves with Prozac, but hedonism is my high.

As I walk past the doorman into the club, I bump

straight into Rochester, who is talking excitedly on his mobile. He motions for me to hang around until he finishes his call and hands over his glass of champagne for me to swig on in the meantime.

'It's all going off tonight,' he says gleefully as he hangs up. 'This is going to be *one of those nights.*'

'Why?' I ask, starting to walk down the stairs with a growing sense of anticipation.

'Well, Celebrity Z is here – can you believe it? She must have heard I was hosting a night and looked me up.'

'Much as I admire your self-belief, it's probably more to do with the fact her PR knows it's the hottest night in town,' I laugh, leading him into the main room.

'Yeah, yeah – whatever! Anyway, Johan is coming and he's bringing the Divorcee here for us to meet. She's booked a private room upstairs so we can all hang out, have cocktails and get to know each other. How cool is that? Apparently she's the spitting image of Audrey Hepburn, totally beautiful.'

'So it's really serious, then? I was worried she'd have tired of him by now. Can't wait to meet her and find out what she's like,' I reply, intrigued at the thought of seeing them together.

As we arrive at the bar, Celebrity Z totters over, winks at Rochester, throwing her arms round his neck, then disentangles herself to shake my hand and say hello. She's obviously 'refreshed' and enjoying the fact that she knows the party's host, Rochester. As quickly as she appeared, she whoops and skips off to dance as a floor-filler comes on, waving her arms wildly in the air and looking for all the world like a demented princess.

'She's certainly in a better mood than when I last saw

her,' grins Rochester, running his hands through his hair with his black-painted fingernails. 'I've got a feeling that I'm going to have a fun night – even if I am just used and abused by her in a drunken state.'

'Look, there's Johan,' I say, pointing to the door as he lowers his six-foot frame down the stairs, wearing an expensive overcoat and matching trilby, a mature outfit that is a striking contrast to his beautiful baby face.

Behind Johan, illuminated in the blue-tinted light is the Divorcee, her head bowed slightly as she follows him, watching her step as she does. Her skin is the palest shade of olive, though the overhead light gives it a slight ghostly cast. Her thick auburn hair is scraped back into a glossy chignon, the curve of which seems to extend along her high cheekbones, artfully shaded with just a touch of crimson blusher. She is elegantly dressed in a simple black cocktail dress, worn with ankle boots for a modern twist. As she nears us, I can see her beautiful brown eyes blinking in the light like a dewy foal; the upward curve of her eyelid is accentuated with a sleek line of black. Her lips are full and sensuous, barely shaded in, just highlighted with a slick of tinted gloss. She is absolutely stunning, and not at all what I expected: somehow, knowing she is a millionairess divorcee, I thought she would be older, and sharper round the edges. She is breathtakingly beautiful and feminine, and has millions in the bank. No wonder Johan is head over heels in love. He has done a romantic somersault and landed firmly on his feet. It also explains his medication-necessitating paranoia. Until seeing her, I had thought that she provided the funding and he provided the pretty face, so he would need never fear her straying eye, but now it's clear that, with or without money, she would be coveted by any man, so the danger is doubled.

Instead of heading to us for an introduction, Johan, his arm proprietoraly round the Divorcee's waist, swerves towards the other set of stairs, to take her up to the private members' room.

'Shall we follow?' asks Rochester, eager to get an introduction.

'Why not?' I say, making my way to the stairs and looking forward to this little soirée.

We walk into the private members' room and a delightful sight greets us. In contrast to the crowded chaos of downstairs, the room is calm and sophisticated. There is a warm yellowish light, and a waiter is busy pouring drinks from a massive magnum of champagne, while another is chilling by the side of the solid oak table.

The Divorcee is holding court in the central seat, with Johan at her side looking admiringly on as she talks animatedly to Byron and Valentino, who are sipping on champagne and looking as if they have already been seduced by the charms and witty conversation of the star attraction.

On seeing us, Johan stands up and proudly introduces us. As we shake hands and kiss once on each cheek, the Divorcee gives us a ravishing smile, full of warmth.

'Lovely to meet you both,' she says as we settle into our seats. 'Johan has told me so much about you.' She motions for the waiter to pour us both a glass of champagne.

'Lovely to meet you too,' I reply, and Rochester tries to break his usual smoulder to return her smile.

'I'd like to raise a toast,' says Johan, again standing up, then announcing, 'We're getting engaged,' at which he raises his glass.

Amid the murmurs of surprise, we all stand up, clink glasses and congratulate them, taking it in turns to hug them both.

'We're really in love, and I just hope you all, as my closest friends, are supportive of our relationship,' smiles Johan slightly nervously.

'Hey, it's like a relay race – did your ex-husband donate the engagement ring?' jokes Rochester to the Divorcee.

Johan's face clouds over with annoyance at the comment.

'Very funny,' laughs the Divorcee, demonstrating an admirable sense of humour. 'You've obviously never met my ex – he wouldn't donate anything if his life depended on it. He makes Scrooge look like a WAG with a spending habit.'

'So why did he give you millions in a divorce settlement, then?' asks Rochester curiously, not having the tact to be discreet about matters of money.

'He didn't *give* me the money; a court *forced* him to pay it to me,' she replies candidly. 'He'd let me rot in a gutter rather than pay me a penny if it was up to him – especially now I'm with a twenty-two-year-old Dior supermodel,' she laughs. 'That's quite a blow to his massive ego.'

'Is that why you left him, because he was a tight-wad?' asks Rochester, once again oblivious to the finer points of politeness.

'Rochester, don't be so nosy,' exclaims Johan in an indignant voice, trying to protect his fiancée from an onslaught of prying questions.

'No, it's fine – I don't mind telling him,' she reassures Johan, then faces Rochester with an open smile. 'It wasn't that he was mean; it was that he used money to manipulate people – me included. Rich men are often arrogant bullies, that's the truth. Having tried it both ways, I honestly think it's far better for women to be with younger men. Rich, older men are control freaks. I'll be honest, at first I thought Johan was just a post-divorce treat, but when I realised – despite the age gap – we were soul mates, I realised this was how relationships *should* be.'

I instantly warm to her honesty, and some of my fears are alleviated. I suppose I find it hard to believe love can blossom in such unlikely circumstances, but the genuine affection that they seem to share is starting to convince me.

Seeing them together, not just with each other for snatched momentary pleasure but committing to spending their lives together and sharing a home, brings all the complications of my situation with Charlotte rushing in. But for us, it is even more complex, because neither of us has millions sitting in a bank account waiting to treat us to a life of luxury and leisure, and I don't know if I have it in me to forsake this lifestyle for love. I hate to admit that to myself, because at heart I am a hopeless romantic who thinks he would die for love, but I don't know if I could endure a living death for love – life in a semi in suburbia, tired from a job in which my CV doesn't hang off my cheekbones, struggling for money. Could love survive that? Especially after the things I've seen: sunsets in Miami, orgies of indulgence, celebrity hotel suites where you're so cushioned from reality you can live from any fantasy script you want. Like an idle prince regent, I've been spoiled rotten to the core, and my blessings are also a curse, casting the evil eye over my love life.

'So where will you live as a married couple?' asks Rochester, breaking my reverie.

I look towards them. They are holding hands under the table, and I smile fondly at the thought of them playing house together, mixing their beauty and wealth into the perfect recipe for happiness – a two fingers to a world that often says you can't have it all.

'I recently bought a Georgian town house in Hampstead,' explains the Divorcee. 'I've been living there for a few months now, but Johan is moving in tomorrow. I tell you what, why don't you all come round for dinner in the evening? It'll be like a house-warming for Johan, a way of welcoming him into his new home.'

Clever, I think to myself. She must truly love him. By having us in the house on his first night, she will cushion his transition from one of us to 'him indoors'. It will be a soft landing, so he won't feel like he's suddenly playing grown-ups in the big house, and being child and master all rolled into one.

'That sounds great. I'd love to come for dinner,' I reply, and the others all chime in their grateful acceptance.

'Don't worry, Rochester.' His face looks less convinced than the rest of ours and she leans forward and puts her hand on his as she continues, 'It won't be too early. I know you're a creature of the night – Johan's told me all about you!'

We laugh, and Rochester sits back smiling and looking instantly more relaxed. The last time he saw daylight he was probably sitting his GCSEs. Early engagements do not suit his temperament at all.

Like a dog with a bone, though, he can't let go the thorny subject of the Divorcee's previous marriage and starts up with his interrogation again, asking, 'If your ex was such a bastard, why did you marry him?'

Johan groans and throws his head back in despair at Rochester's lack of tact.

'I met him when I was very young and innocent and hadn't had any other relationships. He loved the fact that I was this naïve little thing he could control, and that I looked up to him no matter what,' the Divorcee replies. Her candour is amazing, but I figure she must be keen not to look like she's hiding secrets.

I look at Johan's sweet little face and try not to draw parallels. The Divorcee catches my almost imperceptible glance and, giving me a meaningful look, continues, 'It's no crime to want to be with someone innocent, even if you are far more worldly-wise, as long as you're good to them,' she says, squeezing Johan's hand. 'But as my ex-husband's bank balance got bigger so did his ego, and he treated me like I was an object he owned. If he thought I'd been "bad", he'd punish me by cancelling my credit cards or stopping my money. One Christmas he took my car off me so I couldn't drive to my parents' to drop their presents off. But what could I do? I could hardly move back into my cramped bedroom at my parents' – I hadn't lived there for over fifteen years and it wouldn't have been fair on my mum and dad . . .' The Divorcee trails off and looks sadly into the distance.

I feel instantly sorry for her and all my fears that she is some ball-breaking, high-maintenance bitch disappear. 'That's awful,' I say. 'How could anyone be so cruel?'

'Yeah, what a dog – I hate him already!' exclaims Rochester.

'So how did you escape?' I ask, noticing that we have all leaned close in. We're on tenterhooks to hear how her story ends and have expressions of sympathy written on our faces.

'Look, I'll save the second instalment for our dinner party tomorrow,' she laughs, sipping her champagne. 'Let's not spoil our fun tonight talking about evil ex-husbands.'

'I second that,' says Johan, kissing her tenderly on the lips and looking as if he wished the ex would never get a mention again.

Later, Johan tells me as an aside, 'He's worth at least twenty million. Ugly as a pig, but rich as hell. You don't think she thinks I'm not successful enough, do you?'

'No way,' I reassure him. 'She clearly adores you. I admit I had my reservations at first, but I'm more and more convinced. I think there's a moral you need to take from her story, though.'

'What do you mean?' he asks with a worried expression.

'I do believe she'll take care of your heart, but that doesn't mean you have to give it to her wrapped in fancy paper with a bow round it. You need to keep some power for yourself or the relationship will be out of balance.'

Johan looks thoughtful and says, 'Yeah, you're right. But what do I do? I'm mad about her.'

'Look, she says her ex would never let her follow her dreams because he was so controlling, but she's not that kind of person. Take this relationship as an opportunity to do something with your life, something you've always dreamed of.'

'You're right. You know I've always been into painting? Well, I'd love to do more of it and maybe even have an exhibition. That's what I'll do! Then if I'm a successful artist, there's no way she'll leave me.'

Our conversation is interrupted by a very drunken Celebrity Z making an appearance at the doorway, marshalled by two scary-looking bouncers.

'Excuse me,' says Rochester. 'I've got some business to attend to, or else the columnists will be out of work.' And with that he heads towards Celebrity Z with a swagger that spells trouble.

The next evening I get ready for the Divorcee's dinner party, debating which shoes to wear with my Ozwald Boateng jacket. I have a strange sense of anticipation about the evening. Usually if I'm on my way to a £1 million mansion, it's to serve up more than dinner, and it feels a little odd to be invited as a bona fide guest, no strings attached. Our 'partners' are also invited, which elicited a snigger from Rochester as it was said, even though I kicked him under the table. Once again the first person to come into my mind is Charlotte. The thought of us all sitting round the table like ordinary couples having a civilised dinner gives me a strange sense of satisfaction. But of course as soon as the reality encroaches on the fantasy I realise it is untenable. I just couldn't see her making small talk with Rochester, who could easily slip up with an outrageous anecdote. It just wouldn't work. Also, how would I explain my relationship with Charlotte to the others? They just wouldn't get it. So instead I call Trustfundista. A dinner date in the home of a wealthy divorcee is just up her street. She'll fit in perfectly, especially since beginning her new life as a career girl, which seems to have matured her and given her a confidence boost.

Trustfundista picks me up in her car and we drive down the wealthy streets of north London until we pull up outside a beautiful town house. The Divorcee greets us at the door and instantly hits it off with Trustfundista, who recognises the origins of a rare antique sideboard in the hallway.

The high ceilings create a grandiose impression, further accentuated by the ornate white cornice and the elaborate chandeliers featured in every room, which cast a sparkling light throughout. As we walk towards the dining room, I'm amazed by the number of rooms I glimpse as I make my way down the hall: a book-filled study with an imposing desk and leather reading chair; a reception room filled with delicate antiques and old society portraits; a conservatory with floor-to-ceiling French doors revealing a wild country garden, which is a calming mix of green laced with the red leaves of autumn.

The dining room is lit by a dimmed chandelier and the three large candelabras on the massive oak dining table, which could easily seat twenty. Trustfundista and I are the last to arrive and the party already seems to be in full swing. Rochester, still hung-over from the previous night, is indulging in hair – well, entire coat – of the dog and pouring liberally from a champagne bottle. This is a life he could get used to, I can see. He'll just have to whisk a rich divorcee down the aisle first.

We say hello to everyone and sit down. 'Carry on telling us about the great escape,' says Rochester, when the Divorcee settles herself back in her seat.

'OK, Rochester wanted to know how I finally left my husband,' she says for our benefit, and then continues, 'Two things persuaded me to divorce him. Firstly, I decided I wanted to go back to school and study for a degree in theatre and he dismissed the idea out of hand, even though at that point he was away on business all the time and I was mostly left in the house on my own. Secondly, he started talking about having children. For him, it was just another box to tick, but as soon as he said it I knew I could never have him as the father of my child. Imagining that ego-maniac as a dad was the final straw! So I plotted to leave. I sold all my expensive jewellery – including Cartier watches worth fifty thousand pounds each – to create an escape fund and then, one day when he was out, packed my bags and moved into a hotel, one where he would never think of looking for me.'

'Did you leave him a note to explain?' I ask, wondering how it felt to be on the receiving end of such a bombshell.

'Why bother? He'd only have given it to his lawyers to use against me,' laughs the Divorcee. 'Instead I just wrote, "I'm leaving you. See you in the divorce courts," in lipstick on the living-room mirror. I couldn't write anything longer: I didn't have enough lipstick left! Of course he went mad, cancelled all my credit cards, tried to take me to the edge of poverty so he could bribe me back to him. But that sense of freedom and exhilaration when I left him was so amazingly intoxicating I would have crawled over glass rather than return to my old life.'

'But it all turned out OK in the end,' comments Rochester, gesturing to our opulent surroundings with his expensive Viennese crystal champagne glass.

'I got my happy ending,' she smiles, putting her arm round Johan and kissing him on the cheek. 'The judge was very good to me in the divorce case, let's put it that way. But meeting Johan has been the best thing. He's made me happier than anything money could buy.' She blushes as she finishes her speech, and Johan gives her a massive hug.

I feel rather moved by what she's said and a slow tinge of sadness spreads through me.

A few hours later, the party wraps up. Trustfundista has to go home to get a good night's sleep as she has an important meeting in the morning. I don't feel like going home to my empty bed, in my poky little apartment, but Rochester is off on another rendezvous with Celebrity Z, and the others all have engagements to go to. Loneliness is a terrible emotion for a gigolo to feel, but tonight it consumes me. I feel like the proverbial orphan looking through the window at the happy family, condemned to a life of solitude.

With perfect serendipity a message beeps through. It's Miss Stripper. 'We're having an after-hours party at the club. Come along – I'd love to see you. x.' I immediately cheer up and order a cab, waving goodbye to Johan and the Divorcee, who stand on the doorstep to see me off, like the perfect hosts. I look through the cab's rear window to see them walk back inside, no doubt chatting about the night's events and discussing us all. They're the picture of perfect domesticity. For the moment, it's a dream I can't afford to dwell on.

The scene that greets me at Miss Stripper's club is a world away from what I have just left behind in the well-to-do suburbs. The strippers are having a party with a few specially chosen customers and friends. I walk in to see them chasing down tequila shots with champagne, carousing on the stage, giving impromptu performances, and generally being rowdy and boisterous. It's actually really eye-opening to see them being so silly, compared with their usual studied sexiness.

Miss Stripper bounds up and gives me a hug. 'Why the downcast look?' she immediately says, and I'm impressed by her perceptiveness, as I am deliberately trying to appear happy.

'I'm fine. How are you, my gorgeous?' I reply, not wanting to burden her with my woes, as that certainly isn't part of our business arrangement.

'Look, I know you don't want to break your façade for me, but I understand, you know I understand. I'm asking you as a *friend* – is everything OK?'

Her tone is so warm I decide to confess all. I tell her about my dilemma with Charlotte, the scene of domestic bliss I have just left behind and how I don't know if it's something I will ever have – or even want.

'I know exactly how you feel,' says Miss Stripper sympathetically. 'But the truth is, it's never too late to change. When the moment comes for you to move on, you'll just know and everything will fall into place. Until then, just have fun, make the most of this incredible life you're leading and don't worry about the future. In these professions living for the moment is a must.'

'You're right,' I say, with a sudden determination not to dwell on things. 'My life is amazing and I should just enjoy it.' As I finish my sentence, a couple of the girls get on the stage and start yelling for a third person to join them to do a can-can strip.

Before anyone else can even think about replying, I leap up on to the stage, giving Miss Stripper a broad grin. She waves and then falls about laughing as the music kicks in and I start a comically tantalising strip. The two girls onstage immediately fall into a routine as my 'glamorous assistants', and the whole place erupts in whistles, catcalls and wild applause. It seems the strippers like it when the audience entertains *them*.

I get down to just my pants and begin to fear there might be a stage invasion. When I attempt to exit the stage, and finish with a degree of decorum, a gaggle of the girls block my way. A slow clap starts from the floor and the chant 'Get them off!' is picked up with gusto. Miss Stripper is laughing her head off at the front. She's already seen my full-frontal show and seems in no mood to deny the rest of her colleagues the pleasure. I take centre stage again and give the ladies what they want. After all, what else is there left for a gigolo to do?

Chapter 14

Paris and Pretty Patrons

After my star turn taking off my clothes, it only seems fair that my next assignment involves getting dressed up. Paris Fashion Week beckons, and I'm in the mood to strut around the most stylish capital in the world, wearing exquisite finery befitting a dandy who's living on his wits and beyond his means. Trusty old Trustfundista is my VIP pass to a week of glittering folly and frolics – she calls to say she's flying from Monaco to Paris and would love me to join her. I pick up my Eurostar tickets, along with a new tailor-made suit from Savile Row.

Regardless of all my first-class plane journeys, I still find taking the train – especially the Eurostar – infinitely more exciting. I stand on the platform feeling like Cary Grant in some old-time black-and-white Hollywood movie. Today I'm wearing a stylish suit, light-blue Miu Miu shirt, black

winkle-pickers, a long, black Crombie coat, Marc Jacobs
sunglasses and leather gloves. My vintage Gucci suitcase
contains my new suit, and all the other paraphernalia a
modern dandy needs to get through a week of drinking
and decadence.

As I board the train, I look back over the sea of
commuters as they shuffle along beneath a remorselessly
grey London sky. T. S. Eliot's line 'I had not thought death
had undone so many' comes into my mind. I settle into
my seat, carefully folding my coat and feel that strange
rush of exhilaration that comes with a new adventure.
One day I may have to join that tide of everyday folk, I
figure to myself, but until then I'll enjoy my champagne
existence – before the fizz fades out to the mother of all
hangovers.

As the green countryside streaks past, and provincial
bakeries make way for Continental patisseries, I think
about Johan and the Divorcee. Johan usually takes the
Parisian catwalks by storm during fashion week, his angelic
face lit up by the endless stream of paparazzi and style
photographers, but this year he couldn't be bothered to
appear. 'Nah, I'm too old for it now,' he told me dismissively, at the tender age of twenty-two. Maybe models
have a hyper-speed life, with twenty being to them what
thirty is to most of us – their youth and vitality squeezed
out of them in their teenage years after endless globe-
trotting, which garners extra life miles, not just Air Miles.
The life of a gigolo is similar – overexposure to excess is
a fast track to burnout. Ultimately it is impossible not to
become jaded by pleasure, which makes a man need to
devour life even harder to get the same highs. I have a
feeling Paris, whore of Europe, will be the perfect place to

push the boundaries of indulgence and give a hedonism junkie a better hit.

Disembarking at Gare du Nord, I walk round the corner to a little café I know to get a coffee and wait for a taxi to come by. I cannot bear to stand in line with the tourists at the railway queue – snobby, I know. Within five minutes I hail a cab and instruct him to take me to the boutique hotel Trustfundista is checked into, just off the Champs-Elysées.

A smile spreads across my face as we pull up – it is quintessentially French, a small but perfectly formed establishment that seems to be pleasantly stuck in the past. As I walk up the winding wooden stairs to Trustfundista's suite, I feel like the spirit of Baudelaire is following behind me.

The room is what can only be described as 'eccentric luxury'. The bathroom is beautifully decorated with white porcelain tiles and ornate gold trim; a large, traditional overspill bath is framed against a rickety window looking on to the pale-blue Parisian sky. The other rooms are charmingly furnished in an eclectically bohemian mix of 1920s, 1940s and 1950s pieces. The overall feel is one of elegant chaos – like a boho designer pulled the look together after a night out on the absinthe in Pigalle. I walk towards the white French shutters and pull them open. A tiny balcony, guarded by ornate cast-iron railings, looks out on to the bustling street. I see people going about their business. No doubt their lives are just as humdrum as those of Londoners, but when you're in a foreign city everything is cast with romanticism, and I imagine everyone is rushing to an illicit assignation with a lover, rather than just going back to work. I think to myself that for all its debauched reputation, Paris is essentially a city for falling in love, not just fucking.

The bedroom door is closed and I wonder if Trustfundista is having an afternoon siesta. I know she arrived last night and went to a few fashion parties that I got some of my contacts to line up for her. Even if I'm not there, I still do my best to please.

Without thinking, I gently push open the door, hoping not to wake her. The sight that greets me is far from sleepy. Wearing only black stockings, suspenders and some very high patent heels, Trustfundista is straddling the slender body of a youthful boy who has an other-worldly face with aqua eyes and sharp cheekbones. I can barely tell if they're having sex or taking part in the latest Nick Knight shoot, so stylised and beautiful do they look together. I stand at the doorway, spellbound for a few seconds.

Trustfundista looks up at me like a mischievous school-girl who's been caught out and says naughtily, 'Oops, I put my hand in the Dior-model cookie jar again.'

Obviously, after our little sojourn in London, where I tactically set her up with one of the young models, she has developed a taste for them. And fair play to her. Her eyes glitter with excitement at the situation: caught out by Daddy. The sexual scenario probably couldn't get any hotter for her.

'I'll wait in the living room until you're finished,' I tell her with a stern tone – an affectation of course. I'm not bothered in the slightest, but I know she's about to have the most mind-blowing orgasm of her life, riding a Dior model and knowing that Daddy is outside, darkly dis-approving. Sure enough, within minutes of me pouring a drink and gazing across the city I hear her obscenely noisy climax.

After five minutes the model shuffles out, mumbling that Trustfundista is taking a shower. I offer him a beer and his eyes light up. 'Thanks, dude,' he replies with the international English accent most of these models have. We sip in silence, a strange male camaraderie between us, a silent acknowledgement that we are just stunt cocks in this fearsomely feminine world.

'Golden,' Trustfundista shouts from the bathroom.

'I've been beckoned,' I say knowingly to the model, handing him my beer. 'Probably best if you're gone by the time I'm done,' I tell him.

'Sure, dude,' he replies, giving me the rock 'n' roll sign and smiling in a resigned manner.

I start to unbutton my shirt as I open the bathroom door and see Trustfundista naked under the hot stream of water. 'You've been very naughty,' I tell her, without a hint of comedy in my voice, just chastisement.

She giggles coquettishly and starts to touch herself as I undress. I make her bend over the bath and am amazed at how quickly she comes again. No doubt she'll play this scenario over in her head for a long while to come. I smile to myself as I realise that she probably set it up. I love her style. She may like to be dominated, but no one is more into control of her pleasure than Trustfundista. Elaborate fantasies aside, she's the real boss.

Afterwards, we go to get something to eat on the rue de Pontière. With the streetlights picking out the fog of twilight, I feel utterly seduced by Paris: the sense of history stalking every cobbled street; the corner cafés with their ghosts of Sartre and de Beauvoir philosophising over cheap red wine; the self-conscious arrogance of a city that knows it is a cut above the rest of the world. The whole place feels lost in time. A dandy's true spiritual home, with a lineage of penniless poets and princes hoping to make their fortunes in the salons of society's most beautiful and licentious ladies.

We sit down and order chateaubriand steak to share with potato gratin and a nice bottle of '82 Margaux. We don't mention me catching her with a young male model. It has been sealed in her mind as the perfect fantasy and words would only ruin the effect. Her phone rings and a cloud of annoyance crosses her face as she answers it and tersely agrees with the person at the other end of the phone, although she is clearly unhappy with what has been requested.

'Dammit,' she says, slamming her phone on the table. 'Having a job sucks.'

'Why, what's happened?' I ask, reaching for her hand to calm her down.

'It was Daddy. I have to fly back tomorrow. Something's come up at work and he says swanning around in Paris isn't the way to solve it.'

The perfectly preserved bubble of her fantasy bursts when the commander-in-chief calls, it seems. Well, we all have to answer to someone. Whichever way you look at it, there's always a paymaster – be it the wealthy woman keeping you, a rich father or husband, or a corporate employer. Who of us is really free? Thinking of it like that makes my prison seem quite cushy.

The following evening I sit alone in the hotel, watching the early evening sky turn from lilac to deep velvet blue to black. Trustfundista has gone, but has kindly settled the bill for a week's stay anyway. My evening is already planned and in an hour I will be enjoying the spoils of the best parties fashion week has to offer. With time to kill I pour myself a glass of wine and sit in blissful silence. There is something soothing about this hotel room and this city. Unlike the high-octane wealth of New York, I feel happy to just hang out – with or without a benefactress to keep me busy. There is a spirit of freedom here. Unlike America, where money talks, in Paris the cultural conversation is based on something far more cerebral, and the sum of your worth cannot be calculated by your bank statements. It's easy to see why it's been a magnet for artists over the centuries. Part of me wonders if this would be a good place to start again – maybe with Charlotte. I could play piano in bistros to get by and work on my compositions. The romantic ideal of the poverty-stricken artist, I laugh to myself, as I enjoy an expensive bottle of wine in an exclusive hotel. Maybe money *always* talks – it's just that here in France, it's somehow lost in translation.

An hour later I am walking along the cobbled streets to meet my friend Mr Paris, a nightclub owner who is hosting the hottest party in town. He greets me at the door in a wine-red suit with a slight sheen, a black shirt, a trilby hat and a pencil-thin, ink-black moustache. He is everything you would expect from a Parisian impresario and more. Unlike the manic queues of London and New York, heavily policed by power-crazed door whores, the entrance here is far more low key. People are leaning against the wall smoking roll-ups made with black papers, and a few dishevelled youths are sitting on the pavement playing guitar, singing aimlessly in beautifully whimsical French accents.

As Mr Paris walks me downstairs, the stairwell is littered with models elegantly wasted on champagne, adjusting their long legs, smoking and trading stories of the day's events on the catwalk. Expensive dresses hang off bony shoulders, and there is a slightly affected air of jaded knowingness alongside the understated glamour of those young and beautiful enough for everything to feel effortless. I know a few of the girls from London, and they wave listlessly and mouth, 'Hi,' as I walk past, their pale faces heavy-lidded with fashion fatigue, then turn back to their murmured conversations. The difference between the wild energy and eager enthusiasm of the Miami glamour models and the studied boredom of the European catwalk models instantly strikes me – almost like they symbolise the polarities of the new and old world. One continent still wearing its push-up bra to impress, full of the optimism of making good, and the other sated on past excess and laden with world-weary cynicism.

The club, fittingly called Paris Paris, is decked out in erotic reds and flush pinks, and bizarrely features a six-foot statue of Mickey Mouse wielding a huge erection as he looks implacably over proceedings. Neon signs, also in pinks and red, flash the word 'Paris' – like the flickering nameplate of a brothel – just in case any guests imbibe too much champagne and forget the great city they owe their overindulgence to.

As I make my way to the bar, I notice a beautiful French girl sitting alone, reading in one of the booths on the left-hand side. She looks like a heroine of alternative French cinema – glossy black hair with a heavy fringe pushed off her forehead, chalk-white skin, a delicate nose, full lips and darting, intelligent eyes. She has a 1940s-style black hat on and a black pencil skirt. I am immediately intrigued by her – she looks like she's stepped out of a scene painted by a Parisian artist. In all my vast experience I don't think I ever recall seeing a beautiful girl sitting alone reading in a busy club before. Only in Paris!

My friend notices me glance in her direction and gives a low, knowing laugh. 'She's beautiful, yes?' he asks me rhetorically. 'And very rich – heiress to a famous French family fortune. Would you like me to introduce you?'

I nod, so he does an about-turn and we head in her direction. An heiress indeed – it seems this dandy might have found his Parisian patron after all. As we reach her table, before either of us can say anything, she looks up at me with large, black, glassy eyes and says in a thick French accent, 'Pick a page.'

I don't question her and take the book out of her hands and randomly select a page. As I hand it back to her, I note that it is a collection of Shakespearian sonnets, rather than the expected Rimbaud or Mallarmé.

She opens the page at Sonnet 116 and reads out in a throaty voice, 'Love is not love which alters when it alteration finds, or bends with the remover to remove. O, no! It is an ever fixed mark that looks on tempests and is never shaken.' She laughs deeply, looks into my eyes and says with a flourish, 'Now that is your sonnet.'

The irony of the sonnet I have picked is not lost on me – 'Love is not love which alters when it alteration finds' – beautiful words, but sadly not true for a gigolo, who will find that lust alters by the hour, especially when it finds alterations it no longer likes. It is as if by Fate, random chance, whatever you will, one poem has summed up all my inner turmoil about my chosen profession and my feelings for Charlotte.

'Now sign your sonnet,' commands Miss Heiress, interrupting my thoughts with her beautiful voice. She hands me a quill pen, which she has produced from somewhere, and passes me the book to sign the page I have picked.

My youthful obsession with antique pens and calligraphy finally pays off as I write my name in perfectly crafted letters that would not be out of place in an eighteenth-century love letter. Who would have known that an eccentric teenage pastime in the Isle of Wight would come to fruition here in a Parisian club with a glamorous heiress?

She smiles approvingly and turns her head slightly to one side to appraise me, then lowers her lashes slowly, as if to signal I have passed her test. Sitting down next to her, I ask if she is alone.

'No, no, I have friends here somewhere.' She gestures carelessly, as if she is indifferent either to their company or to being alone.

For the next few hours we sip champagne together and talk half-understood nonsense about art, literature and music, while making eyes in each other's direction and punctuating our conversation with flirtatious touches of hands. Every so often, following a passionate monologue, her heavy fringe falls across her eyes and I brush it gently aside. I discover she has the distracted, tangential mind of someone who has never had to pin a thought down in her life or fully explain herself. Her existence is one of beautiful whims and carefree crushes.

As the night crosses the midnight threshold and the

lethargic models seem to kick-start themselves into debauched revelry, Miss Heiress suddenly stands up, preparing to make a dramatic exit. 'Let's go now,' she tells me with a dreamy expression.

I follow her as she stalks up the stairs, her hand fluttering in the air as if thoughtlessly saying goodbye to any friends she may be leaving behind.

'Let's go back to mine,' she says, hailing a taxi and holding her hat on with a ghostly-white hand, guarding against the brisk breeze that has picked up.

I go to speak, but she turns, with a little twirl, to face me and kisses me, holding her hat on with one hand and pulling me in close with the other. I return her kiss with passionate abandon, almost waiting for the art-house film director to yell, 'Cut!' Instead the taxi driver mutters moodily in French, and Miss Heiress lets out a brittle laugh as she pauses our embrace and steps inside the cab.

The deserted Parisian streets seem endless as we drive through the heart of the city, making our way to the wealthy arrondissement where she lives. Side by side with only our fingertips touching, the silence seems to highlight a growing sense of longing between us.

I hold her hand as we walk up the dark, twisting stairs to her apartment, which is right at the top, in the eaves of an historic-looking Parisian building. Her apartment is littered with unfinished canvases set up on wooden easels. The paintings are a mixture of modern, abstract and textural – obtuse faces peering out of random shapes, imperceptible to the eye at first, but on closer inspection looming out ominously.

A large set of French doors open up on to a charming terrace that overlooks the rooftops of Paris. The angular shapes of misaligned roofs are like an abstract painting set against an Impressionist sky of luminous stars painted on darkest midnight blue. I take a deep breath, feeling utterly enchanted by the romance of the situation, and not a little bit intoxicated from the champagne.

I turn my back on the Paris night to see Miss Heiress discarding her pencil skirt, dancing gracefully so the contours of her lithe body are silhouetted against the wall in dim orange lamplight. An old-fashioned gramophone is turning out the ethereal sounds of Puccini.

'I love Puccini, don't you?' she asks, closing her eyes and swaying in time to the music.

I don't reply. Instead I walk inside and take off my jacket. Slowly, with her help, I undress too, and we dance together, naked, to the strains of Puccini. After a while our dancing slows and our bodies become more and more entwined. Silently she places her arms round my neck and I pull her up, wrapping her legs round my waist. I kiss her softly as she starts to move her hips backwards and forwards. The motion gets faster and faster, but never frenzied. Even her orgasm is elegantly done, with a graceful finesse.

Afterwards, me still standing, her still with her body wrapped round mine, she whispers in my ear in her heavy French accent, 'The stars were watching over us.'

Like her obtuse paintings, I don't quite understand what she means, but sometimes romance is best when it doesn't have to be spelled out. It sounded good, after all – why spoil the illusion with something as mundane as making sense?

Later, as I fall asleep in her arms, I find it hard to believe this world really exists. It is so far removed from reality. Even the Trustfundistas of this world at least seem to be accountable to some kind of everyday life. Miss Heiress is so rich she is disconnected from anything that doesn't read like it came from a bohemian novel about how to live a romantic life. I love the experience, but it is a little disorientating – I miss the earthiness of regular women, who are more grounding.

The next day Miss Heiress decides we should spend the day together indulging in the finer things in life. We walk together down the cobbled street she lives on towards a restaurant she assures me is one of the best in Paris. When we arrive, it is closed and her eyes look downcast, but without a hint of petulance. The owner, who obviously knows her, is profoundly apologetic and gesticulates wildly with his hands as he explains the situation to her. Eventually she smiles and asks him something, but their French is too fast for me to understand. He smiles graciously and minutes later comes out with an expensive bottle of vintage champagne all wrapped up for us. No money exchanges hands, but I'm imagining it isn't a freebie – more like she has an ongoing tab, probably one that her wealthy family settles for her. It's as if money doesn't even exist in her little world.

'We shall eat at mine,' she tells me with a charming smile. 'An indoor picnic.'

She looks absolutely beautiful and is wearing a rose-pink dress and large, wide-brimmed hat trimmed with pink ribbon. I smile back at her, kissing her on the lips.

Holding hands, we walk around the narrow streets, calling in at various epiceries and patisseries, picking up such delicacies as quail's eggs and looking for all the world like young lovers who are infatuated with each other.

On the way back to the apartment, she tells me that 'we' have guests coming over that evening, a painter and his wife. I don't know how she has made the arrangements because I haven't once seen her with a mobile phone. It's like the modern world never happened.

Back at the apartment, Miss Heiress floats around, playing classical music and changing outfits, while I prepare our feast. I catch her round the waist and give her a deep kiss, but she is obviously driven by something less base than sexual instinct. It appears that she is enjoying the fantasy of playing at being the beautiful young couple in love, rather than any explicit desire to make the most of my gigolo talents. I almost get the feeling that she is such an aesthete that even sex has to be part of a perfectly crafted moment, rather than a purely sweaty, primitive desire. Last night, against the starlit sky, with Puccini playing and my signature on a Shakespearean sonnet, all the prerequisites had been met. There would be nothing as pedestrian as an afternoon tumble while the quail's eggs were cooking. I am happy either way. Filthy sex or highbrow fantasies – both have their recommendations and are part of my résumé.

When the guests arrive, Miss Heiress is clearly excited that she has her beautiful young dandy by her side to complete the picture of bohemian life. I am rather touched by the attention to detail she has displayed in creating this ideal existence. As we sit on the terrace, the painter smoking filterless cigarettes and philosophising about the role of art in personal redemption, Miss Heiress sets about fixing us all a drink. As she walks in carrying vodka tonics with little ice straws and seahorse ice cubes, I have to smile to myself at the ingenuity of her vision. Rochester claims he's never tasted vodka from a glass as he always swigs it straight from the bottle, and here I am, like Little Lord Fauntleroy, sucking on seahorse ice cubes that taste of premium vodka.

The four of us sit on the roof terrace watching the sunset, eating fine cheese and bread, and taking in the ambience of the city. As darkness overtakes the skyline, the lights of the Eiffel Tower come on, sparkling in the distance like a millennium display. Miss Heiress comes over to sit on my knee and we kiss and hold hands and look out into the night.

After the painter and his wife leave, we sit on the roof terrace for a while longer, but I sense this little romance is about to come to an end. The table where our picnic had been beautifully laid out is now a mess of half-eaten remains and empty glasses – I can see the look of disdain on her face. She likes the idea of us playing house and creating an exquisite spread, but she doesn't like the reality of having to clear up together afterwards: it doesn't fit in with her vision. Eventually she calls me a cab from a large, black vintage phone in the hallway, with its wire coiling round like a grass snake. I kiss her softly without speaking and she smiles a grateful smile that I'm going along with her little charade until the end. After all, a gigolo never asks questions.

In the taxi driving back to the hotel, I feel like I've just woken up from a romantic interlude, like a half-dream of unreality. I can truly say I have never met anyone like Miss Heiress before. She's obviously never had to worry about anything in her life and has absolutely no understanding of money. She's so blissfully unaware of the real world she doesn't even understand the concept of using money to manipulate people. Most wealthy people are aware of the power their cash gives them over other people, but Miss Heiress lives in a little make-believe bubble. She can't deal with reality; it would kill her. I imagine she'll end up with a fabulously wealthy husband, another avant-garde bohemian, probably a painter who will drift off into the land of make-believe with her, never tied down by the shackles of having to make money or earn a living.

Seeing this world makes me realise how different I am from these types of people. Even though my lifestyle as a pianist-turned-gigolo is bohemian, I could never be part of their world, even if I had money. I would always be a working-class boy, just one who had happened to make his fortune. I can't help but put a pricetag on everything. Maybe this is why my attraction to Charlotte is so strong – with her I feel like I belong.

For some reason, my thoughts turn to Rochester, another working-class hero, taking a ride with the rich and famous. In a way our lives mirror each other's, which is why we have such a polarised relationship – me the rarefied dandy and him the rock 'n' roll beast. Underneath, we are the same person; it's just that we created different façades to get by – both of us live with the knowledge that no one really wants to get to know the person beneath the party guy. We are trapped in the web we have spun for ourselves.

A conversation we had one night a few months ago plays on my mind. It seems to sum up our differences but also emphasise our underlying similarity. Earlier that week I'd been to a performance by a brilliantly talented pianist, who dedicated himself to music in a way I had failed to. After a long, impassioned speech about the futility of the gigolo existence – working the same clubs, sleeping with countless women who discard us – I turned to Rochester for his opinion, expecting a moment of existential connection over our shared plight. Instead he poured another glass of champagne, shrugged his shoulders and said to me, 'Well, it could be worse. At least we don't have to pay for our drinks.'

There it is, the bottom line, the thread that unites us. I try to airbrush my life into a fairytale, like Miss Heiress, but Rochester is not afraid to see the blemishes and admit that the gigolo life boils down to not picking up the bill. It's that simple.

The day after I return to London, I decide to take a trip home to visit my parents. After my Parisian adventure I feel like I could do with a little grounding – and some of my mum's home cooking.

I get up early so I can reach Portsmouth in time to catch a ferry that arrives in the Isle of Wight before lunchtime. It's one of those dreary days – not even the bleak romance of a rainstorm. The ferry is on time, and even though I don't recognise anyone, for some reason all the faces seem familiar. As I sit peering out to sea, sipping on a cup of tea, I feel like I'm slipping back into my childhood. Paris seems light years away, like the memory of a really good book I read. Places like the Isle of Wight run on their own time – people aren't interested in what some Parisian heiress gets up to; they only care about what's going on in their neighbourhood. I find it strangely reassuring. Like reading the local paper in which the front-page news is about how some vandals knocked down a wall.

The funny thing about going home is that there's no big need to keep my life a secret. When I reach the house, Mum asks what I've been up to and when I reply, 'A trip to Paris,' she nods enthusiastically, but before I have to go into details, she needs to know more important information, like what I want for my lunch. Some things never change. And everyone, even a gigolo, needs something – or someone – consistent in their life. That's just the way it is.

I realise that with a loving family to fall back on, the gigolo road is not the lonely path I sometimes imagine it to be.

Chapter 15

The Joys of Being a Tourist Attraction

I love the Isle of Wight, but after a few days hanging around in a place where nothing much happens, I start to remember that my life in London, belonging to an underworld of dandies, is a privileged position. It's easy to take our secret society of sexual adventures for granted, but when we have visitors to our little circle of sin, I realise how far from the mainstream we are. It's a good thing, I think, to know there are people who aren't subscribing to the norm of what sex should be. I'm not criticising people who fall in love and have monogamous sex, because God knows, there are times when I wish I was one of them – especially where Charlotte is concerned – but deep down I'm proud to be on the bed-hopping fringes, where women are allowed to drop their knickers without implicitly dropping their morals.

As a gigolo, I can feel the hoary breath of society's censure down my neck, even though I'm a man and such sexual licentiousness is almost expected of me. So what must it be like for a woman who wants to indulge in a spot of sexual exploration but doesn't want the slut police to issue a warrant for her arrest?

I realise it must be very tough. Which is why our decadent world of dandies is such a welcome respite from the relentless judgement of a po-faced society that would choke on so much as a blow job. You know what, if you fancy a threesome or a one-night spank, a gigolo is your man. No recriminations the morning after or reshuffling of your place in the pack of cards from virgin to whore.

Of course, I realise there is a time and a place for everything (although there shouldn't really ever be a place for double standards, should there?) and we can't spend our entire lives in a haze of sexual hedonism – even a gigolo doesn't expect that. But we should all have at least one holiday there in our lifetime – annual leave from sexual repression, if you please. Like a booty call on a far bigger scale.

On my return from the Isle of Wight, all refreshed and recharged after my week chilling out, I decide to be more accepting of the down and dirty basics of what I do – I decide to let the spirit of Rochester inhabit me, see things for what they are and be happy with them.

Tonight, as I look into the sparkling, mischievous eyes of Miss Sweden, I realise that my fellow dandies and I are really the fourth arm of the emergency services, called on to provide extreme sexual liberation for those in dire need.

And yes, even the Swedes sometimes need help in that department. God knows, us Brits often need it in spades.

Rochester's dandies and rakes parties are now happening every week, thanks to unprecedented demand. But for all their popularity, they are still a secret traded between people in the know, a real word-of-mouth event, so I'm surprised that Miss Sweden and her friends have stumbled across the place. Having said that, the Swedes have a habit of sniffing out underground scenes and then throwing themselves into them with abandon. Miss Sweden is mesmerised by the atmosphere of decadence and debauchery happening tonight – and clearly wants a fix of it, and fast.

'I can't believe this place exists,' she whispers in my ear, looking around wide-eyed. 'We don't have anything like this where I come from.' Her eyes are darting around the room, taking in the sight of beautifully dressed women wearing corsets, veiled hats, tight pencil skirts and skyscraper heels, surrounded by handsome men, dressed like a corrupt aristocracy of long ago, all flirting, kissing and generally getting filthy with each other.

'So how come you're over here?' I ask, tracing my finger along the back of her neck, underneath her soft blonde hair.

'A holiday. Simple as that.' Miss Sweden smiles. 'We were bored of Stockholm and we'd heard London was a good place to party. It seems like we heard right.'

'What kind of partying did you have in mind?' I ask her cheekily, already holding my own suspicions as to her motivation.

'The kind of partying we can't do in Sweden,' she says with an enigmatic smile, grabbing hold of my hand and squeezing it, while raising one eyebrow in a suggestive manner. 'Have you met my friends?' she asks, changing the subject, or more to the point, lining up the night's activities.

There are four friends with her. One is a tall brunette with an upturned nose and big, full lips, the girl standing next to her is shorter, with large breasts, black bobbed hair and big blue eyes, and almost hiding behind them is a shy little brunette, looking slightly awkward and in awe of her surroundings. The fourth friend, a blonde with her hair in a ponytail, is at the bar. Miss Sweden looks classically Nordic, with shiny blonde hair, a cute nose and a perfect peaches-and-cream complexion – she has hardly any make-up on and manages to look naturally beautiful. But for all her innocent, girl-next-door appearance, when she speaks her voice is surprisingly husky, with a filthy little inflection to her words. As we all make small talk, the girl with the blonde ponytail joins us. She is carrying a tray of tequila shots, and the brunette – who is very loud and outgoing – squeaks with delight and downs one before the rest of us have even had the chance to pick up a glass.

As I'm introduced to them all, I get the feeling that we're going to have a lot of fun together. They hang off my every word and stick close by me whenever I make a move. As soon as the drinks run out, one of them trots off to the bar to get another tray of tequila shots.

I can see Rochester through the crowd, wearing a dishevelled cravat, his shirt almost open to the waist. He's dancing wildly on the bar and I smile to myself. When will this party ever end? I think, remembering Miss Stripper's advice just to make the most of it.

'It feels good to be anonymous,' says Miss Sweden,

knocking back another tequila, dancing provocatively and adjusting her top so she reveals slightly more toned midriff.

'Why, what's it like back in Sweden?' I ask, wondering just how different things could be over there.

'It's so different,' she replies, grinning and pressing closely against me. 'Stockholm might be a cosmopolitan city compared with most places in Sweden, but it's still got that small-town mentality. Everyone knows everyone else's business, and if you misbehave, people will still be gossiping about it six months later.'

Looking at her style – the typical middle-class uniform of light-coloured flared jeans, pointed boots and a cashmere sweater – it's obvious that they're rich, preppy princesses from the suburbs. They are probably over here to have fun and rebel against their reserved Swedish roots for a few weeks, before returning home to settle back down to the quiet life. I feel perfectly happy to act as their temporary tour guide and show them the X-rated sights.

'Look, I don't mean to be forward,' says Miss Sweden suddenly, 'but why don't we all leave and go back to our hotel? We've had fun drinking and dancing, but now I think we need the kind of fun you'd be arrested for having in a public place.'

'Be as forward as you like,' I tell her with a laugh. 'I like forward – it's my speciality. I think it's a brilliant idea – let's take this party home and heat it up. Are all the other girls into the idea too?' I ask, not knowing if Miss Sweden has taken it upon herself to dictate their night's debauchery without clearing it with them first.

'We talked about this kind of thing weeks before we even left for this holiday,' she confesses. 'We want to go wild and do *everything* we've never tried before. This is a

once-in-a-lifetime experience for us girls, and we intend
to make the most of it.'

'Let's go, then,' I say, taking the tall brunette's hand at
the same time.

She gives me a saucy smile and says to Miss Sweden,
'So it's all set up, then?'

The only one looking slightly hesitant is the small
brunette, who it turns out is sober, as the designated driver.
I give her a friendly smile and she smiles shyly back, then
looks away, blushing.

We pile into the car, a convertible Audi, and within
moments of setting off Miss Sweden instructs the small
brunette to lower the roof. The cold London air rushes
into the car, and the cloudless sky sparkles with stars
rarely seen in the capital. Despite the drop in temperature, the girls are clearly getting hotter. The tall
brunette, sitting in the front, turns up the radio. Pumping
house music blares out. Suddenly the girls start stroking
each other's hair and skin suggestively, cooing over how
soft each other feels, then turn to me and start giving
me the same, seductive treatment. I have a girl either
side and one sitting on my lap. They take it in turns to
slowly kiss me, then provocatively tongue each other,
until we are embroiled in a protracted four-way make-
out session.

'I want to join in,' says the tall brunette in the front
passenger seat petulantly, and the girl on my lap leans
over and French-kisses her, then pulls me over to join in.
The small brunette is so shocked by the activities, she
takes her eyes off the road and keeps turning her head
towards the back seat until we find ourselves pulling up
at a traffic light in the wrong lane.

'Watch where you're going!' the girls all shriek, laughing and continuing their marathon petting session.

The driver in a car next to us beeps his horn, and I raise my arms in a gesture of mock helplessness and mouth, 'Sorry.' He starts shaking his head and laughing, and I can just about lip-read him muttering, 'Lucky bastard,' to himself as he drives off.

We arrive at the upmarket, but faceless, hotel near the Thames and pile into the lift, laughing and all holding hands, or twining our arms round each other. It's the kind of large, anonymous establishment where no one cares what the guests are getting up to. Weary Eastern Europeans go about their business, looking at the floor like they couldn't care less about the reputation of their employer as long as they get paid and don't get into trouble. A place like this is the perfect venue for sexual mischief – not seedy, but not so salubrious that your ardour is dampened by the fear of lowering the tone.

We go back to Miss Sweden's room, shared by the tall brunette. They are obviously the main partners in crime. The ponytail blonde tunes the radio into the same house station we were listening to in the car, while Miss Sweden starts to raid the minibar.

The scene must look like a bubble of noise, chaos and fun. We all dance around, drinking wine or vodka from the bottle, until I collapse on the bed. I suspect these girls have never had group sex before – after all, it turns out the ponytail blonde works in a bank back at home! – and so I assume don't know the special dynamics required for such a venture. Sex with one other person, or even a threesome, is a totally different experience to sleeping with four or more people. There are so many more personalities to cater for, and in this situation, where I am one man to five women, so many more orifices to service, with only my one appendage. The trick is to get creative with absolutely every available body part so that you can include everyone at any given moment. As soon as people are left out of the proceedings, even for a few minutes, insecurity kicks in and boots pleasure out of the way. An orgy is almost like a dance, requiring expert choreography and coordination.

'Shall I be team leader?' I ask, to get things started and give direction to the unfolding events. For me, an orgy is almost like writing a piece of music, making sure everything works together and hits the right harmonic note.

'Yes!' they all squeal in unison, excited that I'm taking control.

I notice that the shy, small brunette is hanging back and looking uneasy. I don't want her to get involved with anything she's uncomfortable with. I've noticed a video camera lying on the writing desk, so I tell her, 'We need someone to film us. After all, no point having holiday adventures and not recording them for posterity. Would you mind sitting out for this evening so you can be camerawoman?'

'Of course,' she replies instantly, suddenly beaming.

As I suspected, she wants to voyeur and be involved in some way, but isn't ready to be a fully fledged participant. This way, she can get off on watching, and filming, without doing anything that's beyond her boundaries.

'Now, as for you others, I want you to undress each other,' I instruct them, leaning back and sipping my wine.

Straight away they start excitedly peeling off each other's clothes, like it's Christmas morning.

'Now, kiss her and touch her at the same time,' I tell Miss Sweden, referring to the tall brunette.

They start to kiss, their hands first wandering over each other's breasts, before moving lower down, fingering each other, moving in rhythm with their tongues. As they do, I walk over to the girl with bobbed black hair and start kissing and touching her. After a few moments I tell them to swap places, so I'm fondling Miss Sweden, while the tall brunette gets intimate with the black-haired girl. When I deem that everyone is suitably heated up, I ask Miss Sweden to get on all fours, which she does, still wearing her heeled boots, but naked otherwise. I then tell the tall brunette to position herself underneath, demonstrating exactly which position to assume to get perfect access to Miss Sweden's clitoris. I then suggest to the ponytail blonde that she kneel in front of the tall brunette so she can orally pleasure her, while she is paying it forward to Miss Sweden. When they are in place, like a perverted game of twister, I take my position to enter Miss Sweden from behind, beckoning the black-haired girl to come by my side as I do, so we can kiss and I can pleasure her with my hands and touch her incredible breasts, which she has taken off her black lacy bra to reveal. After ten minutes of surprisingly sophisticated synchronicity – it usually takes a while for newcomers to get the hang of it – we are all moving in conjunction, a writhing mass of moans, sighs and encouraging, breathless entreaties. I look over and wink at the shy, small brunette, who is filming our every move, her cheeks flushed and her blouse tentatively unbuttoned.

I now whisper to everyone that it's time to change positions, so the black-haired girl gets on all fours, Miss

Sweden comes by my side for some heavy petting, and the tall brunette and blonde ponytail girls take up their places as ambassadors of oral sex on their fellow friends. Thanks to their large size, as I start to push inside her from behind, the black-haired girl's breasts swing backwards and forwards so her nipples are gently brushing blonde ponytail girl's hands as she lies underneath her. The combination of me inside her and blonde ponytail girl's tongue on her clitoris and hands on her nipples brings the black-haired girl to an incredible frenzy, with her moans becoming obscenely loud. All the girls start encouraging her, saying her name and begging her to come for them, like a sisterhood of sexual abandon. Her climax when it comes is so loud, mixed in with the frenzied beats of the loud house music still pumping out, that it feels almost tribal.

Afterwards, we all collapse in a heap so we can take a well-earned break, refresh ourselves and gear up for the next instalment.

'Did you get all that on camera?' Miss Sweden asks the small brunette excitedly, cracking open another bottle of wine and starting to pour us all a glass. Orgies are thirsty work, that's for sure.

She nods shyly, biting her lips with repressed sexual tension and reaching for a glass of wine, looking at me with big, longing eyes. I smile warmly at her to let her know that she's in a safe environment and can enjoy herself to whatever limit she feels OK with.

Ten minutes later, lubricated with more alcohol, the atmosphere gets sexually intense again as Miss Sweden starts an impromptu kissing session with the black-haired girl, fondling her breasts eagerly as they embrace.

'Let's go for hothouse orgasms,' I suggest, taking my place in the centre of the bed, while the small brunette takes her filming position on the dark-red chair opposite.

'What's that?' asks the tall brunette eagerly.

'OK, you each take it in turns to be centre stage and have everyone focus on your every whim. You can go first,' I say, guiding her to the centre of the bed and positioning everyone around her.

As a united front, we all start touching different parts of her body, paying particular attention to the essential areas. I whisper filthy words of encouragement in her ear as I stroke her breasts, and the other three girls take it in turns to touch her. Within minutes she is overwhelmed by the onslaught of pleasure. At the final moments, two girls each push one of her legs apart, like seductive sentinels, while I take over with my special oral technique. As she comes, they coax her, determined that she will have the most intense orgasm ever, saying how sexy she is and how much they want her to let go totally. When she is finished, she swaps, so another eager participant can take her place and have her fill of extreme pleasure.

For our finale, I lie prostrate on the bed as Miss Sweden rides me, pleasuring the other two with my hands. Then the tall brunette takes her turn on top. When it comes to black-haired girl's turn, she gets so aroused that after her climax (when I have finally allowed myself to come), she is still eager for more – obviously being multi-orgasmic. She gives me a cheeky smile, lifts herself off me and slides down my legs, maintaining saucy eye contact. Not sure what she is planning, I smile back and at that she pushes my big toe inside her, closes her eyes and starts to move up and down on it, touching her clit and breathing heavily with excitement. I can hear all the other girls gasp in shock and then start giggling. She is oblivious, focusing on riding my big toe like it is a perfectly compact sex toy. As she comes, the girls all cheer and hug her, telling her how naughty she is. She smiles contentedly afterwards and shrugs her shoulders. I laugh and give her a big kiss as I say I enjoyed the novelty.

We all sprawl on the bed, an exquisite fulfilment and exhaustion overcoming us. The minibar is almost empty, and the small brunette, still looking flushed, suggests she get some more bottles from the minibar in her room, then hesitantly asks if I will accompany her. Of course, I comply with her request.

We make small talk as we walk down the corridor, although I can barely hear what she's saying as she looks shyly down at the carpet. As soon as we enter her bedroom and the door closes behind us, she leaps on me like a woman possessed. I try to calm her down while peeling off her clothes. She's already in a state of high excitement, and it appears that the evening's events have been like one giant foreplay session for her.

'I'm sorry I couldn't join in with the others – I'm just too shy,' she tells me in between fluttering kisses, her hands grasping at me.

'You don't have to explain or apologise,' I reassure her, pushing her back on the bed. 'You deserve your own private session for all your hard work as camerawoman.'

She comes violently within minutes of me entering her, such is her state of arousal, and then as she slowly starts to recover, I treat her to a softer, gentler oral sex session, so she can linger over her pleasure and enjoy it properly. As she approaches her second orgasm, she flips over so she is lying on the bed face down, looks over her shoulder and tells me she'd like to finish with anal sex. Always the quiet ones, I laugh to myself.

When we walk back in the room holding hands, her clothes in a state of disarray, clutching a few bottles of wine, all the girls squeal and leap up to hug her as she beams a smile at them. 'I'm a bit shy, but I got there in the end,' she laughs.

I smile enigmatically as she's made me promise not to mention our naughty finale.

Within an hour we all fall asleep on the bed together, wrapped in each other's arms.

The next morning everyone feels delicate, though in good spirits – if not slightly self-conscious about the previous night's indulgences.

'I can't believe what we did,' exclaims Miss Sweden, shocked but with a hint of pride.

'We can *never* tell anyone back home,' says the tall brunette, laughing.

'What goes on tour stays on tour,' I joke, calling down to room service to bring up breakfast and a bottle of champagne. 'We need to celebrate – and to seal your pact of silence.'

The girls are now in just their underwear, and I am still naked with a white sheet wrapped round me. A chink of sunlight is starting to spread through the slats of the closed blinds. Somehow it feels like we're coming to the end of a voyage, but we're not quite ready to embrace the real world just yet.

'I would never dream of doing this with my boyfriend,' says Miss Sweden, looking at me contemplatively.

All the other girls nod in agreement.

'Why?' I ask, plumping my pillow and resting back.

'He's a nice middle-class boy, and he thinks I'm a nice middle-class girl – which I am. It's just that sometimes I get bored of being a "nice" girl and want to do something wild. He wouldn't understand. But really, I wouldn't *want* him to understand. It would ruin our relationship somehow. After all, I could never have a relationship with a gigolo like you, who has this kind of sexual experience all the time.'

'Oh, I get it,' I laugh teasingly. 'He's the nice boy you'll marry, but I'm the slut you can have crazy sex with.'

'Yes,' she agrees with a broad smile. 'A gigolo is for fun, not for ever!'

'I'll try not to feel too used,' I joke. 'I admit I'm hardly marriage material, although you'd be guaranteed a good wedding night.'

All the girls fall about laughing, then pounce on me to tickle and pinch me.

Eventually I get dressed and wave them goodbye, and they thank me for a night they won't forget in a long time. 'The pleasure was all mine,' I tell them, kissing them in turn as I leave the room.

Walking out of the hotel into the sharp clarity of the day, with a hangover fraying the edges of my nerves, I ponder Miss Sweden's words about my unsuitability as a boyfriend. I know she's right, but strangely it bugs me. I can't help but wonder what it feels like to be the man women share their lives with rather than the gigolo they share their wildest fantasies with. Then it strikes me, with Charlotte I *could* be that man.

Well, I could be if it was somehow possible to press 'delete' on my entire past.

The Divorcee is throwing a party to celebrate her

engagement to Johan next week, and we've all been invited – again, 'with partners'. Maybe I should invite Charlotte. Before I can change my mind, or come up with a million reasons why it won't work, I dial her number on my mobile.

'Hey, how are you?' she answers, a hint of surprise in her voice.

'Really good,' I reply, for once at a slight loss as to what to say. Instead I make mindless small talk that would shame my gigolo alter ego. 'So what's happening with you?' I ask, trying to build myself up to inviting her to the engagement party.

'Not much, working at the café mostly,' she tells me, then adds, 'I went to the jazz bar last night, though. It was really great.'

Without stopping to think, I ask who with, imagining it might be a fellow jazz musician.

'Oh, just this guy I've started dating,' she replies, almost shyly. 'I met him at the café and we've seen each other a couple of times . . .' She trails off.

I'm stunned and don't know what to say. With the typical selfishness of a man, I've spent all my time dwelling on my own dilemmas and never stopped to think that she could meet someone in the meantime.

'That's great,' I say with forced enthusiasm. 'Really great. Good he likes jazz too.' I'm aware I'm babbling in an unbecoming manner. If I could switch to my gigolo persona, I would be fine: in that mode I can hide anything behind my mask. But in this circumstance I can't, and I'm struggling. 'Anyway, I was just calling to say hi. Well, see you in the café sometime,' I say, feeling like a dumbstruck teenager all over again – something I haven't felt for many years.

'Yeah, see you there . . . sometime,' she replies, obviously a bit baffled by my call.

As I hang up, I think how it always happens that when you can't have someone, you finally realise how much you want them. I'm starting to fear my life is lived in a gilded cage – one that doesn't have room for two. Which might be fine, if it wasn't for my feelings for Charlotte. But what can I do now she's met someone else?

Trustfundista is away on business with her newfound career, so instead I call Miss Stripper and invite her to the engagement party. After all, us professionals must stick together.

Chapter 16

Where Gigolos Go to Die

I'm having one of those mornings. First, I can't be bothered to get up. Then, when I finally make it out of bed, I slump on the sofa, unable to find the energy to leave the house. It's not so much that business is slow as that I'm failing to broadcast on that special gigolo frequency that attracts clients along the psychic sexual highway. In a way, professions such as mine are an extension of showbusiness – it's just smoke and mirrors. We're all performers projecting an image, selling a sexual ideal to people who've probably overdosed on too much reality. But what happens when *we* feel that reality is paging us with a message we can't ignore? Even if we'd like to . . .

No one wants a depressed gigolo. It's almost worse than a crying clown. No one wants to see tears streaming down your face when all they're interested in is what's tucked in your trousers. So, in true showbiz tradition, the show goes on and you plaster a smile over the cracks. I think this is what bothers me: I'm losing the ability to discern between what's real and what isn't. The only things that seem to remain still in the orbiting craziness of people and places that surround my life are music and Charlotte. Make that just music. Because Charlotte may be real to me, but I'm a fake with her, and if she knew the truth, she might never speak to me again.

The thing is, in this line of work it's hard to define what it is to be a fake – well, a *real* fake. As I lounged in bed this morning, a strong black coffee on the table beside me, spiralling steam into the cold air of my bedroom, I decided to attempt to count the number of women I've slept with. I stopped attempting to remember names at a hundred. I stopped attempting to remember altogether at 500. I'm not ashamed one bit of the generosity of numbers in my recollection. But it did get me thinking about the nature of what had occurred during all those sexual encounters. I had catered to a fantasy figure of what a chivalrous, charming, attentive, attractive man should be. But can that man ever really exist outside the construction of a gigolo's identity? The reality is, probably not. I've never faked it with any woman I've been with. I've *genuinely* enjoyed their company, I've loved having sex with them, my charming manners have been authentic, and my compliments have come from the heart. But could I sustain that over a long-term relationship? Not likely. So in a way it is fake – or maybe just not the full story.

Relationships are perfect when they are gift-wrapped into a short, finite space of time, but maybe what the human heart *really* craves is imperfection: the moody, insecure, needy person who is in it for the long haul, flaws and all. Because while my finely crafted gigolo persona is like the sex-crazed, loved-up honeymoon, what really counts is the marriage that comes after it. As Miss Sweden pointed out, I'm not even in the running for that part of the proceedings. If I were, I wouldn't be a gigolo. I'd still be myself of course, but not the man I am at the moment. A new Golden Boy.

I look at Johan and I see that rebirth happening in front of my eyes. He looks identical to the supermodel playboy he was, who fraternised with women who would have paid thousands just to get one strand of his perfect DNA, but he is an altogether different man now. He does DIY. He goes into supermarkets. He hangs around the house, and enjoys it. It's like he folded away a cardboard cut-out of his previous larger-than-life character and started to become the real him. Inevitably, his model looks will fade, and this person is all that will remain. Does his wife-to-be love him as he truly is? It remains to be seen, but it's a good start. She could have just picked him up and played with him, putting him back down when it became inconvenient, but she didn't. He shares her home and her life. They are no longer isolated units, playing parts with each other – they're together, seeing the whole picture. Whereas I still feel like I'm a snapshot, a brief encounter of entertainment to be enjoyed and then ultimately discarded.

Not that I'm the victim here. I'm having a good time, living a life of on and off luxury I could never afford on my own, having uncomplicated sex with beautiful women. I chose this life and for the most part I've loved it. So it's not a case of regrets, but of what next?

Contemplating making another cup of strong coffee, hoping

to reboot myself out of this miserable introspection, I walk into the kitchen and catch sight of myself in the hallway mirror: I look *older*. Obviously, I'm not old – I'm not yet thirty – but the passing of time, indiscernible to others, is like a whisper etched on my face that I imagine will one day become a shout. I see it on all our faces: Rochester, Johan, Valentino, Byron. Like our hedonistic bubble, momentarily suspended in time, which will shatter one day, and we'll all fall back to earth. The sunshine outside is dazzling, illuminating fading green leaves still clinging on to branches, while others, charred brown, give in to autumn's pull and descend dreamily from the tree, swaying back and forth in the breeze until they finally hit the ground and the carpet of dull, decayed leaves already trodden underfoot.

I lean on the counter and stare out of the window, mesmerised by nature's dismantling of this year's display. Inspired, I move to my shabby piano and start to play, improvising according to my mood, somehow translating my confusion and the feeling that my life is dragged along by cycles out of my control. Music makes sense of everything, but only for those moments I'm playing. And I can hardly ride off into the sunset on my piano stool, like a musical chariot of possibilities. Or maybe I could.

My phone beeps, interrupting my moment. It's Miss Stripper, with amazing timelines, asking if I would like to join her for lunch. Her stripping sideline of spiritualising must have paid off, as it's like she can psychically sense my need for company. I realise I've never even seen Miss Stripper in daylight before, let alone for a cosy lunch in the suburbs. Mirroring my thoughts, it's as if the constructed relationship we have with each other is crumbling – with daylight and real life filtering through.

'Perfect. See you in an hour,' I text back, grabbing my towel and preparing to jump in the shower. I need at least to *look* the part. No one can deal with *that* much reality.

An hour later I am walking through the streets of middle England. Old ladies are pottering around in overgrown gardens, builders are renovating newly bought family houses, and green-and-yellow Foxtons 'Sold' and 'For Sale' signs are stuck in various gardens, the only indication that there is any movement in these comfortable lives. The sky is a brittle blue, and the air thin and sharp. I breathe in deeply and walk past a young mum struggling with a pram outside her front door, her mousy hair obscuring her face.

'Do you need any help?' I ask like a Good Samaritan, smiling gently in her direction.

'Thanks, that would be great,' she replies, brushing her fringe off her face in a frazzled manner.

As I help her lift the pram down the stairs, it strikes me that to the outside observer, we must look like a family, going about their everyday business. Who would guess that I'm an interloper, a gigolo high on hedonism and the champagne lifestyle? Once again, it's all about illusions. Things are never as they seem.

I arrive at the restaurant bang on time – a gigolo can never lose his dedication to punctuality and rudely keep a lady waiting (unless that's her predilection, of course). The restaurant is dark, in a welcoming, cosy way, and my eyes scan the place trying to spot Miss Stripper. I can't make her out and assume she hasn't arrived yet. Then it occurs to me that I don't actually know if I will recognise her out of a diamanté G-string. A woman is sitting alone at the back, and all I can see is her ruby-red knitted cardigan and the back of her blonde head. She looks like all the other yummy mummies who are hanging out, feeding their kids with plastic spoons and gossiping over pots of tea. Could it be Miss Stripper? Just as I dismiss the idea, she turns round and gives me a broad smile and a wave – it *is* her. She looks somehow younger and fresher scrubbed of make-up and minus her miniscule glittery costume. Not as obviously sexy or striking of course, but more *substantial* – as if I'd only previously met her shadow.

She stands up to greet me, giving me a huge bear hug. 'I don't know why, I just felt I had to see you today,' she tells me, adding, 'and I always follow my gut feelings.'

'I'm glad you did,' I reply, taking off my coat and sitting down. I order a pot of tea and feel oddly touched that Miss Stripper has taken the time out to see me, clearly not on a business matter. That oversized cardie instantly says sex isn't on the cards – and I'm glad. It feels great finally to meet as friends, rather than fuck-buddies.

'You look a bit glum,' she instantly notes, even though I've been doing my best to look sprightly and cheerful. 'You can't fool me with your "gigolo mask",' she laughs. 'I know something's wrong.'

A thought comes to me of what a perfect match she would make with Shiva, should she ever be looking to settle down. Beneath both of their sexual personas, and pasts, beats the heart of a beautiful, spiritual person.

Even now I feel awkward confessing my troubles to Miss Stripper – it's like I've been brainwashed only to conduct one-sided relationships, in which my feelings are filed away.

Jesus, I might have to go in for deprogramming, I think to myself. Becoming a gigolo is almost the same as joining a cult.

'You can tell me,' says Miss Stripper softly, as if reading my thoughts. 'Don't worry, I often feel the same. It's hard to dismantle the façade, isn't it? How do you think I feel when I meet someone and I finally have to swap my Coco de Mer thongs for three-for-two M&S pants!'

I laugh, and stir my spoon in my cup of English breakfast tea. 'I've been thinking a lot about what you said about just enjoying myself and making the most of it while it lasts, but I keep getting this feeling like what if the party's over, but I'm too drunk on sexual highs to notice? As if the lights are up and everyone's gone home to their normal lives and I'm still there, the party guy who's got nowhere else to go.' I stare at the wall and the Clash poster decorating it, frayed round the edges, the singer's face frozen in a scowl of nihilistic scorn. Pictures can suspend time, but what about the subjects whose lives must move on?

'What's brought all this on?' says Miss Stripper sympathetically. 'This sounds like more than just anxiety about your future.'

I sigh, louder than I meant to, and then laugh at my own theatrical misery. 'Look at me,' I smile. 'You know what, I think I've got a case of the sixth-form heartbreaks – can you believe it, a gigolo like me?'

'Even gigolos have hearts,' she replies, giving my hand a squeeze and adding, 'just as strippers do. Whatever has happened in your life doesn't make you exempt from finding love. It's not like a right we signed away in a clause they added in the contract of life. So what's happened?'

'It's Charlotte. Well, it's Johan and the Divorcee too,' I begin in a rather convoluted fashion. 'It started with Johan,' I explain. 'He's fallen in love with the Divorcee and now they're engaged – it seems to be the real thing. We had a cosy dinner party round at theirs the other night, and it just all felt so warm and *real*. Part of me wants that life, but a big part of me still wants *this* life – I just went to Miami recently and had the most amazing time. How can I give all that up? And what would become of me if I did? My CV reads like an erotic novel . . . I can hardly turn up at my local job centre. And making money as a musician is notoriously hard. Anyway, the truth is, what's really made me miserable is that I called Charlotte and it turns out that she's met someone. It was awful. I didn't know what to say . . . I felt, well, devastated.'

'Ah, so that explains why you invited me to the engagement party,' says Miss Stripper with a smile. 'I had been wondering.'

'Oh, no, it's not like that,' I reply quickly, horrified that she would think she was my second choice, even though this is pretty close to the mark. This is what happens when you leave the role of a gigolo behind even for a moment: things get complicated and you say things that get misinterpreted or offend people. 'Please don't think I was using you, that's not the case – I really want you to come, we'll have such good fun and you'll love the Divorcee. She's very similar to you – a totally sorted person.'

'Don't worry, you don't have to explain. I'm just glad you felt like I was someone you could turn to.' She smiles at me warmly again, and I think to myself what an amazing person she is. There are no ego- or insecurity-riddled complexes with her. It's sad to think that the outside world will probably pigeon-hole her because she's a stripper.

'Actually, it's really flattering that you feel like I'm someone you can talk to about these things because . . .' She pauses and looks at me hesitantly, then drops the bombshell: 'I'm hanging up my G-string and quitting stripping to train as a psychotherapist. I've been saving up for years, and I just felt the time was right. My course starts in a few weeks.' She sips her tea and looks over the rim of the cup with expectant eyes.

'That's amazing,' I exclaim, reaching over the table to give her a congratulatory hug. 'You'll be a fantastic therapist, I just know it. Wow! I'm stunned – it's such good news.'

I look closely at her as she thanks me for my encouragement. There is a composure and confidence in her face I've not previously noticed. It feels like I have never really *seen* her before, and in truth, she has probably never seen *me* properly either. I imagine she hardly thought she'd see the man who brandishes a tongue like a weapon of mass seduction moping around like a lovesick teenager, wondering what he'll do when he grows up. It's not appealing, but I suppose it's honest, and that's what Miss Stripper is really after – honesty. As a therapist-to-be the only thing she'll be stripping off in future is the illusions and protective layers we build to protect ourselves from the truth.

'So tell me about Charlotte,' she asks, leaning slightly forward so I have her full attention.

I almost feel like I'm on the couch already. I absentmindedly twist my napkin as I start to explain everything, my comments punctuated by numerous 'So how do you feel about that?' questions from her.

'I suppose part of me wanted to put Charlotte in a box and preserve her for the future, an unspecified time when I *will* be ready to settle down,' I confess to her. 'It never occurred to me that she could meet someone in the meantime. I know that sounds selfish, but I just assumed that she'd always be there, waiting for me in the Literary Café.'

'OK, so what stops you from making that future happen now?' asks Miss Stripper with a frank expression.

'God, it sounds so old-fashioned, but I feel like I need to sort myself out so I can provide for her. Does that sound stupid? I'm a gigolo; women support me – how can I flip that round? If I have a serious relationship, I can't be cavorting around with other women, so what will I do with my life? How will I support myself, let alone anyone else, if I ever get married and have kids?'

'Whoa! Aren't you getting ahead of yourself? You haven't even kissed the girl yet,' laughs Miss Stripper, beckoning the waiter and ordering another pot of tea.

All this talk of settling down has made me feel thirsty and I order a pina colada to bring a taste of Miami to the sleepy suburbs. As the waiter brings our order over, the incongruous sight of the gaudy cocktail umbrella perched in the pea-green drink brings a smile to my face. Taken out of its sun-kissed party context, there is a touch of the ridiculous about it. It's a good-time drink that, like me, doesn't quite fit in with all these decent folk.

Sipping on my cocktail, the slut of drinks, I feel more myself. 'That's the thing about being a gigolo,' I explain to Miss Stripper. 'I can't creep my way into a normal life – it has to be a crazy, kamikaze jump over the cliff to get there. Anyway, I've never had a normal life since I left home – I don't even know if I'm suited to it.'

'I think you're making everything too complicated,' says Miss Stripper with a twinkle in her eye, like she finds my excessive agonising endearing. 'Let's make things simple. With no thoughts to the future, what's the one thing that stops you going into the Literary Café today and telling Charlotte how you feel about her?'

'Apart from her new man?' I ask, trying not to sound jealous as I say the words. 'I don't know . . .' I trail off, thinking hard about what it really is that's preventing me from making a move. My mind seems to be a whirl of fears and doubts – and a desire to escape them in the simplicity of hedonism and momentary pleasures. 'I suppose the most immediate obstacle is the fact that I've lied – well, not so much lied as evaded the truth – about what I do with my life . . . I'm scared she won't want anything to do with me if she knows.' I mumble the last bit, draining my cocktail and absentmindedly dismantling the cocktail umbrella and discarding the pieces on the table.

'OK, now we're getting somewhere,' says Miss Stripper with a satisfied sigh, sipping her tea and looking at me with smiling eyes. 'Right, so you haven't told the truth, but you haven't explicitly lied either. And let's face it, you haven't slept with her, or even kissed her, so what you do with other women is none of her business at this point. You haven't promised her anything, so you haven't betrayed her. So all that leaves to consider is this – is she the type of girl who could deal with the fact that you're a gigolo? Now that's a tough one, because I won't lie, some people can't cope with our type of profession. Take me, I'm a stripper – I take my clothes off for money, *all* my clothes.

Some men can't handle this. They don't care that I practically know the *Bhagavad Gita* off by heart, or that I used the money I earned stripping to fund an education that I didn't have the luxury of getting when I was growing up. They can't see past the fact that I take my pants off for a living. I can't change their opinion. But I tell you something, it doesn't matter to me, because those types of narrow-minded people who like to judge everyone else and put them in a box don't interest me one bit. I'm not interested in *them*, let alone their opinion of me or what I do for a living. So it comes down to this: what kind of person is Charlotte? And if she's the type to judge you and ignore all the things she loves about you just because one aspect of your life doesn't fit in with her vision of who you should be, do you *really* want her in your life?'

Her words take time to sink in, but they make a lot of sense. Even if I give up being a gigolo, I'll never *regret* being a gigolo. I don't think it's morally wrong, and I'm a big advocate of sexual freedom, for both men and women. So if Charlotte is the kind of person to be small-minded and judge me over it, could I ever be happy with her? Probably not.

'You're right,' I reply to Miss Stripper, aware that I'm experiencing a sudden revelation. 'I should tell her and get it out in the open – whatever happens, at least this way I'll know.'

'Exactly,' she agrees. 'If she's fine with it and you start a relationship, *then* you can worry about your future as a gigolo. If you find out she can't accept it, then you know there was never a chance for you and her, and you can carry on having fun as a gigolo without having anything to worry about.'

I suddenly realise that the best way to deal with problems is to take them one step at a time, rather than getting crushed under a huge weight of amalgamated woes.

'What should I do, then?' I ask, already knowing the answer to my question, but looking for reassurance.

The restaurant has emptied and the staff are busy clearing tables and chatting among themselves. The whole atmosphere seems heavy with the sense that a mess needs to be cleared up.

'You know what you need to do,' scolds Miss Stripper affectionately. 'You need to go to the Literary Café now and confess everything – your feelings and your illicit profession. If your relationship is meant to be, it's never too late. This guy she's dating is probably just someone to pass the time because she thinks you're not interested. Go now,' she urges me, passing her card to the waiter to pay the bill.

'Shouldn't we go halves?' I ask, aware that I haven't given her anything for her money on this occasion – in fact, I've virtually had a free therapy session.

'You've not retired as a gigolo yet,' she laughs. 'Anyway, you're like a guinea pig I'm practising on for my new profession.'

'Glad I'm still of some use,' I reply, laughing too. 'So—'

'No more talking – just go,' she instructs me. 'And if I have to go to that damned engagement party with you, I'll be very disappointed,' she tells me as I grab my coat and head out into the fresh air of the fading afternoon.

I stand by the side of the road and hail a taxi – Miss Stripper has also kindly donated travel expenses to my fund. A mission like this cannot be entrusted to public transport.

★

I pause as my hand rests on the door of the Literary Café. Walking in is something I've done countless times before, but this time I'm aware I'm crossing an altogether different threshold. Taking a deep breath, I stride through. Everything is comfortingly familiar: the hazy lighting, the shabby furnishings and Charlotte, hair tied back, lounging behind the counter. Everything is the same, yet in a few moments everything could be different – changed for ever. If things don't work out, I don't think I can ever return. My stomach lurches at the thought of never sitting at the piano again or pouring a glass of red wine, watching passers-by as Charlotte chatters on, making idle conversation.

'Hey, what are you doing here?' says Charlotte, looking surprised as I walk towards her.

'Oh, I was just passing and thought I'd pop in,' I lie, desperately trying to pluck up the courage to start the conversation. I mean, how hard can it be? Tougher than I'd imagined, that's for sure. Her quizzical face just makes me want to turn right round and walk out, like a true coward, but I gather all my gigolo steel – the part of me that is used to being in control of situations – to keep things ticking along.

'The usual?' asks Charlotte, picking up a bottle of Bordeaux and smiling, which makes her eyebrows arch in a very becoming way.

'Why not?' I reply, settling myself on the barstool. A drop of truth serum certainly won't hamper the situation, I figure.

We banter with each other about music and other such rubbish and I studiously avoid mentioning her new man. That omission alone should indicate my feelings to her, but I imagine her mind is not thinking in that direction.

After a glass of wine has warmed my insides and my nerve, I suggest we play the piano. Somehow I hope that proximity will create the impetus I need. We sit down next to each other. I can smell her perfume and feel the warmth of her body. She starts playing, but I'm so preoccupied that I struggle to follow the notes. She laughs at me and jokes that the wine has rendered me incompetent as a pianist.

'Actually, it's not the drink,' I say suddenly, stopping mid-note and turning to face her. 'I wanted to have a chat with you.' All I can focus on is her face, and the beautiful lines of her bone structure. It's like the rest of the café has faded to black.

She looks taken aback, confused and a little bit uncertain, like I'm about to break bad news.

'I wanted to talk about us,' I carry on, deciding to just bomb the situation with confessional information and then see what happens in the aftermath of the explosion. 'I think I'm falling in love with you. I've thought it for a while, but nothing seemed to happen . . . and then you met someone.'

She just looks at me for more moments than I care to count, trying to reconfigure her face from the shock of my announcement.

In her silence I decide to continue – dig myself deeper, as they say. 'I think about you all the time and I wonder what it would be like if we were together . . . I don't know how you feel about this new guy you've met, but I thought you should know how I felt before you made any decisions about him.'

Still there is stunned silence from her as she looks at me, trying to compose herself. I don't have anything left to say, so I just sit and stare at the piano, waiting for her response.

'I don't know what to say,' she replies eventually.

It's not the response I wanted and I can feel the atmosphere around me get heavier, like it's trying to drag me away.

'It's just such a shock – I never knew you felt that way,' she says, looking directly at me, trying to make eye contact, but I look away, imagining the worst and trying to console myself with the fact that at least I gave it a go. 'Sorry I seem so, I don't know, not together about this . . . It's just that I thought you had a girlfriend . . .' She trails off and this time she looks down at the piano to conceal the emotions playing on her face.

'What?' I exclaim, looking at her. 'What made you think that?'

She looks up, and for the first time since my confession, our eyes meet. I feel myself relax and something like relief washes over me.

'You just seemed so secretive. Sometimes we'd spend time together and I'd think we were getting close, and then you'd just withdraw from the situation, like you had something to hide. In the end I gave up. I figured you must have a girlfriend and that you were just playing with me, flirting and then backing off if you thought anything would happen.'

I want to kiss her, but I know that it wouldn't be the gentlemanly thing to do before I reveal the second part of my confession. Like Miss Stripper said, at this point in time all I've got in my favour is that I haven't deceived her properly so far – I can't blow that now with an over-enthusiastic embrace.

'I've got something else to confess,' I say slowly, getting up to fetch the bottle of wine. We'll probably need a stiff drink for this one, I think. I pour us both a drink and then sit directly facing her. 'There is no easy way to say this,' I start, searching for the right words to express what I want to say. Instead of the eloquent explanation my mind is reaching for, a simple statement escapes my lips: 'I'm a gigolo. That's why I've been so secretive. I thought you'd hate me if you knew – and I never suspected you took that to mean I'd got a girlfriend. It just never occurred to me.'

I look up at her, anxiously waiting for her reaction, squeezing my hands to alleviate the tension. Part of me expects her to slap my face and storm out. Instead she throws her head back and starts pealing with laughter, before collapsing over the piano, her shoulders shaking with the force of her mirth. I sit there, stunned. She looks at me, tears of laughter streaming down her face, before squeezing out an apology, and then carrying on laughing. Every time she tries to say something, giggles overtake her.

'I'm imagining that's a shocked response,' I joke uncertainly, knocking back the remainder of my wine. In all my imagined outcomes, this certainly wasn't one of them.

Eventually she stops laughing and kisses me on the lips, her hands resting tenderly on the sides of my face. This response stuns me as much as the uncontrollable laughter. Even with all my expertise in the opposite sex, women never cease to amaze me.

'I'm sorry,' she says finally. 'I just can't believe that was

it all along. I never for a minute thought you were a gigolo
– didn't they die out when Richard Gere went grey and
discovered Buddhism?' she asks, still laughing and looking
amazed at my revelation.

'Very funny.' I smile, glad that at least she has a sense
of humour about the situation.

'OK, now I don't want to be naïve here, but what does
a gigolo actually do? On second thoughts, scrub that – I
know what one *does*, but how does it work?' she asks,
suddenly looking serious about the situation.

'I'm like a host,' I venture cautiously. 'I entertain women
at clubs, at hotels, in their homes . . . I spend quality time
with them, giving them whatever they want – affection,
attention, interesting conversation and –' I hesitate '– *other
services*, and in return I get to live an exciting life, drinking
champagne, hanging out in the best places, travelling first
class.'

'So you're like a male hooker?' she asks, looking at me
pointedly.

'Not at all,' I reply, tapping my finger on the piano,
trying not to be insulted. 'I suppose the closest thing you
can compare it with is a trophy girlfriend, but with a more
straightforward transaction going on – but not so straightforward that I'm hiring out a hotel room by the hour.'

'I suppose lots of single men sleep around,' she says,
trying to figure it out in her mind. 'It's just that you're in
such demand the women have to woo your favours.'

'That's just how it is.' I smile, reaching for her hand
and feeling heartened when she lets me hold it. 'It's a
different world out there from when our parents were
growing up. Women have the purchasing power now –
it's their turn to have a little fun on their expense

accounts. Up until now I've never had a reason not to oblige them.'

'I'll be straight with you,' says Charlotte suddenly, as if she's come out of a trance, like the shock has finally worn off. 'I thought you were a struggling musician honourably suffering for his art, not some libertine party guy living off the favours of wealthy women.' She withdraws her hand and my heart sinks. I knew this would happen. 'But what I hate is deceit, I just find that unforgivable,' she continues, taking a swig of wine.

I've blown it, I think to myself. I should have known a gigolo can never reform.

'For me, the biggest betrayal is when men cheat on their girlfriends. I thought you were in a relationship and betraying her by flirting with me, not to mention leading me on. In the end I hated you for it. That's why I started seeing that other guy. Obviously, I'm not overjoyed you're a gigolo – it hardly ranks on my preferred previous careers for a boyfriend – but at least it means you aren't deceiving anyone. I can forgive you for being a gigolo, but I wouldn't have been able to forgive you for having a girlfriend. A decadent life is better than a deceitful one.'

With that she looks up at me, her wide eyes shining in the candlelight. I lean forward and kiss her. A kiss full of soft sweetness that contains a tenuous quality that a gigolo embrace never has – because love, unlike procured sex, has no certainties, only possibilities.

A week later I am standing on the doorstep of the Divorcee's beautiful town house, arm in arm with Charlotte, ready to attend the engagement party. 'Hello, you two,' says the Divorcee warmly as she opens the door, kissing us both and taking our coats. 'You make a beautiful couple,' the Divorcee whispers in my ear as we walk up the corridor to greet Johan, Rochester and the rest of the dandy clan.

'Thank you,' I reply, as it finally sinks in that I've found someone who won't leave me when the fun ends and the future begins.

The door closes behind us and I think to myself that to the outside world it will appear as though I'm attending an ordinary dinner party, full of ordinary couples, happy and in love.

I hope, for once, that appearances aren't deceptive.